KIM SHAW

PAY ANY PRICE

ALSO BY JAMES RISEN

*State of War: The Secret History of the
CIA and the Bush Administration*

*The Main Enemy: The Inside Story of the CIA's Final
Showdown with the KGB* (with Milt Bearden)

Wrath of Angels: The American Abortion War
(with Judy L. Thomas)

PAY ANY PRICE

GREED, POWER, AND
ENDLESS WAR

JAMES RISEN

Houghton Mifflin Harcourt

Boston   New York

To Penny

www.hmhco.com

Library of Congress Cataloging-in-Publication Data
Risen, James.
Pay any price : greed, power, and endless war / James Risen.
pages cm
ISBN 978-0-544-34141-8 (hardback)
1. War on Terrorism, 2001–2009 — Economic aspects — United States.
2. Iraq War, 2003–2011 — Economic aspects — United States.
3. Abuse of administrative power — United States.
4. War and emergency powers — United States. I. Title.
HV6432.R56 2014
973.931 — dc23
2014012010

Book design by Greta D. Sibley

Printed in the United States of America
DOC 10 9 8 7 6 5 4 3

"I've come back," he repeated; "and I was the King of Kafiristan—me and Dravot—crowned Kings we was! In this office we settled it—you setting there and giving us the books. I am Peachey—Peachey Taliaferro Carnehan, and you've been setting here ever since—O Lord!"

I was more than a little astonished, and expressed my feelings accordingly.

"It's true," said Carnehan, with a dry cackle, nursing his feet which were wrapped in rags. "True as gospel. Kings we were, with crowns upon our heads—me and Dravot—poor Dan—oh, poor, poor Dan, that would never take advice, not though I begged of him!"

RUDYARD KIPLING
The Man Who Would Be King

CONTENTS

A NOTE ON SOURCES

Many people have criticized the use of anonymous sources. Yet all reporters know that the very best stories—the most important, the most sensitive—rely on them. This book would not be possible without the cooperation of many current and former government officials and other individuals who were willing to discuss sensitive matters only on the condition of anonymity.

PROLOGUE

On April 9, 2009, near the start of the first Obama administration, former Deputy Secretary of Defense Paul Wolfowitz attended a modest ceremony at Arlington National Cemetery marking the sixth anniversary of the fall of Baghdad. Fewer than fifty people were gathered that day in Arlington's section 60, where the dead of the Iraq war lay buried, to mark the fact that on April 9, 2003, American tanks had rumbled into downtown Baghdad, and the statue of Saddam Hussein in Firdos Square had been toppled. For Wolfowitz and the ardent advocates of the invasion of Iraq, April 9 was Iraq Liberation Day, and they didn't care that by 2009, most Americans were exhausted by Iraq and eager to forget that the war had ever been fought.

Wolfowitz listened to speeches by a representative of the American Legion, a Gold Star mother, the Iraqi ambassador, and Viola Drath, an aging Georgetown socialite who was the organizer of the event. Never mind that the invasion that ousted Saddam Hussein in just three weeks had turned into a prolonged and brutal war of attrition, or that the Iraqi weapons of mass destruction which had been the predicate for the invasion had turned out to be illusory, or that on that same sixth anniversary in 2009, an estimated thirty thousand Iraqis poured into Firdos Square in Baghdad to angrily protest the continued American occupation of Iraq, while the anniversary went largely unmarked in the United States save for this small gathering in section 60. None of that mattered. Wolfowitz, one of the architects of the Iraq war, was upbeat. After the ceremony, he and I walked and chatted together through the cemetery, from section 60 back to Arlington's entrance, engaging mostly in small talk and pleasantries. But it was clear that Wolfowitz seemed happy that Iraq had turned out so well, at least in his view, and that the global war on terror was still going strong under the direction of a new president who was then in the process of extending and validating many of the Bush administration's most contentious policies.

And there was no end in sight. Wolfowitz was long gone from the Pentagon, and in the 2008 elections, Americans had swept the Republicans from power. Perhaps Barack Obama's greatest political strength was that he seemed as different from George Bush as any politician could be. His campaign offered the promise of light following eight years of Dick Cheney's fondness for operating on what he called the dark side.

But executive power, once accumulated, is a hard thing to give up, and Obama quickly succumbed. He announced that he was determined to "look forward, not back," and that he opposed any broad new investigations of the Bush administration's use of torture, extraordinary rendition, domestic spying, or other potential crimes. After issuing an executive order to close the prison at Guantánamo Bay on his first day in office, Obama changed course and kept it open. He surrounded himself with advisors who had been deeply enmeshed in the Bush administration's most contentious national security policies. He expanded the use of drones in so-called targeted killings around the world, continued the use of military tribunals to try terrorism suspects, allowed investigators to question such suspects captured in the United States without reading them their *Miranda* rights, and approved the nonjudicial killing of American citizens who joined al Qaeda. He did virtually nothing to rein in widespread contracting abuse in Iraq, Afghanistan, or the broader global war on terror.

He pushed for and won the authority to allow the National Security Agency (NSA) to continue to conduct broad electronic surveillance on Americans, and he went further, placing the NSA in charge of cybersecurity, giving the spy agency broad new access to the domestic Internet. Senators from his own party soon began to warn that Obama was secretly expanding the government's surveillance powers even beyond those authorized by Bush. Obama allowed the civil liberties panel that was supposed to provide oversight of the government's war on terror to remain idle and only partially staffed for years. His administration launched a draconian crackdown on the press, spying on reporters while prosecuting more leakers and whistleblowers than all previous administrations combined.

And it paid off for Obama by taking the edge off longstanding Republican critiques that Democrats were soft on national security. Obama performed a neat political trick: he took the national security state that had grown to such enormous size under Bush and made it his own. In the process, Obama normalized the post-9/11 measures that Bush had implemented on a haphazard, emergency basis. Obama's great achievement — or great sin — was to make the national security state permanent.

Half a century earlier, President Dwight Eisenhower had warned of a new "military-industrial complex"; under Bush and Obama, a parallel "homeland security–industrial complex" has been born. The rise of the military-industrial complex had been fueled by fears of Communism. Now, another abstract fear was driving hundreds of billions of dollars a year into building the infrastructure necessary to wage a permanent war on terror, and it had grown like kudzu around the CIA, FBI, Department of Homeland Security, Treasury Department, Pentagon, and dozens of other smaller offices and federal agencies. The post-9/11 panic led Congress to throw cash at counterterrorism faster than the FBI, CIA, and other agencies were able to spend it.

One 2012 estimate concluded that the decade of war had cost Americans nearly $4 trillion.

Greed and power are always a dangerous combination. In wartime, power expands and greed can easily follow. The more our counterterrorism infrastructure has grown, the harder it has become to control. The traditional military-industrial complex was at least partly visible to outsiders; it comprised mammoth defense contractors that built airplanes, ships, and rockets, as well as high-tech firms that pioneered computers and advanced electronics. There were often public, aggressive congressional debates about spending on big new weapons systems, and major defense contractors frequently felt compelled to take out advertisements in newspapers and on television to generate support for their projects.

The new homeland security–industrial complex operates differently. It is largely made up of a web of intelligence agencies and their contractors, companies that mostly provide secret services rather than large weapons systems and equipment. These contractors are hired to help Washington determine the scale and scope of the terrorist threat; they make no money if they determine that the threat is overblown or, God forbid, if the war on terror ever comes to an end.

The growth of this homeland security–industrial complex has come at the same time that outsourcing and privatization have become the new watchwords among management consultants working both in corporate America and inside the government. Now, contractors perform functions once considered inherently governmental, particularly in defense and intelligence. War-zone contractors eventually outnumbered American soldiers in Iraq and Afghanistan.

Today, the CIA relies so heavily on outside contractors that many case officers have learned that the way to get ahead is to quit — and then come back the following week to the same job as a contractor making twice as much money.

As bureaucrats dream up new counterterrorism programs in order to spend the money, they have turned to new companies that seem to sprout mysteriously in the office parks that dot the Dulles Toll Road and other commercial centers in northern Virginia near the CIA and Pentagon. There were more than 1,200 government organizations and nearly 2,000 private companies working on counterterrorism, homeland security, and intelligence programs, the *Washington Post* found in 2010, and more than 850,000 people in America had top-secret clearances, producing 50,000 intelligence reports a year. The U.S. intelligence budget alone has at least doubled since 2001, and by 2013, stood at more than $70 billion a year, including both civilian and military intelligence spending.

It is no accident that seven of the ten wealthiest counties in America are in the Washington, D.C., metropolitan area. A 2012 report by Reuters found that income inequality in Washington was greater than in almost any other city, thanks to the massive amounts of money flowing to lobbyists, contractors, and others benefiting directly or indirectly from federal spending.

America has become accustomed to a permanent state of war. Only a small slice of society — including many poor and rural teenagers — fight and die, while a permanent national security elite rotates among senior government posts, contracting companies, think tanks, and television commentary, opportunities that would disappear if America was suddenly at peace. To most of America, war has become not only tolerable but profitable, and so there is no longer any great incentive to end it.

Thus, the creation of a homeland security complex at a time of endless war has bequeathed us with the central narrative of the war on terror — modern tales of greed joined hand in hand with stories of abuse of power. It was inevitable that those wise in the ways of the world would flock to Washington to try to cash in on the war on terror gold rush — and they have. This book offers just a few of those stories. But those trying to monetize America's obsession with terrorism are not the only ones who have sought to exploit 9/11.

Opportunism comes in many forms and is driven by more than just greed. Ambition and a hunger for power, status, and glory have become great engines of post-9/11 opportunism as well. The more troubling stories here concern abuses of power that have extended across two presidencies for well over a decade. After 9/11, the United States deregulated national security, stripping away the post-Watergate intelligence reforms of the 1970s that had constrained executive power for thirty years. The results are morally challenging—and continue to this day.

In May 2013, almost exactly two years after Osama bin Laden's death, President Obama gave a major national security address declaring that it was finally time to reassess the war on terror and recognize that it could not last forever. He vowed to place new limits on drone strikes and to try once again to close Guantánamo, but he offered few details and left himself plenty of room to continue his counterterrorism policies largely unaltered. In fact, his speech came just one week after Pentagon officials testifying before Congress said that the war on terror was likely to go on for another ten or twenty years, and that the 2001 Authorization for the Use of Military Force, the original congressional resolution providing the broad legal underpinning for the nation's counterterror policies under both Bush and Obama, continues to give the government the right to prosecute the war on terror anywhere and everywhere, from Boston to Pakistan.

Obama's speech, filled with soaring rhetoric about the dangers of endless war, offered little evidence that he planned to follow through with any significant actions to rein in his own policies. It seemed designed to quell a growing restlessness within his liberal Democratic base without actually implementing significant change. The address was inevitably met with skepticism from national security legal experts. "If there was a unifying theme of President Obama's speech," wrote Benjamin Wittes on the influential national security blog Lawfare, "it was an effort to align himself as publicly as possible with the critics of the positions his administration is taking without undermining his administration's operational flexibility in actual fact. To put it crassly, the president sought to rebuke his own administration for taking the positions it has—but also to make sure that it could continue to do so." Similarly, Obama's January 2014 speech, in which he said he wanted to reform the NSA, appeared designed to placate Americans alarmed by former NSA contractor Edward Snowden's disclosures of mass surveillance, while actually doing little to limit the NSA's powers. And Obama's subsequent proposal to scale back domestic phone data collection was considered little more than a half measure by privacy advocates.

Washington's global war on terror is now in its second decade, thanks to the bipartisan veneer it has gained under Bush and Obama. It shows no signs of slowing down; hustlers and freebooters continue to take full advantage, and the war's unintended consequences continue to pile up. All too often, things are not what they seem.

Two years after Paul Wolfowitz visited Section 60 at Arlington to attend the Iraq Liberation Day ceremony, Viola Drath, the event's organizer, was found dead in her Georgetown townhouse at the age of ninety-one. Her much younger German-born husband, Albrecht Muth, was arrested for her murder. Muth had claimed to be a general in the Iraqi Army and often wore an Iraqi military uniform to public events in Washington. But after his arrest, the certificate of his supposed appointment by Prime Minister Nouri al-Maliki was found to be a forgery. A receipt from a Washington printing shop for the certificate was discovered in the couple's Georgetown home.

In January 2014, Muth was convicted of first-degree murder in the death of Viola Drath.

PART I

GREED

1

PALLETS OF CASH

Sometimes the federal government gives very important buildings very dull names. The East Rutherford Operations Center of the Federal Reserve Bank of New York is one such place. The three-story building, nondescript and surrounded by a 13-acre compound, fenced off from the outside world, sits in New Jersey's Meadowlands, literally in the shadows of a far more recognizable landmark, MetLife Stadium, the home of the New York Giants and New York Jets football teams—and the 2014 Super Bowl. Nearby is the Izod Center, which hosts huge live entertainment acts, from Bruce Springsteen to Ultimate Fighting. People driving down the New Jersey Turnpike through the flat, gray wetlands just south of New York City would never notice the unmarked semi-tractor trailers pulling onto the turnpike at exit 16W, coming from the operations center just down the street.

But the East Rutherford Operations Center is hiding riches beyond imagining. Deep inside the complex sits a gargantuan vault, measuring 1 million cubic feet. It is filled with U.S. currency, capable of holding as much as $60 billion. And those trucks driving onto the turnpike are loaded with secret cargo — cash. The East Rutherford Operations Center is to paper currency what Fort Knox is to gold.

The New York Federal Reserve Bank has long served as a key operational hub of the Federal Reserve system. It is the hardwired connection between Washington and Wall Street, between the White House and the financial system. And its storehouse of currency in East Rutherford is there to make sure that banks have the cash they need to refill ATMs across the country. But in 2003, East Rutherford's routine was secretly twisted by the White House. It was placed in the middle of one of the most bizarre operations of the entire Iraq war. The scheme was so weird that it seems hard to believe anyone thought it might be a good idea at the time. It was also symbolic of the profligacy that has been the hallmark of America's endless war on terror — the waste, in both lives and treasure, that two successive presidencies have produced. And it was the moment when thievery in the global war on terror achieved industrial scale.

Within weeks of the toppling of Saddam Hussein's statue in Baghdad's Firdos Square in April 2003, a televised event that came to symbolize the ouster of Saddam's regime in Iraq by the U.S.-led military coalition, unmarked trucks started backing up to the loading docks at the East Rutherford Operations Center. There, they were filled end to end with dozens of pallets of shrink-wrapped $100 bills. The trucks then moved out, down the New Jersey Turnpike, carrying billions of dollars in cash. They hauled their cargo of riches past Newark, where nearly one third of the people live below the poverty level.

The trucks stopped at Andrews Air Force Base outside Washington, D.C., where the palletized cash was transferred to the cargo holds of air force C-17 transport planes. The aircraft taxied down the runway and took off for Iraq, making intermediate stops in Germany and Kuwait. Finally, the planes landed at Baghdad International Airport, where the cash was unloaded and counted in the presence of both American and Iraqi personnel.

What happened next is still one of the great unsolved mysteries of the Iraq war.

Between $12 and $14 billion, mostly in $100 bills, was taken from East Rutherford and flown into the war zone of Iraq in 2003 and 2004, with virtually no supervision or safeguards. Another $5.8 billion was sent from the New York Federal Reserve to Baghdad by electronic funds transfers. All told, approximately *$20 billion* was sent to Iraq without any clear orders or direction on how the money was to be used. The controls on the money were so lax that few credible records exist of exactly how much cash there was or where the cash went once it arrived in Baghdad.

Almost certainly, a portion of it ended up in the hands of some of the most powerful Iraqi leaders of the post-Saddam era. Billions of dollars in cash were wasted. And billions more simply disappeared.

Now, there is explosive new evidence that for the first time may help to solve the mystery of the missing cash. Approximately $2 billion of the money that was flown from the United States to Baghdad was stolen and secretly transported out of Iraq in what may be one of the largest robberies in modern history.

American investigators have traced the missing cash to Lebanon. It is believed to have been stolen after it arrived in Baghdad, and then secretly transported to Lebanon, where it has been hidden away ever since. Between $1.2 and $1.6 billion is believed to be hidden in a bunker in a rural village in Lebanon, according to current and former U.S. officials. These officials have received reports that the cash was stolen and stored in the bunker with the knowledge of several of Iraq's most prominent leaders.

At least several hundred million dollars in additional cash is also being hidden in several other locations in Lebanon, according to former U.S. officials, bringing the total amount stolen from Iraq and moved to Lebanon to approximately $2 billion. The figures of how much money was stolen and transported out of Iraq are inexact, but the reality is indisputable. One former American official even reported seeing the cash for himself, stored in the bunker in Lebanon.

In addition to cash, hundreds of millions of dollars' worth of gold was stolen from the Iraqi government and is also being hidden in Lebanon, current and former U.S. officials have said.

The CIA and FBI, along with the Pentagon and State Department, have all been told about the theft of the cash, and have received evidence about the bunker in Lebanon and other locations where the cash is believed to be hidden. But the agencies have not tried to retrieve the money. Nobody went after it during the Bush administration, nor has the Obama administration tried. Instead, the U.S. government has kept the entire matter secret.

The Iraqi government of Prime Minister Nouri al-Maliki has also been given information about the money's whereabouts. But the Iraqi government has not taken any action to retrieve it either. Instead, the Iraqi government has kept the information about the Lebanese bunker secret. Officials in both Washington and the Middle East seem content to let the truth lie hidden.

Like so many things about the Iraq war, the cash flights from New York started with good intentions. But ideology, chaos, and finally greed all got in the way.

Ged Smith was a veteran of the Treasury Department's tiny band of international firemen who make their living rebuilding lost and broken economies. In the 1990s, he worked in the Balkans following the breakup of Yugoslavia and the ethnic cleansing of Bosnia. In the early weeks of 2003, as the Bush administration geared up for war with Iraq, Smith, the director of the Treasury's Office of Technical Assistance, was assigned to figure out how to get Iraq's financial system restarted after the toppling of Saddam Hussein.

He quickly realized that he was facing much different problems than he had ever seen in Sarajevo. He was going to have to deal with a government of true believers who did not want to hear bad news. And that was just in Washington.

Smith's team of Treasury officials was part of a larger postwar reconstruction organization led by retired army general Jay Garner, who had been appointed by President Bush to get Iraq up and running again after the invasion. Garner had been named because he had been in charge of providing food and shelter to the Kurds following the first Gulf War, and the Bush administration believed that it would only face short-term problems, like feeding refugees, before Iraq was back on its feet. The White House and Pentagon thought that Garner's group, the Office of Reconstruction and Humanitarian Assistance (ORHA), would only be needed in Iraq for a few weeks — a few months at most. Bush and Defense Secretary Donald Rumsfeld were convinced that, after a short time, U.S. troops could come home. They neither wanted nor expected an extended occupation; as a result, any plans that assumed a long-term commitment from the United States were dismissed or ignored.

During one of the few interagency meetings on postwar planning held before the March 2003 invasion, Smith briefed a crowd of senior officials in an auditorium at Fort McNair in Washington on Treasury's plans for Baghdad. He warned that because the Iraqi economy was so centralized under Saddam Hussein, taking down the Iraqi government would likely mean the forced closure of hundreds of Iraqi companies and state-owned enterprises. Factory managers would not know what to do without orders from the regime. That meant that tens of thousands of Iraqis would almost certainly be thrown out of work immediately after Saddam lost power.

Smith looked up after he issued this dire prediction. No one in the crowd said a word. No one asked a single question.

At a follow-up meeting at Fort McNair, Smith mentioned that one of the lessons he had learned in the Balkans was the importance of maintaining a government's ability to collect tariffs and customs duties, so it could meet its payroll. This time, someone did challenge Smith. A Republican political appointee stood up in the audience and forcefully argued that the Bush administration was for free trade and that the United States was going to sweep away the remnants of protectionism along with Saddam's regime. "We are free traders in America, and we will be free traders in Iraq." Treasury's actions in the Balkans, the Republican operative said, were not going to be repeated in Iraq. "That's when you started to hear these ideological things coming out, how they were going to remake Iraq," recalls Smith.

His team waited in Kuwait during the initial stages of the invasion, and then raced for Baghdad, becoming one of the first civilian missions to make it into the capital after Saddam's regime fell. While Smith ran things from Washington, his team made its way through a broken Baghdad to the Iraqi Central Bank.

Smith had asked the U.S. military to protect the bank's compound. But when his people arrived, there were no U.S. troops in sight, and looters had already stripped the bank's buildings bare — except in the vault room. Looters and criminals had tried to get into the main vaults, which held both U.S. dollars and Iraqi dinars, but they were unable to break through. The looters stole some bags of cash held in less secure cage areas outside the main vaults but were never able to get to the bank's main deposits.

Still, the looters did set fires in the building. Pipes burst, water cascaded down into the vaults belowground, and before long the vaults were under 5 feet of water. It took weeks of digging out before the central bank could resume normal operations in its own facilities. Planning went out the window.

The Treasury team had to improvise. They had assumed that once Saddam Hussein was ousted, the Iraqi currency used by his toppled regime would be considered worthless. But to Smith's surprise, Iraqis continued to use the so-called Saddam dinar. Treasury officials couldn't find the printing plates used by Saddam's regime to print the currency, however, and didn't even know where the printing presses for the currency had been hidden.

Eventually, Iraq was going to need new currency. But it would take months to develop, print, and distribute billions of new dinars in a newly designed, post-Saddam currency. In the meantime, Iraq had to have an immediate infusion of cash to get the economy back up and running.

The Treasury officials knew where they could get cash fast: the Federal Reserve Bank of New York.

About $1.7 billion in Iraqi government funds that had been frozen since the first Gulf War were held in the United States. John Taylor, the undersecretary of the Treasury for international affairs, arranged for President Bush to sign an executive order authorizing American banks to release those Iraqi government funds to the Treasury Department. The money would be sent to an account set up by Treasury at the Federal Reserve Bank of New York, and then cash from that account would be taken from the East Rutherford Operations Center and trucked to Andrews Air Force Base outside Washington. It would then be flown to Iraq. The cash was to be "used to assist the Iraqi people, and to assist in the reconstruction of Iraq," Bush's March 20, 2003, executive order stated.

The Treasury team decided to start with an initial shipment of $250 million. Smith wanted the currency sent in small denominations, to help get the cash moving quickly through the paralyzed Iraqi economy. But when his team called the Federal Reserve in New York and asked about the logistics of sending $250 million in ones and fives, they were told that it would require six air force transport planes. So they decided to ship most of it in $100 bills, which required just one flight. (Some currency in small denominations was sent on the first flight, but the Iraqi Central Bank refused to accept it, and the Americans had nowhere to put it. Pallets filled with several million dollars in $1 and $5 bills are believed to have sat, untouched, in a U.S.-occupied building in the Green Zone, for months, perhaps years, afterward.)

After that first flight, it took eight more planeloads for the Treasury team to transport the entire $1.7 billion in cash during the first months after the invasion. Once the Treasury team had turned that cash over to the Iraqi Central Bank, Ged Smith believed they had given Iraq all of the dollars it would need to jump-start the country's moribund monetary system.

But that was just the beginning of the cash flights, much to Ged Smith's dismay. What Smith did not realize was that the post-Saddam order being established in Iraq was already becoming deeply corrupt. Worse, the United States was willing and able to keep feeding into that corruption.

Within weeks of the invasion, American troops scouring one of Saddam's palaces discovered aluminum boxes filled with cash. Each box was stuffed with about $4 million in $100 bills. There were many, many boxes.

The cashboxes were collected and secretly flown to a U.S. base in Kuwait, where the bills were counted by military personnel. In order to prevent them from skimming some of the money for themselves, the soldiers were not allowed to wear anything more than gym shorts and T-shirts while in the counting room.

Not long after that, the Treasury team learned from senior officials of the Iraqi Central Bank that just before the fall of Baghdad, Saddam Hussein had issued orders to withdraw $1 billion in cash from the central bank, and that the money had been handed over to Qusay Hussein, one of Saddam's sons, who had arranged to have the cash trucked away. The Treasury officials soon realized that the cash discovered by American troops and flown to Kuwait was the same money Qusay Hussein had taken from the central bank.

Undersecretary John Taylor and his aides at Treasury said that the money belonged to the Central Bank of Iraq. He argued that the U.S. military should send it back to allow the central bank to maintain steady foreign currency reserves to help stabilize Iraq's shaky economy. Taylor even went to the Situation Room in the White House to argue with top administration officials that the money legally belonged to the central bank and that it should be shipped back immediately. But the White House, the Pentagon, and the newly created Coalition Provisional Authority (CPA), the U.S.-led organization that had just taken over the occupation of Iraq from Jay Garner's ORHA team, did not agree. The U.S. officials decided that they were simply going to keep the money.

"We made the case that the money should go back to the Iraqi Central Bank," said Taylor. "That recommendation was rejected."

The Coalition Provisional Authority decided to dole it out to American military commanders as cash that they could use as they saw fit. The money became the original basis for what was known in the U.S. military as the Commander's Emergency Response Program, or CERP funds, used by American officers to pay for local reconstruction projects — or to pay off local officials to keep them from siding with the insurgency.

The Bush administration never publicly admitted that they simply had taken money that some top U.S. officials argued belonged to the Iraqi Central Bank, nor did the administration reveal that there was an internal high-level argument about whether to give the money back to the central bank. Instead, American officials came up with alternative explanations for the money's origins in order to justify taking it. A lengthy article in the U.S. military's *Joint Forces Quarterly* by Lt. Col. Mark Martins, a senior military lawyer, described the funds as "ill-gotten Baathist Party cash discovered by U.S. forces." In the article, he said that the American seizure of the cash complied with international law because it could be defined as "safeguarding movable Iraqi government property." Somehow, that movable property became the coalition's, to be used as military commanders saw fit.

The CPA and the U.S. military soon began to spread the cash around Iraq promiscuously, doling out bricks of $100 bills to military commanders with scant recordkeeping, receipts, or controls. CERP quickly became the most popular program among U.S. officers in Iraq. But it also placed unimaginable temptation right in front of American soldiers in the field. The money quickly began to disappear into the rucksacks and footlockers of the officers and enlisted personnel who had access to it; some was mailed home to wives and girlfriends. The stealing in Iraq reached epic proportions.

Maj. Mark Richard Fuller — a Marine, pilot, and family man — was assigned to Fallujah, Iraq, in 2005. Rather than fighting insurgents, the reserve officer from Arizona spent his days counting cash. Assigned as the contracting officer for the Marines in Fallujah, Fuller was in charge of doling out stacks of crisp, newly printed $100 bills to American and Iraqi contractors for reconstruction projects in the blasted city.

There was so much cash that Fuller likely realized that there was no one looking over his shoulder, no one checking where the money was really going. In fact, no one seemed to care. The money was disappearing into a dark hole anyway, and the Iraqis he was paying were simply pocketing the cash. They were not rebuilding their country.

There was no conclusive evidence that Fuller stole any of the money he was managing during his opportunistic time in Fallujah, but when he got back to Arizona, Fuller began depositing cash in banks all over Yuma. The FBI later determined that he had made ninety-one separate deposits, carefully seeking to stay below $10,000 each time, the level at which banks are supposed to report cash transactions. He sometimes made large cash deposits at two or three banks in a single day. All told, he deposited more than $440,000 in fresh $100 bills.

Fuller was a pilot, not a money laundering genius. He didn't realize that repeatedly depositing large amounts of cash in amounts just below the $10,000 limit is considered suspicious by banks, especially when the money is all in uncirculated, large-denomination bills. Fuller was arrested. Yet there was not enough evidence for federal prosecutors to prove that Fuller had obtained his money illegally through his work in Iraq. He agreed only to plead to purposefully seeking to structure deposits in federally insured financial institutions to avoid the $10,000 limit. He agreed to pay a $300,000 fine and to spend about one year in jail.

Army Capt. Michael Nguyen served as a civil affairs officer in Iraq in 2007 and 2008. He was in charge of $11 million in cash, which was supposed to be used for payoffs to Iraqi Sunni militias in Anbar Province. The U.S. Army was willing to pay Sunnis who decided to switch sides and fight the extremist group al Qaeda in Iraq instead of the Americans.

A West Point graduate, Nguyen later admitted that, each day, he would skim cash from the piles of dollars he was handing out for reconstruction projects. He would hide his cash in a box at the end of each shift; later, he sent the cash home to Oregon. No one in the army even noticed that nearly $700,000 had simply disappeared.

But when he got home to Oregon, Nguyen repeated Fuller's mistakes. He started making deposits of just under $10,000 apiece in banks all over Portland. He also began spending extravagantly. He couldn't resist. He spent $200,000 in cash for a BMW, a Hummer, and other fancy toys before he was finally arrested.

During the darkest years of the Iraq war, between 2004 and 2008, there were at least thirty-five convictions in the United States and more than $17 million in fines, forfeitures, and restitution payments made in fraud cases in connection with the American reconstruction of Iraq. But the midlevel officers, enlisted personnel, contractors, and others who have been caught account for only a tiny slice of the billions that have gone missing in Iraq.

The biggest thieves have been far more elusive.

Throughout the summer and fall of 2003, the Treasury team scrambled to launch Iraq's new currency. In Washington, the Bureau of Engraving and Printing, the arm of the Treasury Department that actually prints U.S. dollars, awarded a contract to a British firm, De La Rue, to print Iraq's new dinars at seven printing plants around the world. Billions of dollars' worth of new Iraqi dinars were flown to Iraq — enough to fill twenty-seven 747 cargo planes — and the new currency was introduced on October 15, 2003.

The Treasury team believed that they had finally accomplished all that was needed to provide Iraq with financial stability. They had shipped $1.7 billion in U.S. dollars from New York. Although another $900 million in cash that Treasury officials believed belonged to the Iraqi Central Bank had been taken by the United States and doled out to the U.S. military, billions of dollars in new dinars were now in circulation. The new Iraqi currency proved so popular that it quickly began to appreciate against the dollar. Treasury officials saw no reason for any further cash infusion of U.S. dollars flown in from New York.

But the Treasury team did not realize that the Coalition Provisional Authority had other plans. The CPA was about to make the money delivered in Treasury's early cash flights look like spare change.

Paul Bremer, the leader of the Coalition Provisional Authority and the de facto viceroy of Iraq, made a series of sweeping decisions soon after he took over from Jay Garner. Bremer issued orders that effectively purged the Iraqi government of Baath Party members and then disbanded the Iraqi Army, virtually guaranteeing an anti-American insurgency. CPA operatives floated ideas like changing Iraq over to the flat tax — a proposal that had been a right-wing Republican Party talking point in the United States for decades. CPA officials were so busy installing their political agenda that they did not take time to actually manage anything.

Ged Smith's Treasury team saw that there was no oversight, that money was disappearing without a trace, and that nothing was really getting done. And so his entire Treasury team quit in disgust. "All of a sudden the wheels started to come off," recalled Smith. "It got wildly out of control. I had guys who said they had been in government long enough to know that they didn't want to be around there, and didn't want to be part of what was happening."

Ominously, no one seemed to notice or care. "Once our guys quit, it bothered me that no one in Washington or Baghdad seemed concerned that everybody from Treasury was gone, and that the CPA ideologues were now running the show," added Smith. "No one was really concerned that Treasury wasn't there."

It also meant that the Treasury team wasn't there to stop one of the biggest acts of thievery in history.

After 9/11, Basel—an Arab-American financial analyst in Fairfax, Virginia, who asked that his last name not be used—was determined to somehow put his hobby of intensive weapons training to use in the war on terror. It took some time, but by May 2003, he finally arrived in Iraq as a contractor with vaguely defined duties for army intelligence. In the chaos of postinvasion Baghdad, he was still trying to figure out what he was supposed to be doing when he ran into David Nummy, a senior member of Ged Smith's Treasury team. Late one night, Nummy walked through an American-occupied building in the Green Zone and loudly asked if there were any Arab speakers who could help him with an urgent problem. Basel replied that he spoke Arabic, and Nummy quickly led him across the street to a convoy of four cars. The cars were filled with cash that Nummy had just picked up from Baghdad International Airport—the currency from Treasury's first cash flight from the Federal Reserve Bank of New York. Nummy had decided not to take the cash to the central bank, because its main vault was still under water. He was planning to turn the money over to Iraq's two main state-owned banks in the morning. But he needed someone who could speak Arabic to convince his Iraqi drivers to stay with the cash-filled cars overnight. Using a bit of charm and guile, Basel convinced the drivers to stay and then helped Nummy safely distribute the cash to the state-owned banks the following morning. Impressed, Nummy hired Basel on the spot to take charge of security and logistics for the Treasury team.

After Treasury ended its cash flights, Basel kept on working, this time for the CPA, which continued to fly cash in from New York after the Treasury had completed its initial infusion to the Central Bank of Iraq. The Treasury team did not realize it, but their idea of tapping into Iraq's overseas accounts to help the Iraqi financial system had resonated with the CPA and the Bush White House. The CPA quietly arranged to double down on the Treasury plan and started flying in far more cash from New York to Baghdad than the Treasury team had ever considered.

Soon, the CPA gained access to cash held in the Development Fund of Iraq (DFI), a new account created at the Federal Reserve Bank of New York by a United Nations resolution in May 2003. The account held billions of dollars from the Iraqi government's revenues from oil sales. The UN resolution gave the CPA control over the DFI for use in Iraq's reconstruction, but also called for the creation of a monitoring board to make sure that the CPA properly used the money for the benefit of the Iraqi people.

The DFI account was a tempting target for the Americans, and so the CPA, established as the sovereign authority over the government of Iraq, issued orders for the release of the money with no real debate, no real controls, and no real supervision. The monitoring board was largely ignored. Before long, more air force cargo planes filled with more billions of dollars were on their way to Baghdad.

These new cash flights were conducted in a way that kept the Treasury Department in the dark. The senior Treasury officials who had been in charge of the earliest cash flights were never told what the CPA was doing. Both John Taylor and Ged Smith said that they were not involved in the CPA's cash flights, and Smith said he still cannot understand their purpose. Once Iraq had a new currency, there was no need to keep shipping more American dollars, he believed. "We did not know that Bremer was flying in all that cash," said Smith. "I can't see a reason for it. Why was the CPA flying in more money after there was a new currency?"

Between May 2003 and June 2004, the CPA arranged for about $20 billion to be sent from New York to Baghdad, including between $12 and $14 billion in cash flown on cargo planes. The cash continued to be flown into Iraq even as Congress was separately voting to spend tens of billions in U.S. taxpayer money for Iraqi reconstruction each year. Overall, the United States spent $63 billion of its own money on Iraq's reconstruction throughout the war.

For the CPA, one of the big advantages of using the cash from the Development Fund of Iraq instead of money appropriated by Congress was the absence of rules governing how they could use it and the lack of federal regulations or congressional oversight. It was Iraqi money, not American taxpayer funds, and as a result, few people in Washington really cared what the CPA did with it. In effect, it was free cash with no strings attached. And the only Iraqi government leader that the CPA's chief, Paul Bremer, really had to answer to was, well, Paul Bremer.

In an interview, Bremer defended his handling of the cash flights, saying that the money was badly needed to keep Iraqi government ministries in operation. "[The Iraqi government] was broke at that point," Bremer said. "Civil servants had not been paid for about three months. We had to get funds there right away."

"We also needed to get the government started on long-term funding for its regular needs," Bremer continued. He insisted that there was a budget process in Baghdad which determined how much cash was requested from the Federal Reserve, beginning with proposals from each Iraqi government ministry.

"All those proposals were reviewed by the minister of finance and the minister of planning. Once those two steps were complete, proposals went before the CPA Program Review Board, and if approved they would submit it to me for final sign-off. Then the chief financial officer would propose it to the Fed." Bremer further explained that the CPA Program Review Board also had Iraqi representatives on it, so they were "involved in the budget process from the beginning."

But the truth is that much of the cash flown from the United States to Iraq was never used to fund Iraqi ministries or to meet Iraqi payrolls or to keep the lights on in Baghdad. Instead, it simply disappeared.

In the changeover from Treasury to the CPA, the one constant was Basel, the man in charge of making certain that the cash safely made it from the Baghdad airport to downtown Baghdad. Once the CPA took over, the flights to Baghdad from New York became so routine, Basel says, that pilots gave them their own nickname—"jingle flights."

Basel became the indispensable figure in the midst of the supply chain, the one man who knew the routine, who knew how to move pallets of cash from the airport down Baghdad's Route Irish and to the CPA in the Green Zone, or to the Iraqi Central Bank, through the teeth of the Iraqi insurgency. In the process, he stored up a headful of weird trivia. He learned, for instance, that a Chevrolet Suburban with a driver and one heavily armed passenger riding shotgun could hold about $96 million in $100 bills — if you flattened the back seats.

Basel took to the cash transport business with relish, planning every trip between the airport and downtown with military precision. He would lead his security and transportation teams to the airport at least twelve hours before each jingle flight was due to arrive, so that he would have the flexibility to alter his schedule or route if there were signs of trouble. After the flight landed, Basel and his detail would drive right up to the cargo plane and meet the U.S. military officer, usually a colonel or lieutenant colonel, who had escorted the cash. Along with Iraqi officials, an American from the CPA's comptroller's office would meet the plane with Basel and witness the delivery. The cash would be counted as it came out of the airplane's cargo hold, and counted again when it arrived downtown.

Basel used sleight of hand to confuse insurgents or criminal gangs trying to ambush his convoys once they left the airport. He would leave the airport at dawn, when there was little traffic, and constantly change the convoy's routes and types of vehicles used to carry the cash. He would rotate from SUVs to garbage or produce trucks; he would often send out a decoy truck first to see if it was attacked. To guard against betrayal by insiders, he would sometimes tell his Iraqi security and transport staff that the convoy was due to leave the airport at a certain time only to change or cancel the delivery at the last moment. "We wanted to be unpredictable," Basel said.

Two platoons of U.S. soldiers escorted each convoy while Basel rode with an ex–Iraqi Special Forces soldier who was his most trusted shooter. One of their most frequent destinations was the Iraqi Central Bank, which was not in the Green Zone, and so Basel would arrange to have Iraqis positioned on the streets nearby to warn him in advance of any signs of an ambush waiting at the bank.

Between May 2003 and June 2004, while the CPA was in operation, Basel was in charge of all the cash flights and said he never lost a single dollar. All of the cash that arrived at the Baghdad airport got to its destination downtown, he insisted. "Absolutely, all the money I guarded got to where it was supposed to go," Basel said, emphatically.

But what happened to it after Basel delivered the cash was another question.

Today, at least *$11.7 billion* of the approximately $20 billion the CPA ordered sent to Iraq from New York is either unaccounted for or has simply disappeared.

During the post-Saddam era, allegations of massive corruption and money laundering have plagued the Iraqi Central Bank, one of the most frequent destinations of the money from the cash flights. Ged Smith, despite his disgust in 2003, got involved in Iraq policy again in 2007 when he went to Baghdad as the Treasury attaché at the U.S. embassy.

In early 2008, fire struck the central bank, the building that had been looted and flooded in the days after the 2003 invasion. Smith rushed down to the bank and quickly realized that it was an inside job. The worst damage from the fire was to the bank's computers and financial records. Although the computer system was fried, the bank was still able to function the next day. The bank's security guard force was present when the fire occurred, but the bank's video cameras did not show who set the blaze. Many of the bank's records, dating back to the postinvasion period under the CPA, were lost. The fire was part of a cover-up of massive thievery and money laundering, Smith concluded.

In October 2012, Dr. Sinan al-Shabibi, the governor of the Iraqi Central Bank, went to Tokyo to attend the annual meeting of the World Bank and International Monetary Fund. On his way back to Baghdad, during a layover in Frankfurt, al-Shabibi called a colleague to see if he had missed anything important in Iraq while he was away. He was quickly told that Prime Minister Maliki was planning to have him arrested when he landed in Baghdad. So al-Shabibi caught a flight to Geneva instead, and has been in exile in Switzerland ever since. Maliki's government issued an arrest warrant for al-Shabibi as part of a wider investigation of corruption and money laundering at the central bank. In a series of interviews from exile in Geneva, al-Shabibi denies the Maliki government's allegations of corruption against him, and instead says that Maliki moved against him because Maliki wanted to consolidate his own control over the central bank and its massive foreign currency reserves.

Al-Shabibi also said that while he knows that questions have been raised about the missing money from the cash flights from the United States, he does not know whether it was all properly accounted for or not. "There were questions raised by Iraqis [about how the Americans had handled the money], and the answer from the Americans was always an answer that this money has been spent for the benefit of the Iraqi people," al-Shabibi said. But he added that management of the central bank was weak in the first year or so following the U.S. invasion. "The central bank was not very well organized in the beginning," he noted. "The early period was a very difficult period."

Stuart Bowen, a lawyer with a patrician ancestry and deep roots in George W. Bush's Texas circles, came to Washington with the bona fides of a true loyalist. He had worked for Bush when Bush was Texas governor, had gone to Florida to help the Bush campaign in the legal fight during the 2000 recount, and then joined Bush's White House staff as associate counsel. He later served as deputy staff secretary in the White House, a position that placed him in the inner ring of trust. And so Bowen seemed to be a safe choice when the White House needed someone who could be counted on to pull his punches and protect the president from the political fallout from the war in Iraq.

Once the war started going badly, and the White House had to continually go back to Congress for more and more money to fund it, frustrated congressional leaders finally demanded that a watchdog post be created to keep track of the tens of billions of dollars they were sending, blindly, to Iraq. The Bush administration reluctantly agreed to the creation of a special inspector general (IG) who would have wide-ranging investigative powers to scrutinize what was happening in the war zone.

But the last thing the administration really wanted was an independent and aggressive inspector general sleuthing around Baghdad. And so White House officials turned to someone they knew was on their side, someone who would say all the right things to Congress but who knew the Washington game of burying problems under a blizzard of rhetoric and paperwork.

Or so they may have thought. Once Bowen was appointed in 2004, it didn't take the White House long to realize their mistake. Stuart Bowen was, indeed, a Bush loyalist, but he wasn't a Bush lackey. Once he was named to the post of special inspector general, he did the unthinkable — he took the job seriously. He became the only American official who cared about the disappearance of the billions of dollars flown from the Federal Reserve Bank of New York to Baghdad — and he launched an investigation to try to find out what happened. When he started getting at the truth, however, he faced powerful resistance in Baghdad and Washington.

Bowen got an early clue of what he was confronting during his first trip to Baghdad after being named inspector general. Walking through the CPA's offices in one of Saddam's former palaces in the Green Zone, Bowen overheard part of a conversation between two CPA officials walking just in front of him. "We can't keep doing this," one CPA official said to the other. "There's an IG here now."

Soon, Bowen and his investigators began to hear bizarre stories about the way the Coalition Provisional Authority was doing business. Bowen's people heard about boxes of cash being carried out of the CPA's offices, with no records of where it went. They heard of contractors being paid millions of dollars for projects that were never built. There were whispers of massive kickbacks and bribes, of foreign workers brought to Iraq in slavelike conditions, of U.S. Army officers slipping cash meant for reconstruction projects into their footlockers to take home. With huge amounts of cash being poured into the war zone, there were signs that the American enterprise in Iraq was being transformed into a vast kleptocracy.

Bowen was stunned to realize that the CPA was a dream world, a bizarre mix of Republican ideologues and freebooters out to strike it rich. As the insurgency intensified and Americans were forced to withdraw behind blast walls in the Green Zone, the CPA's frenzied spending grew worse, not better. In June 2004, in the last two weeks before the CPA went out of business and handed the country over to a new interim Iraqi government under Prime Minister Ayad Allawi, the CPA ordered between $4 and $5 billion in cash to be flown to Baghdad from New York in a rapid-fire series of last-minute jingle flights. More than one thousand contracts were awarded by the CPA that month, according to the *Los Angeles Times*. The CPA was shoveling money out as fast as it could be flown into the country, and there were no controls on where that money went.

As Bowen began to investigate cases of fraud and corruption, his old allies at the White House grew angry with him. Iraq had become a political sinkhole for President Bush, and Bowen's investigations were threatening to make things worse. Working through friendly Republicans in Congress, the White House quietly tried to eliminate Bowen's office and shut down his investigations as soon as he began to ask questions about sensitive topics. But Bowen was tipped off about the effort and was able to warn his own allies in Congress, including Sen. Susan Collins, a moderate Republican from Maine, who blocked the White House effort. By October 2004, she had begun to move to place Bowen's job on more solid footing.

It did not take Bowen and his investigative staff long to start asking questions about the cash flights and the CPA's use of the DFI. Bowen and his staff couldn't believe the amounts of cash that were being flown to Baghdad, and were shocked by the fact that the CPA was unable to account for so much of it.

Bremer now says that he agreed with the inspector general that there could have been better accountability on the spending that took place in individual Iraqi ministries. "The issue is what happened to the money once it was distributed through the Minister of Finance," Bremer said in an interview. "We had a very clear record of funds going to the Iraqi system. The funds were all distributed to the minister of finance. The inspector general implied we should have established better controls in other ministries. That would have been a very nice thing to do but it would have required hundreds of internationally trained auditors. It would have taken us at least three years to set up that system."

For his part, Bowen is dismissive of Bremer's defense of the CPA's actions. Rather, Bowen says he found the CPA's handling of the cash and its distribution arbitrary and capricious. One stunning example came when CPA officials decided that the Kurds in northern Iraq should get a cut.

The Kurds were in the process of carving out their own semi-independent state of Kurdistan in northern Iraq, and they had powerful leaders whom the Americans wanted to keep happy. And so, in June 2004, three Chinook helicopters were loaded with $1.6 billion in cash freshly offloaded from a U.S. Air Force cargo plane. The three helicopters flew from Baghdad airport to Erbil in Kurdistan, where the money was delivered to a branch of the Iraqi Central Bank.

The cash arrived without warning. None of the officials at the bank branch in Erbil knew the money was coming, and they had no idea at first what to do with it. The Americans unloaded it into piles, after which it was stored in the bank building until bank officials could figure out what to do next.

Later, after senior American officials realized that the cash had been left with bank officials who were entirely unprepared to receive it, they called back to the bank branch in Erbil to check on it. The American officials were told that the cash had been taken care of and that everything was fine, according to staffers with Bowen's IG office.

The CPA never saw the money again, never knew where it went or how it was spent.

It almost certainly disappeared into the private bank accounts of powerful figures in Kurdistan.

★

The CPA's management of Iraq came to an end on July 1, 2004, as an interim government was installed under Prime Minister Ayad Allawi. His government was a temporary placeholder until Iraq could hold elections, but there was no doubt at the time that Allawi was the man the United States wanted to become the permanent leader of Iraq. In fact, Allawi was known in Iraq as "the spymaster's favorite" because of his longstanding ties to the CIA.

When the CPA accelerated the cash flights from New York in the final two weeks of its existence, the Americans already knew that Allawi would be taking over as prime minister — and that he would be facing a tough election campaign to keep the job. As an exile who had spent much of his adult life in London, he was far more popular with the Americans and British than he was with the Iraqi people. He was a Shiite but also had a past as a Baathist, and thus lacked solid Shiite support, which was crucial in a majority-Shiite nation.

His popularity in Washington and his political vulnerability in Baghdad raise an interesting question — was the decision to suddenly accelerate the cash flights in the CPA's dying days part of an effort by the Bush administration to give Allawi a financial edge, to bolster him and consolidate his hold on power?

Similar questions have been raised in the past. In 2005, Seymour Hersh, the investigative reporter for *The New Yorker*, wrote that the Bush administration had in the spring of 2004 engaged in a secret debate over whether to provide financial support to Allawi and his political allies while also using American money to stunt the power of more radical Shiite Iraqi figures. The United States feared the Shiite parties and their suspected ties to Iran. The CPA was coming to an end, but the White House wanted to maintain its influence over the Iraqi political process to go along with the massive American military occupation, and Allawi seemed to be its best bet. Hersh wrote that President Bush had secretly authorized a covert action to back Allawi's campaign, but that once congressional leaders were briefed on the plan, Nancy Pelosi, the California Democrat who was then the House minority leader, objected. Hersh reported that Bush then circumvented Congress and Pelosi's objections by arranging an operation "that was kept, in part, off the books" to support Allawi. Hersh wrote that the operation "used funds that were not necessarily appropriated by Congress." If they weren't using U.S. funds, according to Hersh, then it would be much easier to hide the operation from Congress.

In the 2005 elections, despite whatever cash assistance he may have had, Allawi's ties to the Americans damaged his credibility and he was routed, losing to Shiite political leader Nouri al-Maliki. Hersh wrote that there was evidence that Allawi had plenty of money at his disposal during his failed campaign.

Bremer denied in an interview that the cash flights were accelerated at the last minute to help Allawi. "That's nonsense," Bremer said. "We didn't know as of June or May whether Allawi would even be a candidate in 2005. It had to do with the fact that the government would need $5–6 billion until they could get procedures in place with the Fed." Bremer further said the flights were accelerated because the Iraqi finance minister wanted to get the funds, because he was concerned that the new Iraqi government would be unfamiliar with the procedures used to arrange the cash flights, and thus the government might have to go without funds as a result.

"The Iraqi minister of finance contacted us in, I think late May or early June," Bremer said. "[He was concerned] there might be hesitation on the Iraqi side or the Fed side to transfer funds."

For years, Stuart Bowen and his investigators were frustrated that they could not get any answers about what had happened to the cash. They could trace it from East Rutherford to Andrews Air Force Base, from Andrews to Baghdad International Airport, and from the airport to downtown Baghdad. But they had no idea what happened after that; the records were abysmal. Billions of dollars had simply disappeared into the CPA and the Iraqi government

That did not mean it had all been stolen. It meant that no one could prove that it hadn't been, and so Bowen's office did repeated audits of the cash from the Development Fund of Iraq, and with each new report, complained about the suspicious absence of adequate recordkeeping for so much money.

Gradually, Bowen's staff made progress. His office concluded that as much as $1.3 billion from the cash flights had gone into a corrupt deal arranged in 2004 by the Iraqi minister of defense, Hazim al-Sha'alan. The defense minister, working with a key aide, Ziyad Qattan, created a fraudulent defense contract to make it look like the money was being used for equipment purchases to help rebuild the Iraqi Army, Bowen's office concluded. They fled Iraq but were able to move the money out of the country without being detected. They were tried and convicted in absentia in Iraq on corruption charges.

The most explosive investigation Bowen's office ever conducted began in 2010, when Wael el-Zein, a Lebanese American who was then serving as a special assistant and translator for Bowen, relayed highly sensitive information that led Bowen and his team on a secret mission to find a hidden treasure trove of missing cash and solve one of the biggest mysteries of the Iraq war.

Wael el-Zein, who worked for the U.S. Army before joining Bowen's staff, had been told that billions of dollars from the jingle flights had gone missing and was now being hidden in Lebanon. Based on el-Zein's information, Bowen's office opened the most secret investigation that it conducted during the entire Iraq war. Bowen's investigators code-named the case "Brick Tracker." The case has never been previously disclosed.

Eventually, Bowen's investigators obtained information from an informant in Lebanon who identified a bunker there that contained mountains of U.S. dollars, staggering amounts of cash that had been shipped from Iraq for safekeeping and was being carefully hidden. There was between $1.2 and $1.6 billion in cash in U.S. dollars in storage. In addition, there was approximately $200 million in gold — belonging to the Iraqi government. Bowen's investigators were also told that some powerful Iraqi political figures had ties to the bunker and the cash.

Eventually, the special inspector general for Iraq and his team became confident that they had discovered the secret hiding place of a major portion of the U.S. currency that had been missing since the cash was shipped to Baghdad. The investigators determined that there was so much cash that the people hiding it were reluctant to try to move it.

In addition to the cash in the bunker, Wael el-Zein said he later discovered at least several hundred million dollars more in U.S. currency hidden in other locations in Lebanon. Including this cache, the total amount of U.S. currency flown from the United States to Iraq and then stolen and hidden in Lebanon was approximately $2 billion.

Some of the serial numbers on the U.S. currency flown from the United States to Iraq had been recorded by the U.S. government, which would have made it possible to trace. But slipshod recordkeeping in the early days after the U.S. invasion meant that not all of the serial numbers had been recorded by the Americans before the cash departed, and it is not known whether the stolen currency now hidden in the bunker in Lebanon and elsewhere is among the former or the latter, according to former staffers with Bowen's office who investigated the matter. Even with the records of the serial numbers for some of the cash, however, the chances that the United States would ever be able to trace and prevent the cash from being used is remote.

Still, the people controlling the hidden cash have apparently been hesitant to move it in large quantities into the international banking system and so have mostly been spending it in Lebanon. Wael el-Zein said he had received reports that some had been used to buy weapons for backers of several political parties in Iraq. It is believed that several powerful Iraqi political figures have been involved with the stolen cash, and that they still control the money with the help of the Lebanese money launderers who first provided the bunker and other secure hiding places.

Meanwhile, Bowen found to his dismay that no one else in the U.S. government seemed particularly interested in uncovering the truth. By the time Bowen's team discovered the cash-laden Lebanese bunker, most of official Washington had long since forgotten about the cash flights. The Obama administration was in the process of winding down the war in Iraq, and the White House was not interested in opening up old wounds. Since the cash from the Development Fund of Iraq was not American taxpayer money, administration officials were not especially interested in getting it back. The Obama White House wanted to forget about Iraq.

Another possible explanation for the lack of interest in Washington could be that the White House did not want to pursue an investigation which might implicate some of the most powerful officials in Iraq. The United States needed to continue to work with them.

When Bowen's staff met with CIA officials to discuss the cash-laden bunker, agency officials showed little interest and made it clear that they were not going to cooperate with Bowen's staff in any probe of the matter.

(Long before I learned that Bowen's office was also investigating the same case, a former CIA officer told me in an interview that he had learned of the existence of a secret hiding place in Lebanon filled with U.S. dollars shipped from Baghdad to Lebanon by powerful Iraqi leaders. This source said that he had been told about it by a contact in Syrian intelligence.)

When Bowen and his staff tried to conduct an investigation of the missing cash in Lebanon, they also met with resistance from the U.S. embassy in Beirut. U.S. Ambassador Michele Sison denied Bowen country clearance, meaning that he was not allowed to travel to Lebanon on official business. Two of his investigators who did go to Lebanon were also denied permission from the embassy to visit the bunker themselves. Embassy officials told them that it was too dangerous for American government officials to travel to the area. Bowen saw it as another sign of how little interest the U.S. government had in conducting any investigation into the missing cash.

Bowen's staffers were able to meet in Beirut with Lebanon's prosecutor general, Said Mirza, who agreed to cooperate on an investigation. Mirza said that he would conduct a raid on the bunker and help to recover the funds. Bowen would then be able to trace the origins of the cash back to Iraq and perhaps to East Rutherford.

But after his initial promises, the Lebanese prosecutor started dragging his feet, pledging an investigation and raid but never delivering. Bowen eventually realized that the Lebanese prosecutor was unwilling to move against the bunker, and that he may have been pressured to abandon his plans.

Bowen's investigators also discussed the case with the FBI in Washington, but FBI agents told them they did not believe they had any jurisdiction to pursue the matter. The FBI never launched an investigation. Bowen and his staff were frustrated, but they kept their work secret, never mentioning in public that they were on the trail of the missing cash.

During a private meeting in Baghdad in either late 2011 or early 2012, Iraqi Prime Minister Nouri al-Maliki casually asked U.S. Ambassador James Jeffrey what the U.S. government knew about reports of a bunker in Lebanon filled with U.S. currency brought from Iraq. Jeffrey told him that he had heard the reports but did not know any details, Jeffrey said in an interview. Jeffrey told Maliki that the American official who knew the most about it was Stuart Bowen, and that Maliki should talk to him about it.

"He said, hey, I'm hearing all these rumors about this money, what do you know," recalled Jeffrey, who was U.S. ambassador to Iraq from 2010 until 2012. "And I told him to talk to Stuart Bowen." When Bowen met with Maliki in Baghdad in 2013, the prime minister questioned Bowen about the missing cash. Bowen said that Maliki made it clear to him that he knew about the bunker in Lebanon, and Bowen came away from his meeting convinced that the theft of so much Iraqi money after it was so cavalierly handled and shipped by the Americans still angered the prime minister.

Yet despite Maliki's signs of personal interest in the matter, the Iraqi government has not taken any action to go after the cash in Lebanon. The Baghdad government may be paralyzed because no one really wants to pursue the powerful Iraqi figures involved with the theft.

The mystery surrounding the cash and the Lebanese bunker is one that the American government, with all its bureaucratic rules and limitations, was unlikely to ever solve, and it also seems unlikely that the Iraqi government will ever try to get the money back. Most of the original $2 billion in uncirculated U.S. currency is believed to still be sitting in the bunker and other locations in Lebanon, waiting to be spent by powerful Iraqis.

And so, today, the bunker full of cash in Lebanon serves as a fitting monument to the excesses of the American war on terror. It certainly seems like a more appropriate symbol of the American adventure in the Middle East than the half-forgotten statue of Saddam Hussein in Firdos Square that was pulled down on the April day in 2003 when Baghdad fell.

2

THE EMPEROR OF THE
WAR ON TERROR

Greed and power, when combined, can be devastating. In the case of the missing cash of Baghdad, greed tempted Americans and Iraqis alike, while the power of the Coalition Provisional Authority to make fast, sweeping decisions with little oversight allowed that greed to grow unchecked. Billions of dollars disappeared as a result.

Throughout the war on terror, greed and power have flourished just as readily back home in the United States, where the government's surging counterterrorism spending created a new national security gold rush. The post-9/11 panic led Congress to throw cash at the FBI, CIA, and Pentagon faster than they were able to spend it. Soon, a counterterrorism bubble, like a financial bubble, grew in Washington, and a new breed of entrepreneur learned that one of the surest and easiest paths to riches could be found not in Silicon Valley building computers or New York designing clothes but rather in Tysons Corner, Virginia, coming up with new ways to predict, analyze, and prevent terrorist attacks — or, short of that, at least in convincing a few government bureaucrats that you had some magic formula for doing so.

Consider the example of Dennis Montgomery. He provides the

perfect case study to explain how during the war on terror greed and ambition have been married to unlimited rivers of cash to create a climate in which someone who has been accused of being a con artist was able to create a rogue intelligence operation with little or no adult supervision. Crazy became the new normal in the war on terror, and the original objectives of the war got lost in the process.

Whatever else he was, Dennis Montgomery was a man who understood how best to profit from America's decade of fear. He saw the post-9/11 age for what it was, a time to make money.

Montgomery was the maestro behind what many current and former U.S. officials and others familiar with the case now believe was one of the most elaborate and dangerous hoaxes in American history, a ruse that was so successful that it nearly convinced the Bush administration to order fighter jets to start shooting down commercial airliners filled with passengers over the Atlantic. Once it was over, once the fever broke and government officials realized that they had been taken in by a grand illusion, they did absolutely nothing about it. The Central Intelligence Agency buried the whole insane episode and acted like it had never happened. The Pentagon just kept working with Montgomery. Justice Department lawyers fanned out across the country to try to block any information about Montgomery and his schemes from becoming public, invoking the state secrets privilege in a series of civil lawsuits involving Montgomery.

It was as if everyone in Washington was afraid to admit that the Emperor of the War on Terror had no clothes.

A former medical technician, a self-styled computer software expert with no experience whatsoever in national security affairs, Dennis Montgomery almost singlehandedly prompted President Bush to ground a series of international commercial flights based on what now appears to have been an elaborate hoax. Even after it appeared that Montgomery had pulled off a scheme of amazing scope, he still had die-hard supporters in the government who steadfastly refused to believe the evidence suggesting that Montgomery was a fake, and who rejected the notion that the super-secret computer software that he foisted on the Pentagon and CIA was anything other than America's salvation.

Montgomery's story demonstrates how hundreds of billions of dollars poured into the war on terror went to waste. With all rules discarded and no one watching the bottom line, government officials simply threw money at contractors who claimed to offer an edge against the new enemies. And the officials almost never checked back to make sure that what they were buying from contractors actually did any good—or that the contractors themselves weren't crooks. A 2011 study by the Pentagon found that during the ten years after 9/11, the Defense Department had given more than $400 billion to contractors who had previously been sanctioned in cases involving $1 million or more in fraud.

The Montgomery episode teaches one other lesson, too: the chance to gain promotions and greater bureaucratic power through access to and control over secret information can mean that there is no incentive for government officials to question the validity of that secret information. Being part of a charmed inner circle holds a seductive power that is difficult to resist.

Montgomery strongly denies that he peddled fraudulent technology. He insists that the charges have been leveled by critics with axes to grind, including his former lawyer and former employees. He claims that he was following direct orders from both the NSA and the CIA, and says that the CIA, NSA, and U.S. military took his technology so seriously that it was used to help in the targeting of Predator strikes and other raids. Montgomery adds that he is limited in what he can say about his software and business dealings with the CIA and Pentagon without the approval of the Justice Department. The fact that the government is blocking public disclosure of the details of its relationship with him, he adds, shows that his work was considered serious and important. "Do you really think," he asked, "the government invoked the state secrets privilege just from being embarrassed or conned?"

★

The strange tale of Dennis Montgomery and his self-proclaimed plan to win the war on terror begins, appropriately enough, inside the El Dorado Casino in downtown Reno.

Montgomery was an overweight, middle-aged, incorrigible gambler, a man who liked to play long odds because he was convinced that he could out-think the house. He once boasted to a business partner that he had a system for counting an eight-deck blackjack shoe, quite a difficult feat for even the best card sharks, and he regularly tested his theories at the El Dorado and the Peppermill Casino in Reno. He usually came up short but that didn't stop him from playing blackjack on a nightly basis, racking up unwieldy debts that eventually led to his 2010 arrest for bouncing more than $1 million in bad checks at Caesar's Palace in Las Vegas.

Gambling is how he met his first backer, Warren Trepp. Trepp got rich in the biggest casino of them all, Wall Street. He had been Michael Milken's right-hand man in the heyday of Milken's famous Beverly Hills trading desk during the "greed is good" era of insider trading in the 1980s. When a hungry federal prosecutor named Rudolph Giuliani went after Milken for insider trading, he tried to get Trepp to roll over on his boss. Trepp refused, even in the face of a threat that he would be charged himself if he failed to cooperate. Milken went to jail, but Giuliani never could nail Trepp. Instead of facing criminal charges, Trepp became the subject of a marathon investigation by the Securities and Exchange Commission (SEC), which tried to impose civil sanctions for Trepp's alleged part in Milken's insider-trading bonanza. It took nearly a decade, but Trepp finally beat the feds. In 1997, the SEC's case against him was dismissed. He walked away from the Milken years with a fortune.

Warren Trepp may have been able to defeat Rudy Giuliani and a whole legion of federal investigators, but he couldn't outwit Dennis Montgomery.

By the late 1990s, Trepp was living in Incline Village, a wealthy enclave on the Nevada side of Lake Tahoe, where he was shaking off his past and trying to remake himself into a respected philanthropist, theater angel, and canny private investor. And then he met Montgomery.

Trepp was introduced to Montgomery by a casino host at the El Dorado in 1997. Montgomery was on the lookout for somebody to bankroll him, and had put out the word to his friends at the casinos that he frequented the most. A year later, Montgomery and Trepp were in business together. Trepp was one of the first, but hardly the last, to be beguiled by Montgomery's claims that he had achieved breakthroughs in computer technology of historic significance. The two founded a company together and tried to find buyers for Montgomery's alleged miracle software.

Montgomery convinced Trepp that he had achieved a series of major technological advances in computer software that could be worth millions. One was the development of software that he argued provided a new method of video compression, allowing for greater video storage and transmission than was ever available before. Another innovation was stunningly detailed video facial recognition. But the most dazzling claim of all involved software that Montgomery said could identify objects and anomalies embedded in video with unprecedented detail. He claimed that his technology could even find and identify objects hidden inside videotape that were not visible to the naked eye.

How his technology worked was a secret. Dennis Montgomery's computer code became the great treasure behind eTreppid Technologies, the company he and Trepp founded. Later, many of those around Montgomery began to suspect the reason why Montgomery had to guard his technological innovations so carefully. They came to believe that at least some of the technology didn't really exist.

★

To commercialize his technology, Montgomery first tried to convince Hollywood that he had developed a new and efficient means of colorizing old movies. His object identification software, he claimed, could speed the process of deciding where and how to colorize each frame of film. Warren Trepp later told a court that Montgomery had given him a demonstration of his software's ability to identify patterns and images in a video of the 1939 black-and-white classic *Gunga Din*.

But after failing to strike it big in Hollywood, Montgomery and Trepp shifted their focus to the casino industry in Reno and Las Vegas. Montgomery later bragged that he had developed pattern recognition software specifically for casinos that could help identify cheaters. He even claimed he had technology that could identify high-value chips inside piles of chips on gaming tables, to detect when dealers tried to steal from the casinos by slipping valuable chips to friends. Montgomery also said he had developed video compression software that would allow casinos to more easily store thousands of hours of surveillance tapes, rather than erase all of their old footage.

But his technology was never a big hit with the casino industry, either. So Montgomery turned to Washington. There, Montgomery finally succeeded in his new search for clients through a series of coincidences and chance encounters, along with strong political and financial connections that helped to smooth the way. And it all started, like so many other things in his life, in a casino.

In 2002, Warren Trepp arranged for the MGM Grand Casino to take a look at Montgomery's technology. An air force colonel who had heard about Montgomery's work decided to come and see it as well. Impressed, he helped Montgomery and eTreppid land a contract with the air force.

Michael Flynn, Montgomery's former lawyer — who later concluded that Montgomery was a fraud — said that Montgomery had told him that Montgomery had won over the visiting air force officer, who became convinced that Montgomery's object recognition and video compression technologies could help the air force's Predator drone program. The CIA and air force were flying Predator drones over Afghanistan at the time, and they were sending back thousands of hours of video that needed to be analyzed and stored. Just like

Las Vegas casinos, the air force needed a way to maintain the massive piles of video generated by its own version of the eye in the sky. Montgomery's object recognition technology could provide new ways for the air force to track suspected terrorists with the Predator. Montgomery claimed that his facial recognition software was so good that he could identify individual faces from the video camera flying on a Predator high above the mountains of southern Afghanistan.

By the spring and summer of 2003, eTreppid was awarded contracts by both the air force and U.S. Special Operations Command. Montgomery was able to win over the government in part by offering field tests of his technology — tests that former employees say were fixed to impress visiting officials. Warren Trepp later told the FBI that he eventually learned that Montgomery had no real computer software programming skills, according to court documents that include his statements to the FBI. Trepp also described to federal investigators how eTreppid employees had confided to him that Montgomery had asked them to help him falsify tests of his object recognition software when Pentagon officials came to visit. Trepp said that on one occasion, Montgomery told two eTreppid employees to go into an empty office and push a button on a computer when they heard a beep on a cell phone. Meanwhile, Montgomery carried a toy bazooka into a field outside eTreppid. He was demonstrating to a group of visiting U.S. military officials that his technology could recognize the bazooka from a great distance.

After he was in place in the field, he used a hidden cell phone to buzz the cell phone of one the eTreppid employees, who then pushed a key on a computer keyboard, which in turn flashed an image of a bazooka on another screen prominently displayed in front of the military officers standing in another room, according to court documents. The military officers were convinced that Montgomery's computer software had amazingly detected and recognized the bazooka in Montgomery's hands. (Montgomery insists that the eTreppid employees lied when they claimed that he had asked them to fix the tests, and also says that the air force issued a report showing that it had verified the tests.)

Montgomery had a lot of support when it came to dealing with the government. Through Warren Trepp, he had excellent political connections, and in Washington that can take you a very long way.

To help eTreppid get more government business, Trepp brought in Letitia White, a Washington lobbyist with ties to congressional Republicans. She was particularly close with her former boss, California congressman Jerry Lewis. He, in turn, was chairman of the powerful House Defense Appropriations Subcommittee (he later became chairman of the full appropriations committee) and so was able to steer billions of dollars in spending to programs he favored throughout the Pentagon. Letitia White, who had been one of Lewis's closest aides, had left to go to work with the Washington lobbying firm of Copeland Lowery, where she specialized in arranging custom-built earmarks in the defense and intelligence budgets for her clients.

The connections among Lewis, White, and Copeland Lowery later became the subject of a long-running criminal investigation by the Justice Department. The U.S. attorney in Los Angeles probed whether Lewis had steered huge amounts of money to Copeland Lowery's clients in return for large campaign donations from the lobbying firm and from the defense contractors that were its clients. The investigation of Jerry Lewis was ongoing when the U.S. attorney handling the case, Carol Lam, was fired by the Bush administration in 2007, making her one of eight U.S. attorneys pushed aside by the Bush White House in a famously controversial, possibly political decision. The investigation into Lewis and his ties to Copeland Lowery was eventually dropped, but the lobbying firm broke up under the pressure, and Letitia White moved to a new firm. In 2009, Citizens for Responsibility and Ethics in Washington (CREW) named Lewis one of the fifteen most corrupt members of Congress.

But Trepp wasn't finished after hiring White. He convinced another heavyweight Nevada investor, Wayne Prim, to put money into eTreppid. In September 2003, Prim hosted a dinner that brought together Trepp, Montgomery, and Rep. Jim Gibbons of Nevada, a former airline pilot and rising star among congressional Republicans. Gibbons, an influential member of the House Intelligence Committee, almost certainly played a critical role in helping Montgomery to gain access to the Central Intelligence Agency.

Gibbons did not need much coaxing to try to assist eTreppid. Not only was the company based in his home state, but both Prim and Warren Trepp were longtime campaign contributors. After the dinner at Prim's house, Gibbons went to work immediately opening doors in Washington for eTreppid. Flynn said that Montgomery later told him that Gibbons quickly arranged to meet with Porter Goss, then the chairman of the House Intelligence Committee, to discuss eTreppid and Montgomery's technology.

By the fall of 2003, Dennis Montgomery had made a series of impressive moves to gain access to the black budget of the government's national security apparatus. He had the backing of two wealthy investors, had one of the nation's most influential lobbyists scouring the federal budget for earmarks on his behalf, and had the support of a key member of the CIA's oversight committee. After obtaining a series of small contracts with the air force and the Special Operations Command, Montgomery was ready for the big time.

For a few months in late 2003, the technology from Dennis Montgomery and eTreppid so enraptured certain key government officials that it was considered the most important and most sensitive counterterrorism intelligence that the Central Intelligence Agency had to offer President Bush. Senior officials at the CIA's Directorate of Science and Technology began to accept and vouch for Montgomery to officials at the highest levels of the government. Montgomery's claims grew ever more expansive, but that only solidified his position inside the national security arena. His technology became too impossible to disbelieve.

Montgomery's big moment came at Christmas 2003, a strange time of angst in the American national security apparatus. It was two years after the 9/11 attacks, and the war in Iraq was getting worse. Iraq was turning into a new breeding ground for terrorism, and Osama bin Laden was still on the loose, regularly thumbing his nose at the Americans by issuing videotaped threats of further terrorist strikes. The CIA, still stumbling in the aftermath of the two greatest intelligence failures in its history—missing 9/11 and getting it wrong on Iraq's supposed weapons of mass destruction—was desperate for success, a quick win with which to answer its critics.

The CIA's Science and Technology Directorate, which had largely been stuck on the sidelines of the war on terror, saw in Dennis Montgomery an opportunity to get in the game. The directorate had played an important role in the Cold War, but in the first few years of the war on terror, it was still struggling to determine how technology could be leveraged against small groups of terrorists who were trying to stay off the grid.

Montgomery brilliantly played on the CIA's technical insecurities as well as the agency's woeful lack of understanding about al Qaeda and Islamic terrorism. He was able to convince the CIA that he had developed a secret new technology that enabled him to decipher al Qaeda codes embedded in the network banner displayed on the broadcasts of Al Jazeera, the Qatar-based news network. Montgomery sold the CIA on the fantasy that al Qaeda was using the broadcasts to digitally transmit its plans for future terrorist attacks. And only he had the technology to decode those messages, thus saving America from another devastating attack. The CIA—more credulous than Hollywood or Las Vegas—fell for Montgomery's claims. In short, he convinced CIA officials that he could detect terrorist threats by watching television.

By late 2003, CIA officials began to flock to eTreppid's offices in Reno to see Montgomery's amazing software. Michael Flynn, Montgomery's former lawyer, said that Montgomery had dealings with or knew the identities of at least sixteen different CIA officials. These people now joined the senior military officers who had frequented the company since the previous spring, when it first began to work on the Predator program.

Montgomery persuaded the spy agency that his special computer technology could detect hidden bar codes broadcast on Al Jazeera, which had been embedded into the video feed by al Qaeda. Allegedly, al Qaeda was using that secret method to send messages to its terrorist operatives around the world about plans for new attacks. Montgomery convinced the CIA that his technology had uncovered a series of hidden letters and numbers that appeared to be coded messages about specific airline flights that the terrorists were targeting.

Montgomery insists that he did not come up with the idea of analyzing Al Jazeera videotapes—he says that the CIA came to him in late 2003 and asked him to do it. CIA officials brought Montgomery two different versions of al Qaeda videotapes, he claims. They gave him original al Qaeda videotapes obtained independently by the CIA, and then also gave him recordings of the same videotapes recorded as they had been broadcast on Al Jazeera. The CIA wanted him to compare the two, he claims.

But even if it wasn't Montgomery's idea, he ran with it as fast as he could. He told the CIA that he had found that the versions of the tapes broadcast on Al Jazeera had hidden letters and numbers embedded in them. He says that he found that each bin Laden video broadcast on al Jazeera had patterns and objects embedded in the network's own banner displayed with the video recordings.

Montgomery let the CIA draw its own conclusions based on the information he gave them. After he reported to the CIA that he had detected a series of hidden letters and numbers, he left it up to the CIA to conclude that those numbers and letters referred to specific airline flights. He insists that he did not offer the CIA his own conclusions about what the data meant.

By the middle of December 2003, Montgomery reported to the CIA that he had discovered certain combinations of letters and numbers. For example, coded messages that included the letters "AF" followed by a series of numbers, or the letters "AA" and "UA" and two or three digits, kept repeating. In other instances, he told the agency that he had found a series of numbers that looked like coordinates for the longitude and latitude of specific locations.

The CIA made the inevitable connections. "They would jump at conclusions," says Montgomery. "There would be things like C4, C4, and they would say that's explosives. They jumped to conclusions." He added that he "never suggested it was airplanes or a threat."

Montgomery's data triggered panic at the CIA and the White House—and urgent demands that Montgomery produce more. On Christmas Eve, CIA officials showed up at Montgomery's house in

Reno and told him that he had to go back to his office to keep digging through incoming videotapes and Al Jazeera broadcasts throughout the holidays, Montgomery recalled.

Montgomery was telling the CIA exactly what it wanted to hear. At the time, the Bush administration was obsessed with Al Jazeera, not only because of the network's unrelenting criticism of the invasion of Iraq, but also because it had become Osama bin Laden's favorite outlet for broadcasting his videotaped messages to the world. Each time bin Laden released a new video, the American media immediately turned to the CIA for a quick response and analysis of whether the recording was genuine and where and when it had been taped. Each new broadcast on Al Jazeera forced the CIA to scramble to stay one step ahead of Western reporters baying for answers. At first, when bin Laden released videotapes filmed outdoors in what appeared to be the mountainous terrain of northwestern Pakistan, the CIA even tried to conduct a geological analysis of the rocky outcroppings that served as the backdrop for the video, to try to figure out where bin Laden was. His broadcast statements prompted the CIA to look for new methods of analyzing the news network, and also led some American officials to suspect that there was a covert relationship between Al Jazeera and al Qaeda.

Former senior CIA officials say that officials from the CIA's Science and Technology Directorate, including the directorate's chief, Donald Kerr, believed Montgomery's claims about al Qaeda codes. They also convinced CIA director George Tenet to take the technology and intelligence flowing from Montgomery's software seriously. As a result, in December 2003, Tenet rushed directly to President Bush when information provided by Montgomery and his software purported to show that a series of flights from France, Britain, and Mexico to the United States around Christmas were being targeted by al Qaeda. The data strongly suggested that the terrorist group was planning to crash the planes at specific coordinates.

Based on Montgomery's information, President Bush ordered the grounding of a series of international flights scheduled to fly into the United States. This step caused disruptions for thousands of travelers on both sides of the Atlantic, while further stoking public fears of another spectacular al Qaeda attack just two years after the 9/11 attacks on New York and Washington.

Years later, several former CIA officials who eventually pieced together what had happened in those frenzied days became highly critical of how Montgomery's information was handled by Tenet and other senior CIA managers. The critics came to believe that top officials in the CIA's Science and Technology Directorate became fierce advocates for Montgomery's information because they were eager to play a more prominent role in the Bush administration's war on terror. The scientists were tired of being shunted aside, and Montgomery gave them what they wanted: technology that could prove their worth. "They wanted in," said one former senior CIA official, "they wanted to be part of the game."

But former CIA officials blame Tenet even more; the CIA director enabled the overeager scientists. He allowed them to circumvent the CIA's normal reporting and vetting channels, and rushed the raw material fed to the agency by Montgomery directly to the president. Bush himself had no way of vetting the material he was being handed by the CIA. "Tenet made George Bush the case officer on this," said one former senior CIA official. "The president was deciding how this was being handled."

One former senior CIA official said that for two or three months in late 2003 and early 2004, the intelligence from Montgomery was treated like it was the most valuable counterterrorism material at the CIA. Special briefings were given almost daily on the intelligence, but only a handful of CIA officials were told where the intelligence was coming from. "They treated this like the most important, most sensitive compartmented material they had on terrorism," said one former CIA official.

Officially, the CIA still refuses to discuss any details of the episode. One CIA official offered a qualified defense of Tenet's handling of Montgomery's information, saying that the decision to share the threat information with President Bush was debated and approved by the administration's so-called principals committee, made up of Vice President Dick Cheney, the secretaries of state and defense, and other members of the cabinet. Only after the principals agreed did Tenet take the intelligence in to Bush. In other words, Tenet wasn't the only one who appears to have been hoodwinked. Dennis Montgomery's information received the stamp of approval by the entire upper echelon of the Bush administration.

What remains unclear is how Montgomery was able to convince all of them that he had developed secret software that could decode al Qaeda's invisible messages. While he had gotten by a few credulous military officers who came to view his demonstrations, he apparently found it just as easy to persuade the CIA as well.

A CIA official defensively pointed out that the agency did not actually have a contract with eTreppid at the time Montgomery was providing data from the Al Jazeera videotapes. While they were working closely together during the final months of 2003, the CIA had not yet started paying Montgomery, the official said. The agency never finalized a contract with him because agency staff eventually realized they had been conned, according to this official. But that does not diminish the fact that for a few crucial months, the CIA took Montgomery and his technology very seriously.

Montgomery was able to succeed with the CIA in part because senior agency officials considered his technology so important that they turned the knowledge of its existence into a highly compartmented secret. Few at the CIA knew any more than that there was a new intelligence source providing highly sensitive information about al Qaeda's plans for its future terrorist strikes. In other words, the CIA officials working with Montgomery — people who had already bought into Montgomery — controlled who else was told about the man and his technology. By limiting access to the information, they enhanced their own standing within the CIA; they were the high priests in on the agency's biggest secret. There would be no second-guessing.

The fact that Montgomery and eTreppid had such powerful connections in Washington also reduced the incentives for anyone at the CIA to speak up. Raising questions about Dennis Montgomery would almost certainly lead to a grilling in front of the House Intelligence Committee and Jim Gibbons. It might also incur the wrath of Jerry Lewis and the Defense Appropriations Subcommittee, which, along with the House intelligence panel, controlled the intelligence budget.

★

For those few allowed into the CIA's charmed circle of secret knowledge, Montgomery seemed to be providing powerful and frightening information.

The string of numbers flowing inexorably from Dennis Montgomery's computers prompted President Bush to act. One set of flights he ordered grounded were Air France flights from Paris to Los Angeles. French security detained seven men at Charles de Gaulle Airport in Paris for questioning, but then released them after no further evidence of a pending attack was uncovered. Christmas 2003 came and went with no attacks. But that did not make the White House any more skeptical of Dennis Montgomery.

One former senior CIA official recalled attending a White House meeting in the week following Christmas to discuss what to do next about the information coming from Montgomery. The official claims that there was a brief but serious discussion about whether to shoot down commercial airliners over the Atlantic based on the intelligence. The former CIA official said that during the meeting, Frances Townsend—then a counterterrorism official on the National Security Council—discussed with an NSC lawyer the fact that the president had the legal authority to shoot down planes believed to be terrorist threats, and that it might be time to exercise that authority. "I couldn't believe they were talking about it," the former senior CIA official said. "I thought this was crazy."

Townsend denied ever having such a discussion. The former CIA official repeated his version of events after being told of her denial.

Finally, the French brought an end to it. Since Air France flights to the United States were among those that had been grounded, French officials had taken a dim view of the entire episode. They began demanding answers from the Americans. The French applied so much pressure on Washington that the CIA was finally forced to reveal to French intelligence the source of the threat information. Once they heard the story of Dennis Montgomery and eTreppid, French officials arranged for a French high-tech firm to reverse-engineer Montgomery's purported technology. The French wanted to see for themselves whether the claims of hidden messages in Al Jazeera broadcasts made any sense.

It did not take long for the French firm to conclude that the whole thing was a hoax. The French company said that there were simply not enough pixels in the broadcasts to contain hidden bar codes or unseen numbers. The firm reported back to the French government that the supposed intelligence was a fabrication.

At first, CIA officials were taken aback by the French company's findings and did not want to believe that they had been fooled. Montgomery says that CIA officials continued to work with him for months after Christmas 2003, and that CIA personnel were still showing up at his offices in Nevada until late 2004.

Once the CIA officials finally accepted the truth, however, and agreed with the French findings, George Tenet and others at the CIA who had been Montgomery's advocates tried to forget all about him. They never talked about the operation again. Within the CIA, it was as if Dennis Montgomery had never existed.

The CIA never investigated the apparent hoax nor examined how it had been handled inside the agency. No one involved in promoting Montgomery, in vouching for his information to the president, or in proposing to shoot down planes based on his claims ever faced any consequences. Donald Kerr, the head of the CIA's Science and Technology Directorate at the time, was never held to account for the role the CIA's technical experts played in advocating for Montgomery. Instead, Kerr kept getting promoted. He received several other senior assignments in the intelligence community, and was eventually named deputy director of national intelligence. Kerr did not respond to requests for comment.

At the time of the Christmas 2003 scare, John Brennan was head of the newly created Terrorist Threat Integration Center and in charge of distributing terrorism-related intelligence throughout the government. That meant that Brennan's office was responsible for circulating Montgomery's fabricated intelligence to officials in the highest reaches of the Bush administration. But Brennan was never admonished for his role in the affair. After Barack Obama became president, Brennan was named to be his top counterterrorism advisor in the White House. He later became CIA director.

In 2013, while the Senate was considering whether to confirm Brennan to run the CIA, Sen. Saxby Chambliss, a Georgia Republican who was vice chairman of the Senate Intelligence Committee, submitted a written question to Brennan about his role in the intelligence community's dealings with Montgomery. In response, Brennan denied that he had been an advocate for Montgomery and his technology, and insisted that the Terrorism Threat Integration Center was merely a recipient of Montgomery's information and data, which had been passed on by the CIA. He said that the center included Montgomery's data "in analytic products as appropriate." He claimed not to know what had become of the CIA's program with eTreppid, "other than it was determined not to be a source of accurate information."

There was no further inquiry on the matter from Congress. "Nobody was blamed," complains one former CIA official. "Instead, they got promoted."

Even more stunning, after the debacle over the bogus Christmas 2003 terrorist threats, Montgomery kept getting classified government contracts awarded through several different corporate entities. Montgomery's problems with the CIA did not stop him from peddling variations of his technology to one government agency after another. The secrecy that surrounded his work once again worked in his favor. CIA officials were reluctant to tell their Pentagon counterparts much about their experiences with Montgomery, so Defense Department officials apparently did not realize that his technology was considered suspect at CIA headquarters.

In February 2004, just two months after the Christmas 2003 airplane scare, eTreppid was awarded a new contract with Special Operations Command. The contract was for both data compression and "automatic target recognition software," Montgomery's purported technology to recognize the faces of people on the ground filmed in videos on Predator drones. Special Operations Command gave eTreppid access to video feeds from Predator drones controlled from Nellis Air Force Base in Nevada. It is not certain how long officials there tested Montgomery's facial recognition technology before realizing that eTreppid had no secret formula for identifying terrorists from Predator drone video feeds. But eventually, Special Operations Command also began to see through Montgomery.

"The technology didn't meet the requirements for us," said a Special Operations Command spokesman drily. Still, there is no evidence that officials at Special Operations Command ever talked with their counterparts at the CIA to check up on Montgomery before awarding him a contract. Special Operations Command paid a total of $9.6 million to eTreppid under its contract with the firm.

By late 2005, Dennis Montgomery was in trouble. Employees at eTreppid were becoming more openly skeptical of Montgomery and trying to get access to his secret technology to see if it really existed. For years, Montgomery had somehow managed to hide the truth about his secret work for the government from the small number of employees he had hired. He successfully infused a sense of mystery around himself. He was like the Wizard of Oz, but now people were beginning to try to examine the man behind the curtain.

Sloan Venables, hired by Montgomery to be eTreppid's director of research and development, later told the FBI that another employee, Patty Gray, began to suspect that Montgomery "was doing something other than what he was actually telling people he was doing." Venables added in his statement to the FBI that he knew that "Montgomery promised products to customers that had not been completed or even assigned to programmers."

At the same time, Montgomery was arguing with Warren Trepp over money; Montgomery needed cash and claimed that Trepp had shortchanged him on his share of the revenue from eTreppid's contracts. In December 2005, Montgomery asked Trepp for a personal loan of $275,000, on top of the $1.375 million Trepp had already loaned him since 1999, according to court documents. This was too much for Trepp, who finally became fed up with Montgomery.

But Montgomery moved first. Over the Christmas holidays, Montgomery allegedly went into eTreppid's offices and deleted all of the computer files containing his source code and software development data, according to court documents. He broke with Trepp, left eTreppid, and began looking for new backers. Trepp soon discovered that Montgomery had asked yet another casino host at the El Dorado if he knew of any wealthy gamblers who would be willing to invest $5 to $10 million in a new business he was about to launch. Trepp later told the FBI that on his way out the door at eTreppid, Montgomery screamed at one employee, "You're an asshole and I will see you again!"

Trepp was furious. According to court documents, he told the FBI that Montgomery had stolen the software eTreppid had used on secret Pentagon contracts. As federal investigators moved in to investigate the alleged theft of the technology, they heard from Trepp and others that Montgomery's alleged technology wasn't real. Yet they doggedly kept probing Montgomery's theft of secret technology, and even raided Montgomery's home searching for the computer codes, all the while largely ignoring the evidence that he had perpetrated a hoax.

After their partnership broke up, Montgomery and Trepp remained locked in a series of nasty and lingering legal battles. The worst involved Montgomery's allegations that Jim Gibbons, the Nevada Republican congressman whom he had met at Wayne Prim's house, had received bribes from Warren Trepp in return for helping eTreppid to obtain defense contracts. Montgomery's accusations were explosive because they became public just as Gibbons was being elected governor of Nevada. They helped to trigger a federal corruption investigation, but the inquiry was eventually shelved amid questions about whether e-mails that Montgomery claimed showed that Gibbons had accepted money and a Caribbean cruise in exchange for help in winning contracts for eTreppid—and thus supposedly provided evidence of bribery—may have been forgeries. Dennis Montgomery was widely suspected of having fabricated the e-mails in an effort to damage both Trepp and Gibbons.

In 2008, Abbe Lowell, the Washington attorney representing Gibbons, announced that Gibbons had been cleared of wrongdoing and that prosecutors had told him that he would not be charged in the corruption investigation. Lowell said, "It should be crystal clear that the only persons who should be investigated or charged are those who made false allegations of wrongdoing and who tried to fuel this investigation for their own private purposes," according to an account of his statement in the Associated Press. Gibbons added that "today, I am exceedingly pleased that the FBI and the Justice Department have vindicated me from the allegations and claims of Mr. Montgomery."

Montgomery was able to recover from his battle with Trepp once he landed another wealthy patron, Edra Blixseth, the wife of billionaire Tim Blixseth. Tim Blixseth had made his fortune in timber land swaps in the Pacific Northwest, and then turned his focus to developing a mountain resort for the uber-rich in Montana called the Yellowstone Club. Set in the Rocky Mountains not far north of Yellowstone National Park, the 13,600-acre club was said to be the only private ski resort in the world. It attracted jet-setters who were willing to pay to avoid mixing with the rabble at public ski resorts.

Developing the Yellowstone Club helped to secure for Tim Blixseth the ultimate status symbol—a spot on the Forbes 400. Tim and Edra enjoyed all of the perks of the super-rich—among many other things, they owned a private jet, a yacht, and a massive estate in Rancho Mirage, California, called Porcupine Creek, which came with its own private golf course. Their wealth and ownership of the Yellowstone Club also meant that the Blixseths were networking with some of the most famous and powerful people in the world, from Bill Gates to Jack Kemp to Benjamin Netanyahu.

Edra Blixseth was Dennis Montgomery's latest mark. After being introduced to him by a former Microsoft executive and then hearing Montgomery explain his software, she agreed in 2006 to bankroll Montgomery to launch a new company, to be called Blxware. Montgomery needed new government contracts for Blxware, and Edra Blixseth had the money and contacts to try to make it happen. Jack Kemp, the former congressman and onetime Republican vice presidential candidate, was a member of the Yellowstone Club, and in 2006 he helped to arrange a White House meeting for Montgomery to push his technology. Thanks to Kemp, Montgomery met with Samantha Ravich, a national security aide to Vice President Dick Cheney, who was an old friend of Kemp. Montgomery explained his technology to Ravich and then tried to convince her that Cheney should support his bid for more government funding. But unlike other officials who had dealt with Montgomery in the past, Ravich demanded proof. She told Montgomery that she could not do anything for him unless some technical experts in the government vouched for his technology. He was never able to get anyone from the Pentagon to call Ravich on his behalf, and so she dropped the matter. She said in an interview that she never tried to help him obtain any new government business.

Montgomery also sought to convince Israeli officials to use his technology, but, like Samantha Ravich, the Israelis were unimpressed and rejected his offer. Still, Montgomery continued to find ways to get Pentagon contracts. He says that his technology was often used to provide targeting information in raids in Iraq and Afghanistan, and that he was given access to the Predator Operations Center at Nellis Air Force Base — a sign that his work was playing a role in Predator strikes. "Months of testing and validation at Nellis," as well as at other bases, "confirmed the value of the technology," insists Montgomery.

Edra Blixseth refused a request for an interview.

★

Montgomery continued to get defense contracts even during the Obama administration. In 2009, Montgomery was awarded another air force contract, and later claimed that he had provided the government with warning of a threatened Somali terrorist attack against President Obama's inauguration. Joseph Liberatore, an air force official who described himself as one of "the believers" in Montgomery and his technology, e-mailed Montgomery and said he had heard from "various federal agencies thanking us" for the support Montgomery and his company provided during Obama's inauguration. The threat, however, later proved to be a hoax.

Inevitably, Montgomery had a falling out with Edra Blixseth. He then turned to Tim Blixseth to invest and back his operation. By then, Tim and Edra Blixseth were going through an extremely bitter divorce, and Montgomery became caught up in their legal battles. Mysteriously, government lawyers sometimes sought to intervene in their court cases, with vague references to the need to keep classified information stemming from Montgomery's work with the intelligence community out of the public record.

When Montgomery approached him, Tim Blixseth had no intention of giving money to Montgomery, his ex-wife's erstwhile partner. Blixseth was interested in finding out what Montgomery was really doing, however, and so he played along when Montgomery called desperate for money. At one point, Montgomery's wife even called Blixseth to plead for help with bail after Montgomery was arrested for passing bad checks at Caesar's Palace in Las Vegas. (Eventually, Montgomery was forced into personal bankruptcy proceedings.) Blixseth refused to help but kept talking to Montgomery.

In 2010, Blixseth finally went to see Montgomery's latest computer software operation, hidden away in a nondescript warehouse near Palm Springs. Blixseth says that throughout the darkened office, Montgomery had mounted at least eight large-screen televisions, all tuned to Al Jazeera and all tied in to a computer in the middle of the room.

Dennis Montgomery was once again using his top-secret decoding technology to scour Al Jazeera broadcasts. Montgomery had not given up on his secret project, despite being abandoned by the CIA. As Blixseth took in the bizarre scene, Montgomery proudly told him that his Al Jazeera data was all being fed "straight to the Pentagon."

In fact, Montgomery says that his focus on Al Jazeera was unwavering. He claims that he recorded every minute of Al Jazeera's network broadcast nonstop from February 2004 until the London Olympics in the summer of 2012. "That's over 8 billion frames."

Today, Dennis Montgomery continues to argue that he is not a fraud, that his technology is genuine, and that he performed highly sensitive and valuable work for the CIA and the Pentagon. After former NSA contractor Edward Snowden leaked documents about the NSA's domestic surveillance operations in 2013, Montgomery suggested to me that he could provide the documents that would prove not only that he had been telling the truth, but that he had also been used by top U.S. intelligence officials in highly questionable intelligence operations.

But Montgomery has never provided the documents to back up his assertions.*

* Eric Lichtblau and James Risen reported about Montgomery for the *New York Times*. Aram Roston also wrote an excellent story about Montgomery for *Playboy* magazine.

3

THE NEW OLIGARCHS

Dennis Montgomery is, of course, an extreme example of the new kind of counterterrorism entrepreneur who prospered in the shadows of 9/11. But he was hardly alone in recognizing the lucrative business opportunities that the war on terror has presented. In fact, as trillions of dollars have poured into the nation's new homeland security–industrial complex, the corporate leaders at its vanguard can rightly be considered the true winners of the war on terror.

From the sky high above, the outlines of Neal Blue's beachfront estate in La Jolla, California, certainly look impressive. His house sits just a few yards away from the Pacific Ocean. Assessed by San Diego County at $8.4 million in 2012, the house on La Jolla Farms Road is listed on county property records as having more than 10,000 square feet of space, not including a large rectangular pool that is clearly visible from the air.

Still, the images of the estate taken from thousands of feet above the ground cannot possibly do it justice. They show the roof but little else about the home itself. In fact, pulling back with a wider view, it is hard to distinguish Blue's roof from the roofs of the other, equally impressive homes that crowd the Southern California beach. From the air, the home of the chairman of General Atomics, the manufacturer of the Predator drone, the signature weapon of the global war on terror, could be confused with any one of the houses scattered along the beach, like the one two doors down owned by Ron Burkle, the wealthy investor and longtime friend of former President Bill Clinton.

Such confusion doesn't matter in La Jolla, one of the wealthiest and safest enclaves in America. Antiwar protesters from Code Pink once made an appearance outside Blue's house, but otherwise Blue's personal security and privacy have remained undisturbed.

But confusion certainly does matter in Datta Khel, a small village in North Waziristan along Pakistan's northwest frontier, where the Predators and the newer Reapers built by Neal Blue's company do their work. Confusion in the skies above Datta Khel means death.

On March 17, 2011, American drones fired at least two missiles into a gathering in Datta Khel that killed more than forty people. The U.S. government insisted that the drone strike killed a Taliban commander, but villagers later told investigators that the drones had attacked a meeting of local elders gathered to negotiate a dispute over a chromite mine. Many of those killed were men who were both local elders and heads of large families. Their deaths triggered yet another round of anti-American protests in Pakistan. Confusion and angry finger-pointing over the strike reverberated in the United States and Pakistan for a few days, but eventually quieted down. Meanwhile, the drone strikes continued unabated, killing suspected terrorists and civilians alike. The Pentagon and the CIA kept buying more drones, General Atomics kept building them, and Neal Blue kept making money.

After Datta Khel, in fact, the U.S. drone campaign intensified throughout 2012 and into 2013, and a new term entered the language of the American way of war — "signature strikes." These were drone strikes that targeted groups of people that appeared to be military-age males who happened to be in suspicious locations, even when they hadn't been specifically identified as threats. Those strikes reportedly included attacks on rescuers following an earlier drone attack, as well as the targeting of funerals of the dead from previous attacks.

The global war on terror has been very, very good to Neal Blue. He and his younger brother, Linden Blue, the vice chairman of the firm, are the owners of privately held General Atomics. Almost no one outside of the insular world of the defense industry has ever heard of the Blue brothers, but they are the men who ultimately profit the most from America's drone war, from the use of Predators and Reapers, the soulless hunter-killers that circle the skies of Pakistan, Yemen, and other chaotic lands. In fact, the Blue brothers have benefited from the nation's decade-long homeland security binge more than almost any other Americans. In 2012, General Atomics Aeronautical Systems received $1.8 billion in government contracts, up from just $110 million in 2001.

The Blue brothers are among the oligarchs of 9/11, the people who have earned vast wealth from businesses involved in the nation's most controversial counterterror policies and programs. There is an entire class of wealthy company owners, corporate executives, and investors who have gotten rich by enabling the American government to turn to the dark side. But they have done so quietly. They have largely avoided the scrutiny and infamy that dragged down the post-9/11 operators who garnered too much attention, like Erik Prince, the founder of Blackwater. The new quiet oligarchs just keep making money.

They are the beneficiaries of one of the largest transfers of wealth from public to private hands in American history. America's richest discovered that the hottest way to make money was to get inside Washington's national security apparatus. With new regulations, Wall Street is no longer quite as attractive as it was before the banking crisis, so the nation's most clever men have targeted the steady flow of billions into counterterrorism programs. Washington's partisan budget battles have left counterterrorism spending largely unscathed.

One study found that government spending on homeland security has been so excessive that the only way it could be considered cost-effective would be if it funded programs that prevented 1,667 terrorist attacks—each year—like the 2010 Times Square attempted car bombing. That would mean stopping four terrorist attacks in the United States every day.

Neal and Linden Blue have been inseparable their entire lives. After growing up in Colorado, where their mother served as the Colorado state treasurer, both went to Yale and both learned to love to fly airplanes. While still in college in the 1950s, the brothers spent months crisscrossing Latin America in a small plane, garnering publicity and landing themselves on the cover of *Life* magazine in 1957.

They served in the air force, started a plantation in Nicaragua to grow bananas and cacao beans, and got into real estate, construction, and oil and gas in Colorado. Years later, Linden Blue became a top executive at Lear Jet and Beech Aircraft. By 1986, the brothers were in position to acquire General Atomics, which had started as a nuclear technology subsidiary of General Dynamics, the giant defense contractor, but had subsequently become an orphan. General Atomics had been sold and resold and passed around from one oil company to another until Chevron agreed to unload it to the Blue brothers for $50 million. That turned out to be quite a bargain.

Along the way, the Blue brothers became major players in uranium mining and real estate. Their penchant for playing hardball was on display in both. In the 1980s, Neal Blue bought the valley floor area just outside Telluride, the Colorado ski resort. He was determined to develop it, despite the overwhelming opposition of the town of Telluride and many of its wealthy and famous residents. He spent years locked in a costly legal battle with the town, which ended up at the Colorado Supreme Court. Blue lost but still forced his opponents to raise $50 million to buy him out.

Meanwhile, Blue's firm faced investigations because of radioactive pollution spilling from a uranium plant on an Indian reservation in Oklahoma. He also faced complaints about uranium leaks from a closed mine in Golden, Colorado. Another Colorado uranium facility became a Superfund site. In Australia, the Blue uranium empire was accused of trying to mislead customers in order to get out of unfavorable contracts. Even with General Atomics, Blue ran into problems just before 9/11, when it was reported that the firm had been accused of rigging contracts to benefit a company owned by Neal Blue's sons, according to a 2001 story in the *San Diego Reader* as well as court documents filed in the case.

But 9/11 changed everything for the Blue brothers, turning a diverse business portfolio into an empire — thanks to the federal government. The controversies surrounding their business practices were overlooked as the nation's top defense and intelligence officials scrambled to throw money at the brothers as fast as possible.

Neal Blue has said that he first began to think about drones because of Nicaragua. He knew the country from his plantation days. In the 1980s, he became fixated on dreaming up ways to drive out the leftist Sandinistas who had come to power in 1979. (The Blue brothers had a long history of animosity toward Communism in Latin America, dating back at least to 1961, when Linden Blue's plane was forced down in Cuba, where he was jailed for twelve days.) Neal Blue later told a reporter that he came up with the idea of launching explosive-laden, unmanned aircraft to destroy fuel dumps and other targets in Nicaragua. The notion of combat drones stuck with him.

In 1990, General Atomics acquired Leading Systems, a small drone maker. Washington had minimal interest in drones then, and Leading Systems had been struggling financially because it was ahead of its time. Things began to pick up by the end of the 1990s, when drones played a surveillance role in the Balkans — the United States was reluctant to put more American soldiers and spies on the ground than was absolutely necessary, and drones proved a useful substitute.

After the turn of the century, the air force and CIA began to get serious about pushing for drones armed with missiles so that they could shoot whatever they could see. The 9/11 attacks jump-started their development. It wasn't long before a Predator drone carrying Hellfire missiles made its first appearance in the skies over Afghanistan.

The General Atomics Predator was followed by the larger and more powerful General Atomics Reaper, and the air force, a pilot-centric service that had long been dismissive of unmanned aerial vehicles (UAVs), read the writing on the wall and began to convert squadrons of piloted fighters into squadrons of drones. Today, the air force is training more personnel to operate drones than to actually fly manned aircraft. The service has also waged a prolonged turf battle with the CIA for control over the government's fleet of armed drones. In effect, this battle has been over who could give the most money to the Blue brothers. In 2013, President Obama appeared to side with the Pentagon when it was reported that he had decided to shift most drone operations away from the CIA to the air force, but the CIA fought back and refused to relinquish its central role in drone strikes. Meanwhile, the Department of Homeland Security has been getting its own Predators for border surveillance, and General Atomics has been allowed to begin selling unarmed Predators to other nations, even in the Middle East.

Of course, the Blue brothers and General Atomics have also been doing their best to curry favor in Washington. In 2006, for example, the Center for Public Integrity found that General Atomics had spent more than any other company to pay for the travel of congressional staffers.

Yet the Blue brothers do not see themselves as being on the federal dole. In 2011, Linden Blue coauthored a blistering critique of Barack Obama's free-spending ways — even as government contracts to General Atomics were soaring to new heights. In a column published by the conservative Hudson Institute, Blue complained that "many people, far too many people, believe the role of government is to care for them."

Since General Atomics is privately held, the precise figures for the profits earned by the firm—and the wealth generated for the Blue brothers—are not publicly known. But the real costs to the nation of its dependence on General Atomics cannot be measured only in dollars. America's moral standing has been severely damaged by the Obama administration's addiction to drone warfare.

Compared to George W. Bush, in fact, Barack Obama has had a love affair with drones. By 2012, the CIA had conducted six times more drone strikes in Pakistan during the three years of the Obama administration than the agency had conducted under the entire eight years of George W. Bush, according to the Bureau of Investigative Journalism, a British journalism group that has reported extensively on American drone campaigns in Pakistan and other countries. By May 2013, there had been a total of 368 American drone strikes in Pakistan since 2004, killing between 2,541 and 3,533 people, according to the journalism group. Those figures include between 411 and 884 civilians—with somewhere between 168 and 197 children among them. The vast majority of the drone strikes—316—have been conducted during the Obama administration.

The Obama administration acknowledged in 2013 that four American citizens had also been killed in drone strikes overseas, including some who were not intended targets. That admission highlighted the fact that the government was choosing the targets of its drone strikes with secret standards of evidence. There was no legal due process provided to the intended targets, even for American citizens.

As the drone strikes have intensified under Obama, international opinion has finally begun to turn against them. In late 2012, for example, a researcher affiliated with the United Nations launched an investigation of the civilian casualties caused by the American drones. "The exponential rise in the use of drone technology in a variety of military and nonmilitary contexts represents a real challenge to the framework of established international law," said Ben Emmerson, the UN's special rapporteur on human rights and counterterrorism. In October 2013, Emmerson issued a report that identified thirty-three incidents in Afghanistan, Yemen, Pakistan, and other nations in which drone strikes resulted in civilian casualties. The new scrutiny of drones from the United Nations could be the first sign that international restrictions on the use of drones in combat may someday be imposed, much like the limits on chemical weapons or those that have been sought on cluster bombs.

★

More troubling is the resentment against the United States that the drone strikes have stoked in the Muslim world. Many experts warn that anger will mean that the numbers of Islamic extremists will keep growing much faster than the drones can kill them.

That is particularly true since the Obama administration has been employing drones to target suspected militants far beyond the al Qaeda leaders who were the program's original targets. McClatchy Newspapers reported in 2013 that U.S. intelligence reports showed that drone strikes in Pakistan had been used to kill a wide range of Afghan and Pakistani militants, some of whom belonged to groups that didn't even exist at the time of the 9/11 attacks. A number were low-level militants with no identified affiliation. McClatchy also determined that the U.S. intelligence reports it had reviewed revealed that U.S. drone pilots were not always sure whom they were killing.

The International Crisis Group, an independent nonprofit organization, warned that drone strikes were a short-term fix that could not solve the fundamental political problems fueling militancy in Pakistan's northwest frontier region. Pakistan needs to end the second-class status of its tribal areas but is unwilling or incapable of doing so, and America isn't pushing for political reform, the group observed. "Drone strikes alone will not eliminate the jihadi threat in Pakistan's Federally Administered Tribal Areas," the group said in a 2013 report. "Extension of Pakistani law and full constitutional rights to the region is the only long-term solution."

The drone campaign is already having a deep political impact in Pakistan, where it has become an issue of national sovereignty. But it is increasingly seen as a human rights issue as well. In late 2012, Imran Khan, one of Pakistan's most famous celebrities, a cricket star turned politician, led thousands in a protest march against the drones. The march was so large it had to be blocked from entering Waziristan by the Pakistani Army. "The drones are inhumane," Khan said. "Are these people not humans?" he pleaded. "These humans have names."

In a major national security speech in May 2013, President Obama finally acknowledged the growing criticism both at home and overseas of his drone policies, and vowed to impose new limits on drone strikes. In addition to vowing to move drone operations from the CIA to the U.S. military, he discussed ways in which he might make decision-making on target selection more open and transparent. But Obama provided few details, and his vague promises left him plenty of flexibility to continue strikes wherever and whenever he sees fit.

In fact, so little changed that in October 2013, Amnesty International and Human Rights Watch both issued reports claiming that U.S. drone strikes were killing far more civilians than the Obama administration was willing to admit, and that the United States' drone campaign was in violation of international law.

It is never a good sign for a corporation when its chairman has to write a book to defend the firm's reputation — even worse when the book has to refute charges that the company's personnel were involved in torture. But for J. Phillip London, executive chairman of CACI, a defense and intelligence contractor based in northern Virginia, the war on terror has been a battle of extremes. London has fought for years to cleanse his company's reputation from the stain of Abu Ghraib. In the meantime, CACI and London have also been making loads of money.

CACI is a multibillion-dollar defense contractor and Fortune 500 company. It is best known, at least on the Internet, for its infamous role at Abu Ghraib prison in Iraq. After the U.S. invasion of Iraq, CACI sent contractors to serve as interrogators at Abu Ghraib. One of those interrogators was later caught up in the Abu Ghraib torture scandal that broke in 2004 with the release of graphic photographs of abuse of Iraqi prisoners by American guards. While the low-ranking soldiers involved in the scandal faced punishment from the military justice system, the senior military and intelligence officers who oversaw the prison emerged from the scandal largely unscathed. And so did the outside contractors who worked alongside the military and intelligence personnel inside the prison.

But there was still plenty of bad publicity. And prolonged legal action.

CACI was mired in the Abu Ghraib scandal after an army investigation concluded that Steven Stefanowicz, a CACI contractor working as an interrogator at the prison, had played a role in the detainee abuse. In the army report, Maj. Gen. Antonio Taguba determined that Stefanowicz had "allowed and/or instructed MPs, who were not trained in interrogation techniques, to facilitate interrogations by 'setting conditions' which were neither authorized [nor] in accordance with applicable regulations/policy. He clearly knew his instructions equated to physical abuse." Taguba also found that Stefanowicz had made a false statement to investigators about his interrogations and knowledge of abuses.

The involvement of CACI and another contractor, Titan, in the Abu Ghraib scandal raised new questions about outsourcing in the war on terror, and exposed for the first time the degree to which U.S. intelligence was using outside contractors to perform some of its most sensitive tasks. Indeed, the contractors had greater legal exposure to the fallout from Abu Ghraib than did the federal government, which could claim sovereign immunity to avoid lawsuits brought by the victims at Abu Ghraib. Lawyers for those victims skirted the sovereign immunity obstacle by targeting CACI and Titan, turning them into proxies for the government.

J. Phillip London decided to respond to the allegations about Abu Ghraib by going on the offense. Rather than apologize or explain its real role with the U.S. intelligence community, CACI aggressively took on news organizations that wrote about it and Abu Ghraib, and issued statements claiming that the media portrayal of CACI's role was highly inaccurate and biased. In 2008, London even wrote a book, published by a conservative publishing house, that he claimed was designed to correct the record about CACI. It was entitled *Our Good Name.*

The CACI counteroffensive didn't stop the press from writing about CACI, and certainly didn't stop legal actions from being brought against the company. After a drawn-out legal process in the U.S. courts, Titan's corporate successor, Engility, agreed in 2012 to pay more than $5 million to former detainees at Abu Ghraib to settle their lawsuit. But CACI showed no willingness to settle and fought on. Its refusal to settle was finally rewarded in 2013, when a federal judge dismissed the Abu Ghraib lawsuit against it, nine years after the prisoner abuse scandal erupted.

CACI's aggressive attempts to change the public's narrative about the firm apparently did help with the government, because CACI's work for the defense and intelligence communities continued with little interruption after Abu Ghraib. It has actually grown remarkably ever since. In the immediate aftermath of the scandal, the *Los Angeles Times* reported that the government might ban CACI from further contracts. But by August 2004, just months after the Abu Ghraib scandal erupted, CACI reported sharply higher profits. A company executive told the *Washington Post* at the time that Abu Ghraib had generated "a lot of noise," but that it had not had a significant impact on CACI's bottom line.

The negative headlines have faded since Abu Ghraib, and CACI has boomed since. By 2012, revenue had surged to $3.7 billion, up from $2.4 billion in 2008. London is almost certainly not as rich as the Blue brothers, but he does own more than 192,000 shares in CACI stock as of 2012, according to the firm's SEC filings. He has thus benefited handsomely from the firm's post–Abu Ghraib resurgence.

★

Robert McKeon was a man of Wall Street, not the Pentagon or the CIA. He was a New Yorker, a graduate of Fordham University who went to Harvard Business School and made it big in private equity, founding his own firm, Veritas Capital. But while he wasn't a creature of Washington, McKeon was smart enough to realize that the war on terror was throwing off cash in a big way. There had to be a play in that. And so Veritas, which had started investing in defense contractors in the 1990s, went after Dyncorp International.

Dyncorp was not a sexy buy, but it had a steady flow of revenue from large government contracts for police training in Afghanistan and other mundane tasks. One of Dyncorp's biggest assets was that it wasn't named Blackwater, and so it stood to benefit when Blackwater became radioactive in Washington.

To be sure, Dyncorp had its share of controversies, and in fact had been in trouble long before Blackwater landed in headlines about contractor scandals. When Dyncorp worked on a State Department contract to handle police training in Bosnia in the late 1990s, its personnel were accused of involvement in sex trafficking—a scandal so rich that it later formed the basis for a movie starring Rachel Weisz. Yet despite its track record, Dyncorp was given contracts to provide police training in Afghanistan and Iraq. In Afghanistan, Dyncorp was caught up in another scandal when its contractors reportedly paid for young "dancing boys" to entertain Afghan policemen, an incident that was described in a State Department cable released by WikiLeaks.

But fortunately for Dyncorp, these allegations of misdeeds by its personnel were overshadowed by Blackwater. After Blackwater's guards were involved in a 2007 shooting incident in Baghdad's Nisour Square in which at least seventeen Iraqi civilians were killed, pressure mounted in Washington for the government to dump Blackwater and give its business to other firms. Dyncorp was there to pick up the pieces.

McKeon's private equity firm, Veritas Capital, acquired Dyncorp in a leveraged buyout in 2005. *Forbes* magazine, which provided excellent coverage of McKeon and Dyncorp, later called it "the most lucrative deal of the wars in Iraq and Afghanistan." (But precisely because Dyncorp was such a sweet deal, it led to a split between McKeon and one of his closest business partners and friends, who accused McKeon of squeezing the partner out in order to keep more for himself, leading to acrimony and lawsuits.)

McKeon was able to ride the surge in spending by the State Department and Pentagon in Iraq and Afghanistan, and then adroitly sold the firm for a huge profit just as the American involvement in Iraq was winding down in 2010. When McKeon sold out to another Wall Street player, Stephen Feinberg of Cerberus Capital, *Forbes* once again lauded McKeon's move, saying that, "for all the talk about Blackwater and Houston oil industry firms connected to Dick Cheney, it took a Wall Street player to truly figure out how to play the war game." *Forbes* estimated that McKeon reaped a windfall, turning his own $48 million initial investment into as much as $320 million.

Sadly, for whatever reason, it wasn't enough for McKeon. In 2012, just two years after scoring one of the biggest paydays of the war on terror, McKeon committed suicide at his multimillion-dollar Connecticut home. No explanation has ever been made public. In 2013, McKeon's estate began selling off his holdings, offering a glimpse into the glittered world of the oligarchs of the war on terror. McKeon's estate sold two homes in Darien, Connecticut, with a combined price tag of more than $13 million; listed a Fifth Avenue co-op apartment in Manhattan for $11.5 million; and sold a 10,000-square-foot beachfront home in the Hamptons for $60 million.

More than a decade after 9/11, the war imperative, the war economy, and the war lobby all remain powerful in Washington. The transfer of power from one political party to another seems to have had little effect. But the homeland security gravy train will someday have to come to an end. With trillion-dollar annual federal deficits and a mountainous national debt, the country cannot sustain this spending on counterterrorism, and political leaders in Washington will eventually have to say "Enough."

In late 2012, just before he resigned his post, Jeh Charles Johnson, the Pentagon's general counsel, gave a speech at Oxford University. It was one of the first efforts by a top American official to raise the possibility of bringing the war on terror to a close. Johnson's speech presaged the themes that President Obama used in his national security address in May 2013. Al Qaeda's leadership has been so decimated, Johnson said, that the United States should begin to think about when it can call off the war on terror. Victory could be declared, and the remnants of al Qaeda could be dealt with as a law enforcement problem. That would mean returning to a pre-9/11 normalcy.

"I do believe that on the present course, there will come a tipping point—a tipping point at which so many of the leaders and operatives of al Qaeda and its affiliates have been killed or captured, and the group is no longer able to attempt or launch a strategic attack against the United States, such that al Qaeda as we know it, the organization that our Congress authorized the military to pursue in 2001, has been effectively destroyed," Johnson said. "At that point, we must be able to say to ourselves that our efforts should no longer be considered an 'armed conflict' against al Qaeda and its associated forces; rather, a counterterrorism effort against individuals who are the scattered remnants of al Qaeda, or are parts of groups unaffiliated with al Qaeda, for which the law enforcement and intelligence resources of our government are principally responsible, in cooperation with the international community—with our military assets available in reserve to address continuing and imminent terrorist threats."

"'War' must be regarded as a finite, extraordinary and unnatural state of affairs," Johnson added. "War permits one man—if he is a 'privileged belligerent,' consistent with the laws of war—to kill another. War violates the natural order of things, in which children bury their parents; in war parents bury their children. In its twelfth year, we must not accept the current conflict, and all that it entails, as the 'new normal.' Peace must be regarded as the norm toward which the human race continually strives."

★

President Obama's national security address five months later hit many of the same themes. He said that "America is at a crossroads" in its fight against terror, and warned that the nation "must define the nature and scope of this struggle or else it will define us. We have to be mindful of James Madison's warning that no nation could preserve its freedom in the midst of continual warfare."

The speeches by Obama and Johnson raised an intriguing question—wealth can't be generated from the war on terror forever, can it?

But nervous defense and intelligence contractors put on edge by the Obama administration's rhetoric could rest easy. In October 2013, just five months after Obama's speech, General Atomics was awarded a contract worth up to $377 million to build twenty-four more Reaper drones for the air force. That same month, Obama named Jeh Johnson to be secretary of the Department of Homeland Security—less than one year after Johnson's speech in which he tried to imagine an end to the war on terror.

PART II

POWER

4

ROSETTA

New York. Humid, overcast July weather. The narrow streets of lower Manhattan are nearly empty. In courtroom 21D of the U.S. District Court for the Southern District of New York, in the Daniel Patrick Moynihan Federal Building at 500 Pearl Street, the Honorable George B. Daniels presiding, a patent case drones on.

The arcane case has an unusually large audience of esteemed lawyers listening in, but only because they are waiting patiently on the back benches of the courtroom for the next case on Judge Daniels's docket, *In re Terrorist Attacks on September 11, 2001, MDL 1570.*

Judge Daniels, a balding man with glasses, a moustache, and a gravel-voiced New York accent, spars with the patent lawyers, and then, having exhausted the minutiae of patent law, calls for a break. When he returns, he says he will hear about September 11, and so the lawyers in the back of the courtroom spring to life. More than a dozen file awkwardly forward to their familiar tables. They know their places from long practice. They have all been here many times before.

America has spent the long years since the September 11, 2001, attacks exhausting its soldiers and its treasury fighting wars in Iraq, Afghanistan, and a global war on terror. But here in courtroom 21D, time seems frozen. A lawsuit brought in the heated aftermath of 9/11 (now consolidated into a larger legal action), pointing the finger of blame at the financial elite of Saudi Arabia, accusing them of financing al Qaeda and the terrorist strikes against New York and Washington, and seeking a trillion dollars in damages, still shambles through the American legal system. Progress, any movement at all, is barely perceptible.

Many of the original targets of the lawsuit were dismissed from the case years ago. Even Al Baraka Investment and Development Corporation, a Saudi-based financial services firm that gave its name to the main 9/11 lawsuit, *Burnett et al. v. Al Baraka et al.* (now consolidated, along with several other 9/11 lawsuits, into *In re Terrorist Attacks on September 11, 2001*) was dismissed from the case in 2005.

But the case grinds on, just a few blocks from the World Trade Center site, and a trial in the case, if it ever happens, is still years away. It may never go before a jury. On this day, the two sides were conducting painfully drawn-out arguments over procedural issues, including discovery, the process to determine whether the lawyers for the plaintiffs (in the *Burnett* case, there are 4,733 plaintiffs, representing 2,762 victims) can obtain the documents and other information from the defendants that they say they need to pursue their case.

George Daniels has displayed time and again why he has earned a reputation as one of the slowest federal judges in the nation. In 2010, lawyers representing the 9/11 victims took the unusual step of asking an appeals court to remove Judge Daniels from the case because he was moving too slowly. He wasn't taken off the case, and nothing changed.

And so almost everyone, undoubtedly including many of the lawyers who have trudged to lower Manhattan in the summer doldrums to attend Daniels's courtroom, have largely given up hope that the lawsuit will ever achieve its original objective — to gain justice for the victims of 9/11.

For a court case like *In re Terrorist Attacks on September 11, 2001*, which has occupied the federal docket for so long, there is remarkably little legal activity once the hearing actually gets under way. Daniels's great achievement for this day in July 2011, just two months short of the tenth anniversary of 9/11, is to issue an order on something called a Rule 54(b) motion, formalizing a long-since-accepted fact that one particular defendant is being dismissed; this ruling briefly excites the assembled lawyers, apparently in the hopes that they can now chew on the issue all over again in some different way.

The judge is about to gavel the hearing to a close when a hulking, broad-smiling New York lawyer stands up. It is Jim Kreindler, one of the lawyers for the 9/11 victims in *In re Terrorist Attacks*. "Your honor, I thought I might tell you where the case stands," Kreindler explains. "We've been working on this case for ten years, without getting paid, and that's been difficult. Ten years has been a long time. But I wanted to tell you that an end is in sight." Kreindler's bold statement is met with silence, save a ruffling of papers at the lawyers' tables.

"As you know, South Sudan has declared its independence, and I think it is now likely that the United States will remove Sudan from the list of state sponsors of terrorism," Kreindler says. "And I think both the United States and Sudan will then want to reach a settlement of all outstanding civil litigation. If Sudan settles and pays a significant amount, that will be a huge event in this case."

As Kreindler speaks, the frustration in his voice is clear. He is a man desperately looking for a way to cut the Gordian knot that now ensnares *In re Terrorist Attacks*. The possibility that an independence movement in Sudan could provide a way out of the 9/11 legal thicket entices him. Like a thirsty man who sees an oasis just up ahead, he is calling out to his comrades to join him and drink.

The other lawyers ignore Kreindler. They act as if they have heard it all before, the dreams of a final resolution of a case that has now consumed a good portion of their legal careers. They look the other way, like members of an extended family who have just witnessed a crazy uncle give his annual rant over a holiday dinner.

Only one lawyer bothers to stir, ever so briefly, to express his disappointment that he had not been informed of this "diplomatic issue" before Kreindler chose to share it with the whole court.

Kreindler takes his seat.

Judge Daniels responds as if Kreindler has not said a word. "Okay, let's continue to make progress and I'll see you all on January 13th."

The judge has just declared that the next hearing won't take place for another six months.

As the hearing ends, and the lawyers pack their papers, one lonely 9/11 widow sits quietly in the back benches of the courtroom, taking notes.

★

The fate of *Burnett v. Al Baraka* has become a depressing tale within the legal profession, but it is one with a bizarre backstory. It is a case study in how unintended consequences and the search for money and power have become the hallmarks of the war on terror.

The story begins with a legal campaign against the financiers of 9/11 launched by a brilliant Southern lawyer. It ends with controversy, finger-pointing, and unanswered questions amid evidence of strange and secretive intelligence ties between investigators hired to support the legal campaign and the Pentagon, the FBI, and the Drug Enforcement Administration.

The story shows how, during the war on terror, greed and ambition have been married to unlimited rivers of cash and the sudden deregulation of American national security to create a climate in which clever men could seemingly create rogue intelligence operations with little or no adult supervision. It is also a story of the potential abuse of power: how federal agencies, including the Defense Department and the FBI, may have perverted the American legal system. American officials who prosecuted the global war on terror in the name of the victims of 9/11 may have enabled and cooperated in the hijacking of their efforts to seek justice.

Crazy became the new normal in the war on terror, and the original objectives of the war got lost in the process. One of the unintended consequences has been to deny the families of the victims of the 9/11 attacks their day in court. Their lawsuit has been idling in court for years. In fact, more than a decade later, one of the few things the families of the 9/11 victims have to show for their trillion-dollar lawsuit is an Afghan drug dealer sitting in an American prison. He was lured to the United States through an intelligence operation conducted for the U.S. government by the people who were also acting as investigators supporting the 9/11 case.

Above all, this is a story about a mystery, one that reflects the confusion that has become all too common in the American national security apparatus. Since 2001, the United States has poured billions of dollars down one rabbit hole after another, searching for the magic bullet to battle terrorism. The years since the 9/11 attacks have been a time when it is often difficult to determine what is real—and what is concoction.

On the morning of September 11, 2001, Deena Burnett was up early with her three daughters when her husband, Tom, an executive with a medical device company who was returning home to California from a business trip to New York, called from his seat on United Airlines flight 93. In a few rushed words, he told her that his plane had been hijacked and asked her to call the authorities. During a series of frantic conversations, Deena told Tom about hijacked planes crashing into the World Trade Center and Pentagon, and he told her that he was planning to fight back against the hijackers with a group of other passengers. On their fourth call of the morning, Tom Burnett told his wife: "We're going to do something." He never called back.

In the aftermath of the 9/11 attacks, most Americans were not searching for justice. They were in the mood for retribution and revenge. The Bush administration quickly threw out any notion of using the American legal system to arrest and prosecute those responsible for the attacks, despite the fact that the criminal case involving the biggest al Qaeda attack prior to 9/11, the 1998 suicide bombings of two

U.S. embassies in East Africa, had been successfully prosecuted in federal court in New York a few months before September 11, with convictions and life sentences for four al Qaeda operatives.

The U.S. legal system had put together a remarkably successful track record on terrorism — especially on cases involving al Qaeda. By the time of the 9/11 attacks, the FBI's New York office and the U.S. Attorney's Office for the Southern District of New York had become the government's leading experts on targeting al Qaeda. They already had an indictment of Osama bin Laden waiting to be used if he were captured and brought to the United States for trial.

But for the Bush administration, using the courts was never an option. It smacked of the 1990s, of the Clinton administration, and of a new phrase — "pre-9/11" thinking. Bush brushed aside the FBI and Justice Department, and turned instead to the Pentagon and Central Intelligence Agency to launch a global war, both overt and covert, on terrorism. Bush reached for a national security answer to terrorism rather than a law enforcement solution. That would turn out to be the crucial decision that would alter the history of the next decade.

Deena Burnett was one of the first Americans to be shocked into the war on terror. But once she recovered from the immediate trauma of losing her husband, she had the courage to find her voice and become a leading spokeswoman for the group that would become known as the 9/11 families. Despite Bush's declaration of war, many of these families were eager to seek accountability through a more conventional path. In particular, Tom Burnett's father was driven by a determination to sue anyone responsible for funding or supporting the terrorists who had murdered his son. And so, in November 2001, Deena Burnett called Ronald Motley, a South Carolina lawyer famed for securing the largest class-action settlement in U.S. history with a victory over the tobacco industry.

At the time, Ron Motley was like a shark out of water. In the late 1990s, no lawyer in America had been more celebrated, more triumphant. He had won the largest legal victory ever in the United States, bringing Big Tobacco to its knees through a $246 billion settlement with a group of states' attorneys general. But in the years since that historic victory, he had been restless, and by September 11, 2001, he was searching for his next big case.

Motley took Deena Burnett's call and agreed to fight a legal battle against terrorism, much to the chagrin of Joseph Rice, the partner who kept an eye on the bottom line at their firm, Motley Rice. Rice knew how difficult it would be to ever repeat their tobacco success.

But Ron Motley would not be swayed. He was going to take on Saudi Arabia, the richest oil kingdom on earth, a country with more political influence in Washington than almost any other foreign power. It was also the native country of fifteen of the nineteen hijackers on 9/11, and there was a widespread belief in the United States that wealthy Saudis had been financing terrorism for years. The Saudis, Motley was convinced, were behind 9/11, and he was going to hold them accountable.

On August 15, 2002, at a Washington press conference, standing with Deena Burnett and other 9/11 family members by his side, Motley announced that he had filed a trillion-dollar lawsuit — *Burnett et al. v. Al Baraka Investment and Development Corporation et al.* — accusing Saudi banks, charities, and even members of the Saudi royal family of financing Osama bin Laden's reign of terror.

Now all Ron Motley had to do was prove it.

Motley realized that in order to jump-start his massive legal assault on the Saudi elite, he would need evidence to prove that the defendants had actually financed terrorism. He would have to back up his claims that there were significant ties between the Saudi financial elite and al Qaeda.

To help him in the hunt, Motley decided he needed to hire his own investigators. He wanted to create his own intelligence service, built from the ground up, to unlock the secrets of 9/11. He was determined to bring together the greatest collection of antiterrorism experts outside of the CIA, experts who were willing to take on the oil-rich Saudis in a way that the Bush administration was not. But Ron Motley could never have guessed what he would end up with instead.

★

As he started to assemble his investigative team, Motley first turned to a French writer and analyst who claimed to have ties to French intelligence.

The 9/11 attacks brought a sudden burst of notoriety for Jean-Charles Brisard. Just two months after the attacks, he published one of the first books to deal with 9/11, one that made sensational accusations against the Saudis. In *Forbidden Truth,* published in France in November 2001, Brisard named banks, charities, and individuals in Saudi Arabia that he claimed were responsible for funding al Qaeda. He took particular aim at one of the richest men in Saudi Arabia—Khalid bin Mahfouz.

Brisard devoted an entire chapter of his book to bin Mahfouz, whom he dubbed "the Banker of Terror." "The bin Mahfouz financial and charity network is one of the most active in facilitating Osama bin Laden's activities," Brisard wrote. In a separate paper he published in 2002, which he said was submitted to the president of the United Nations Security Council, Brisard named bin Mahfouz as one of seven prominent Saudis who were the "main individual sponsors of terrorism."

For Ron Motley, who knew virtually nothing about Saudi Arabia, *Forbidden Truth* provided a road map to follow as he put together his case in 2002. Motley took the Saudi organizations and individuals identified in Brisard's book—including Khalid bin Mahfouz—and named them as defendants in the *Burnett* case. *Forbidden Truth* became Ron Motley's bible.

Brisard said that he first met with the Motley Rice lawyers in June 2002, before the 9/11 lawsuit was filed, during a trip to Washington to testify before Congress. Jodi Flowers, a Motley Rice lawyer and one of Motley's key lieutenants, contacted Brisard and arranged for him to meet with Motley and a group of lawyers at a Washington hotel where they talked about terrorism financing for three hours. At the end of the session, Motley asked Brisard to work for him. As Motley Rice was preparing its lawsuit, Brisard helped the lawyers to identify potential defendants, he recalls.

"They were basing the names of the defendants on my writings," said Brisard. "I was participating in the selection process of defendants." Soon, Brisard set up a five-member team in Paris to launch a global hunt for documents that could establish financial links between wealthy Saudi institutions and al Qaeda. He began reaching out to his contacts in governments throughout Europe, seeking access to their files on al Qaeda. Brisard's biggest coup was acquiring what became known as "the golden chain," a document that was to become a key part of Motley's case as well as one of the most widely disputed pieces of evidence of Saudi complicity in terrorism financing.

In 2002, Bosnian police, working with the CIA, raided the Sarajevo offices of Benevolence International Foundation, an Islamic charitable organization. There, on a computer they found a document that purported to identify early financial backers of Osama bin Laden and al Qaeda. The Justice Department used the document as evidence in a criminal case against Benevolence International in Chicago, and a key al Qaeda defector and informant, Jamal al-Fadl, testified that it was authentic and dubbed it "the golden chain."

Brisard traveled to Bosnia in 2003 to try to get the golden chain and other Benevolence files from the Bosnian government. He was armed with formal legal requests from U.S. District Judge James Robertson, the federal judge in Washington who was then presiding over Motley's lawsuit against the Saudis. The Bosnians were willing, but the Justice Department wanted the documents to be used exclusively for its criminal case in Chicago. The Justice Department finally agreed only after the president of the Bosnian Supreme Court issued an order asking the Americans to share the documents with the Motley Rice team.

The biggest problem, however, was that it was virtually impossible to prove whether the golden-chain document was genuine. No one could say who wrote it, exactly when it was written, or what the list of names really meant. It was supposedly a list of donors to bin Laden's efforts to support Arab fighters in Afghanistan in the late 1980s. Yet at that time, support for anti-Soviet mujahideen in Afghanistan was official American and Saudi policy. So, it was difficult to show whether the golden-chain document was really a smoking gun identifying al Qaeda's founding financial backers.

Meanwhile, Brisard's work came under scrutiny in Saudi Arabia. Khalid bin Mahfouz was not amused by *Forbidden Truth* or by the fact that Brisard's book was now providing the blueprint for a massive American lawsuit blaming him for financing 9/11. Bin Mahfouz was an angry billionaire with plenty of lawyers, and by 2003, he had decided to sue Brisard for libel. Other defendants in the *Burnett* case followed his lead and also filed libel cases against Brisard. Soon the French investigator was fending off lawsuits in Belgium, Switzerland, France, and Britain.

To Brisard and Motley, the libel suits against Brisard's book appeared to be a Saudi counterattack on the 9/11 lawsuit. "No one sued me until I started working for Motley Rice," said Brisard. "It was obvious they were targeting me as the lead investigator for Motley Rice."

Ultimately, Brisard was able to fend off the libel suits in every country — except Britain. There he didn't put up a fight, other than to argue that he had not authorized the publication of his book in England. The libel laws in Britain at the time were notoriously difficult for authors, so he defaulted. As part of a settlement with bin Mahfouz, Brisard issued an extensive apology and recanted many of the assertions he had made in his book and in the report that he said he had submitted to the president of the UN Security Council.

Brisard also had to acknowledge that he had done some editing of the golden-chain document. Among the names of purported al Qaeda financiers listed in the document was someone named "bin Mahfoodh," and Brisard was forced to admit in his court-ordered apology that in the English translation of the document he had amended the name to read "Khalid bin Mahfouz." He said he had changed the name because he believed that it made the document more accurate. "I inserted the forename Khalid before bin Mahfouz in the amended translation, but I accept that the reality is that the name Khalid is not contained within the original Arabic document," Brisard admitted.

In fact, Brisard had to make a series of admissions of error — including that he had gotten it completely wrong when he wrote that Khalid bin Mahfouz was Osama bin Laden's brother-in-law. It was a brutal setback not only for Brisard but also for Ron Motley.

But Ron Motley wasn't willing to give up. He hired Michael Asimos, a bearded, long-haired former army officer and stockbroker who at first seemed perfectly suited to roam the world and hunt down the smoking gun Motley so desperately wanted in order to take down the Saudis.

Years later, it was difficult for the Motley Rice lawyers to explain exactly how Asimos had arrived at their doorstep. It was also difficult for them to describe who he was, or why he had come. To this day, they aren't certain whom he was really working for. Like the itinerant soldier in *The Return of Martin Guerre*, Asimos could become whatever people wanted him to be.

In that, Asimos was hardly alone in the post-9/11 world. He was one of many dream weavers who flourished in Washington's global war on terror, cashing in on the counterterrorism gold rush. What the stock market and the Internet bubble were to the 1990s, the counterterrorism bubble was to the first years of the new millennium, and there was a cadre of men willing and able to take advantage.

Asimos was tall, broad-shouldered, bright, and articulate, with a presence at once friendly yet slightly conspiratorial, as if just being with him lets you in on a secret. When he met Ron Motley and the other lawyers involved in the 9/11 case, he struck them as a secret agent straight out of central casting. For tort lawyers whose idea of combat was a long day in a courtroom — lawyers who had learned most of what they knew about war from the movies — Mike Asimos seemed like Rambo come to life. He was the kind of guy they all wanted to be in high school. To Motley Rice, he appeared to have come out of nowhere at just the right time.

Born in 1961, the son of a Greek owner of a diner in York, Pennsylvania, Asimos went to West Point, where he joined the Arabic language club and was jokingly nicknamed "the Envoy" in his West Point yearbook because of his interest in the Middle East. The yearbook suggests that, even while in college, he had already developed a reputation for being a little bit mysterious. "Whether it was drill, intramurals, or a DPE [physical education] test, 'As' wasn't there," read his yearbook inscription. "The 'book' grew throughout the years, but a whole chapter was needed to explain how 'the Envoy' missed finals for another Middle East vacation. If he wasn't in the air assisting the U.S. resolve the Middle East crisis, he was on the road cruising to good times in his car — if it wasn't loaned out! Mount up!"

Asimos graduated from West Point in 1984, and by 1987, he was assigned to the staff of the John F. Kennedy Special Warfare Center at Fort Bragg, the training center for army Special Operations, according to his military records. In 1989, he received a meritorious service medal for his work on Special Operations training programs. He left active duty in July 1989 with the rank of captain. He remained in the reserves until 1998.

While he was in the army, Asimos experienced a strange firsthand encounter with an al Qaeda mole inside the U.S. military. At Fort Bragg, Asimos met Sgt. Ali Mohamed, a former Egyptian Army officer who had briefly been in contact with the CIA, which was interested in recruiting him as an asset. Mohamed had later immigrated to the United States and enlisted in the U.S. Army. After the 1998 bombings of two U.S. embassies in East Africa, Mohamed was arrested and charged with conspiracy to aid terrorism. It turned out he was secretly Osama bin Laden's chief of security, and had come to the United States in order to infiltrate the army and get to know American security tactics and methods.

Asimos was quoted by the *New York Times* in its first story disclosing the existence of the government's case against Mohamed. In a

1998 article Ben Weiser and I coauthored, Asimos recalled how, while he was stationed at the Kennedy Special Warfare Center in 1988, he had given Sergeant Mohamed some unclassified maps of Afghanistan for a trip he said he was planning to take on his own time to Afghanistan to fight with the mujahideen against the Soviets. "I remember Ali coming back at some point in 1988 and telling me how much Ahmad Shah Massoud [an Afghan rebel leader] was pleased that I took him some maps," Asimos said in the *Times* article. Asimos also told the *Times* that in 1988, he had been running a classified war game at Fort Bragg, and that he warned participants to be careful what they said in front of Mohamed, who did not have a security clearance.

After Asimos left active duty, he attended the Fletcher School of Law and Diplomacy at Tufts University in Medford, Massachusetts, and received a master's degree in 1991. In the early 1990s, Asimos worked as a stockbroker, but he left behind a messy paper trail exposed by the Securities and Exchange Commission in 1994. According to an SEC report, the agency found that in 1992 and 1993, Asimos had convinced both his friends and family members to turn over large amounts of money so that he could invest it on their behalf. He claimed to have gained access to a special program that would allow small investors to put their money into the same high-earning investment vehicles normally reserved for institutional investors and wealthy individuals. He told his clients that their money would be held in his name, but he said that was the only way they could take advantage of this special offer.

The only problem was, the special deal didn't exist. Asimos forged documents to make it appear as if he had invested his clients' money in the special program, according to the SEC report. In reality, he had simply deposited the money in his own bank accounts and used some of it to pay off his own debts, according to the SEC report. But Asimos was so sloppy that he was eventually caught and forced to return the money to his clients in order to avoid more serious trouble. He admitted to the scheme, cut a deal with the SEC, and was barred from acting as a stockbroker for at least three years.

Despite his past trouble with the SEC, Asimos was able to move back into the financial industry in Charleston, where he opened his own firm, Atlantic Financial, specializing in advising small companies on mergers and obtaining lines of credit. In 1999, his company was purchased by Seaboard & Company, a local bond trading firm, which made the acquisition primarily to hire Asimos, according to a business executive who was involved with Seaboard at the time.

But the partners in Seaboard eventually became concerned about Asimos because he frequently talked vaguely about having secret, ongoing connections to the U.S. military's Special Operations, according to the business executive. Asimos often suggested to the Seaboard partners that he had another life in the shadows, beyond the world of finance, the business executive said. Seaboard's staid bond traders did not want any part of that and eventually split with Asimos.

When the 9/11 attacks occurred, some of Asimos's erstwhile colleagues in the financial industry told each other they were happy that they had nothing to do with the world of shadows in which he seemed to revel. By contrast, Mike Asimos was reborn on 9/11. In the process, he became one of the most intriguing figures of the post-9/11 age.

Mystery and unanswered questions have enveloped Asimos's post-9/11 life. After 9/11, Asimos has said that he began to look for a way to get involved in the new global war on terror. Although he wasn't interested in rejoining the military, he wanted to be in on the action, and later told me and others that he went to Afghanistan sometime after the 9/11 attacks. It appears that Asimos did go to Afghanistan for the government in some capacity soon after the attacks. He told his wife that he was going to Afghanistan and left his home in Charleston for an extended period. When he came back in early 2002, he also told others that he had been in Afghanistan. But it remains uncertain exactly who sent him, whom he was working for, and what he did while he was there.

After he returned, Asimos began working as an investigator on the 9/11 lawsuit for Ron Motley and his law firm, Motley Rice. Exactly how and why that happened is still a matter of dispute that says a lot about the bizarre nature of the global war on terror.

Over the course of several years, Asimos repeatedly told me and many other people that he had been secretly assigned by top Defense Department officials to, in effect, infiltrate the Motley Rice lawsuit and use his job as an investigator as cover for a clandestine Defense Department intelligence operation, a kind of off-the-books covert action program. In some interviews, Asimos said that he had been secretly sent to Motley Rice by then Deputy Defense Secretary Paul Wolfowitz; at other times he said he was sent by senior Defense Department officials close to Wolfowitz. Asimos said that Wolfowitz wanted him to turn the lawsuit into an intelligence operation through which all of the information gathered by the law firm would be turned over to the Pentagon. What's more, he said, he was tasked to conduct clandestine missions for the government while working for Motley Rice.

Asimos told me that he had met with Wolfowitz, who wanted him to arrange a meeting with Ron Motley. Wolfowitz, Asimos said, wished to secretly enlist Motley and his law firm in the Bush administration's fight against terrorism. Pentagon officials, according to Asimos, wanted access to all the information that Motley Rice would acquire in its pursuit of the Saudis, using Asimos's role as an investigator for Motley Rice as cover, essentially turning the 9/11 families' lawsuit into an intelligence-collection enterprise for the Pentagon. That would allow Wolfowitz to conduct operations far outside the normal intelligence channels of the U.S. government.

After Asimos had told me this story, with only slight variations, a number of times over several years, I learned that he had told essentially the same tale to a number of other people. After I told him I was going to write about it in this book, he sent me a letter denying that his work for Motley Rice had been a cover for a Pentagon operation and that anyone who had told me that was wrong. In a subsequent statement, he wrote that "a small group of people opposed to the

9/11 litigation have repeatedly made false claims about the research effort—its origins, funding goals, etc. I believe a close examination of the current situation with Mr. Risen would show many of these individuals to be his principle sources." Asimos has refused follow-up interviews for the book, warning that writing about him would put him and his family at risk. His New York lawyer, Kelly Moore, has not responded to questions.

When asked in an interview whether he believed that Asimos had arranged a secret relationship between the Pentagon and his law firm, Ron Motley said that he had never heard of such an idea. (Motley subsequently died in 2013.) But despite Motley's statements, several others working on the 9/11 lawsuit said that they suspected that Asimos was operating as a clandestine agent of the government while he was working for Motley Rice. Harry Huge, a co-counsel on the *Burnett* case, said that he thinks there was some kind of secret relationship between Asimos and the Pentagon while Asimos was working with Motley Rice. "I began to have suspicions that he was working for the government," recalled Huge. "I came to believe that things weren't what they seemed."

Patrick Jost, who worked with Asimos as an investigator for Motley Rice, said that Asimos made it clear to him on several occasions that he had a secret relationship with the Defense Department. A former analyst at FINCEN—the Financial Crimes Enforcement Network at the Treasury Department—Jost was considered one of the government's leading minds on *hawala,* the Islamic money transfer system. Short, stout, and with strong opinions, Jost could not have been more unlike Asimos. The two came to detest each other.

Jost said that his suspicions of Asimos grew after he received a strange phone call one day from the Pentagon. A man who identified himself as an army officer started asking questions about a memorandum Jost had just written, a confidential analysis produced for lawyers on the *Burnett* lawsuit. Jost was stunned that the army officer had the memo and quickly got off the call. Jost phoned Mike Elsner, one of the Motley Rice lawyers handling the *Burnett* case, to warn him that the Pentagon had obtained privileged materials intended for the lawsuit. Elsner responded that he was sure Asimos was passing documents directly to the Defense Department, Jost recalled. Elsner told Jost that he should be careful about sharing documents in the future.

★

In an internal Motley Rice document related to Asimos and the 9/11 lawsuit, the firm says that it discovered in October 2003 that Asimos was sharing Jost's strategy and analysis memos with officials at the Defense Department (DOD). "I think I knew he was doing work on a freelance basis for DOD," recalled Elsner. "There were certain projects for DOD. I don't know if he was sent to us by DOD. I suppose I had a sense he had an involvement in a private intelligence operation."

Ansar Rahel, an Afghan lawyer hired by Motley Rice for the *Burnett* lawsuit, said he worked with Asimos when he was first hired as an investigator. Rahel said that Asimos told him and others at the law firm that he had been sent by the Pentagon to keep an eye on the case. "Mike told me that he was reporting to Wolfowitz," recalled Rahel, who now lives in California. "He said he worked for him, or reported to him. He said they wanted him to keep an eye on things on the lawsuit. I assumed that was Wolfowitz's office."

"Asimos would joke about it," Rahel remembered. "He would say, make sure you give me these documents, so I can get them over to them. It was kind of known that he was turning over everything to the DOD."

Joe Rice, Motley's partner, said in an interview that he believes that Asimos was working for the Pentagon, and that the Defense Department took advantage of Motley Rice and used the firm's lawsuit for intelligence-gathering. "I think he was working for the government all along and they just used us," said Rice. "He was using us to get stuff for the government and we got stuck with the bill. They knew we were dedicated to investigating the 9/11 suit, and they used us."

For his part, Paul Wolfowitz denies knowing anything about Mike Asimos or a secret plan to hijack the 9/11 lawsuit in order to turn it into a Pentagon intelligence operation. No one at the Defense Department has been willing to corroborate reports of an extensive formalized intelligence-sharing relationship between the Pentagon and Motley Rice. Steve Ganyard, who served as one of Wolfowitz's military assistants at the time, acknowledged that he did meet with Asimos and Deena Burnett once, because they wanted to arrange a meeting with Wolfowitz to discuss greater cooperation between the law firm and the Pentagon. But he said that, as far as he knew, nothing ever came of it. Douglas Feith, who served as undersecretary of defense for policy and was one of Wolfowitz's top lieutenants, also denied knowing anything. Patrick Jost said that he met Feith and other Defense officials through Asimos, although Asimos has repeatedly disputed Jost's credibility, and Feith denies ever meeting with either man.

Was Asimos just making idle boasts? One person he confided in, Mark Heilbrun, was a Capitol Hill staffer working on the Senate Judiciary Committee at the time. Heilbrun had gotten to know Asimos because the judiciary committee's chairman, Sen. Arlen Specter of Pennsylvania, had decided to try to investigate terrorist financing, and so Heilbrun was interested in what Motley Rice was finding out about the Saudis.

In several interviews, Heilbrun said that Asimos had told him about his secret relationship with Paul Wolfowitz and the Defense Department. Heilbrun also says he received confirmation that the special relationship existed. He said that Asimos further told him that his point of contact was an old friend from the army, Col. Steven Bucci, a Special Forces officer who had risen to the position of military assistant to Secretary of Defense Donald Rumsfeld. "Asimos would tell me that he was working with Paul Wolfowitz," recalled Heilbrun. "He said the guy to call is Steve Bucci. I probably had a dozen conversations with Bucci. I talked to Wolfowitz once about this."

Bucci was described to him as the conduit to Wolfowitz on this off-the-books operation, Heibrun recounted. "Bucci would tell me, yes, I'm working with Asimos. And then things would get done. There was no doubt that Bucci was the action officer, and that Asimos was on the same team as DOD. I've never seen that before. There was never any question that Asimos was working for Wolfowitz." A Motley Rice internal document says that on March 8, 2003, Bucci wrote an e-mail to Asimos thanking him for "the large quantity of stuff you and your friends have provided." He added that "quite a bit of it is becoming more and more valuable."

In an interview, Bucci apologized for having a fuzzy memory on many specifics but asserted that the only thing he did to foster a relationship between Motley Rice and the Pentagon was to connect Asimos with the Defense Intelligence Agency (DIA). Bucci said he had known Asimos in the army, and said that Asimos came to him sometime after he started working with Motley Rice. By that time, Asimos had acquired an Afghan document that was a directory of foreign fighters who had registered weapons with the Taliban government, Bucci recalled. Asimos told Bucci that, in addition to the weapons registry, the Motley Rice investigation had acquired a significant cache of materials extraneous to the lawsuit that they would be willing to turn over to the government.

Bucci said that he walked the weapons registry into the office of Lt. Gen. John Abizaid, who was then the director of the Joint Staff at the Pentagon, and explained the opportunity to acquire additional information from Motley Rice. Abizaid seemed impressed by the registry and directed Bucci to deliver the document to the director of the DIA, who would determine if the agency wanted to establish a relationship with the law firm. Shortly afterward, Bucci said, the law firm delivered "a truckload" of documents to the DIA. "It was at that point, I understand, that they got interested in Mike's connections, and the people he knew in the Pakistan/Afghanistan area, and they started a relationship and sharing information." In a follow-up e-mail, Bucci stressed, "Once I connected Mike to DIA, I was not privy to who was managing the effort, or what it produced."

As for Heilbrun's account that he had spoken to Bucci about Asimos on a dozen or so occasions, Bucci said, "I don't have any remembrance of that. I'm not denying it, but I don't have any recollection of it. I mean if somebody did call, I think I probably would've said, 'Yeah, he's doing good stuff.' I hadn't gotten any negative feedback from any of the intel people. . . . So if somebody had called me from the Senate and said, 'Is he one of the good guys? Is he trying to do something positive?' I probably said yes. But I don't recall the conversations, and I'm pretty sure I wouldn't have said 'Yeah, he's working for us,' like he's on the payroll and we're giving him his marching orders."

Analysts from the Defense Intelligence Agency also flew from Washington to Charleston to review the document database the law firm was constructing at Motley Rice's headquarters. In a December 2003 e-mail to Motley Rice lawyers, Asimos wrote that he had just gotten off the phone with Capt. Art Jones, assistant to DIA director Vice Adm. Lowell Jacoby, who told him that the DIA wanted to "get moving aggressively on working with us, including formalizing the channels for share of information, analysis, and field operations." DIA officials have since confirmed that analysts met with Motley Rice in Charleston to review its collection of documents.

When asked whether it was common practice for the DIA to encourage American citizens to participate in collecting raw intelligence on behalf of the agency, Bucci explained, "DIA lives and dies on voluntary interactions. . . . Additionally, America had just been attacked and lost 3,000 people, and we were about to invade two countries, and pursue an international enemy. There was a lot of, 'Let's get help wherever we can' going on."

Indeed, Ron Motley was willing to share information with the Defense Department — up to a point. "I think Ron just cared about winning the lawsuit," Ansar Rahel said. "I think Ron took pride in helping. Wolfowitz wrote a letter to Ron and the families thanking them. Every time he met the families, Motley would talk about how he was cooperating with the government."

The January 23, 2003, letter from Wolfowitz was addressed to the 9/11 families, in care of Ron Motley. "You have responded to President Bush's call for assistance in this national effort that is the Global War on Terrorism," the letter said. "In the midst of your loss, or perhaps because of it, you have never lost the focus that this Nation is at war. Your decision to share the large volume of data, including papers, computer disks, record books and other documents without any request for a quid pro quo is laudable and greatly assisted our analysts."

According to numerous sources familiar with the matter, Motley was open to providing information to the Bush administration but always hoped that the government would reciprocate, perhaps by giving Motley Rice access to classified intelligence reports on Saudi involvement in terrorist finance. The Bush administration, however, never returned the favor. That suggests that Pentagon officials merely accepted the information from Motley Rice and viewed it as nothing more than the voluntary, patriotic contributions of American citizens.

Of course, there is nothing wrong with the 9/11 families' volunteering to share information with the government. But extensive interviews, internal reports, e-mails, recordings, and other materials raise questions that have never been fully resolved over whether Asimos was pursuing sources, investigations, and operations that had as much or more to do with the interests and demands of the United States government than with the needs of the 9/11 families and Motley Rice. His work as reflected in internal reports and communications strongly suggests that some of the research that Asimos was conducting was being guided by the interests of government officials involved in the ongoing war on terror. This wasn't a mere volunteering of civic-minded citizens. The bedeviling question is whether it was, in effect, a hijacking by the government.

For example, while working for Motley Rice, Asimos lured an Afghan drug lord with ties to the Taliban to the United States, where he was arrested and jailed. It was an operation that, in the end, had nothing to do with the 9/11 lawsuit. Whether Mike Asimos was actually doing the bidding of the government during the period in which he was working for Motley Rice threatened to become a major public issue in the federal trial of the Afghan drug lord. A federal judge eventually ruled the issue inadmissible, and the question was never resolved in public.

After being introduced to Mike Asimos by another Charleston lawyer, Ron Motley was sold, and soon began to refer to him by a code name—"the Traveler." Motley seemed convinced that he had found his most daring investigator, a man who could take on the Saudis. No one at Motley Rice seems to have asked too many probing questions about Asimos's background or where he had really come from.

At first, Motley Rice lawyers were so dazzled by Asimos that they did not mind that he seemed to have secretive government connections. When he told Motley Rice lawyers that he would need sophisticated communications gear to operate in the field, he impressed them by showing up with several communications experts of unknown origin. Joe Rice said that the first time he was introduced to Asimos, he had arrived with a handful of "men in suits" carrying high-end communications gear. "I didn't ask who the other guys were," Rice said. "They had encryption machines and untraceable cell phones and other gear. It had enough credibility. We gave them $50 to $100,000."

Asimos decided to begin his investigative efforts in Afghanistan rather than the country that was the focus of the lawsuit, Saudi Arabia. Ron Motley and the other lawyers at Motley Rice did not object. They offered little direction or supervision for Asimos.

At first, Asimos worked with Ansar Rahel, who had been hired by Motley Rice to help with the *Burnett* case, Rahel said. He had grown up in the United States, but his father had been press secretary to the last king of Afghanistan, Mohamed Zahir Shah, who at the time of 9/11 was living in exile in Rome. Rahel was hired by Motley Rice in 2002 when Ron Motley was still casting about trying to figure out how to investigate 9/11 and the Saudis.

Rahel said that he helped Asimos to make contacts with prominent Afghans in Kabul, just as the new Hamid Karzai government was taking control. Afghanistan seemed suited to Asimos, Rahel believes, because he was far from any supervision by Motley Rice. But he still had Motley Rice's extravagant financial backing. "I'm not sure anybody else knew exactly what he was doing, and that's the way he liked it," Rahel said. "In Afghanistan, there were these huge spaces where no one had any real information about what was going on, and he would exploit that."

One foreign correspondent who reported from Afghanistan recalled having first met Asimos through Brian Mallon, a former Immigration and Naturalization Service agent from New Jersey who was then working in Afghanistan for a new mobile phone company. Mallon joined up with Asimos and became his trusted right-hand man in the field. The correspondent recalls that the two men became fixtures in the Mustafa Hotel, a notorious Kabul hangout for contractors, reporters, and other drifting expatriates who had washed up in postinvasion Kabul. It was often difficult for other people there to figure out what Asimos and Mallon were really doing there. In short, they fit right in at the Mustafa.

Asimos returned to the United States after acquiring the Taliban registry of al Qaeda foreign fighters authorized to carry weapons in the country, which he considered to be an invaluable discovery. The document included names and photographs of al Qaeda foreign fighters who had been in Afghanistan. Although it was not clear what connection the document could have to the 9/11 lawsuit, Asimos saw it as a major coup. He met with the Motley Rice lawyers at the Willard Hotel in Washington, carefully showed them the document, and then told them that the Pentagon wanted it.

Harry Huge, one of Motley's co-counsels, and Chip Robertson, a Missouri lawyer and former aide to Attorney General John Ashcroft who had also joined the lawsuit, agreed to go with Asimos to meet with Bucci to discuss the document. Huge was reluctant to meet Bucci inside the Pentagon because he feared that once they were inside the building with the document, they would never see it again. He wasn't sure whether the al Qaeda weapons registry would ever be of any value to the 9/11 lawsuit, but he also didn't want it to disappear without a trace into the Defense Department.

Instead, they met at the Ritz-Carlton in nearby Pentagon City. They agreed to give Bucci the document as long as they could keep a copy. Huge and Chip Robertson then met privately with Judge James Robertson, the federal judge then overseeing the 9/11 lawsuit, and explained their encounter with the Pentagon. They told the judge that they wanted to be able to have a copy of the document admitted as evidence since they had given the original to the Pentagon. Huge and Chip Robertson agreed to place the copy of the document in an envelope, and then they both licked the envelope before sealing it; that way, they both had DNA proof linking them to the document. Judge Robertson, now retired, said in an interview that he remembers meeting with Harry Huge and Chip Robertson to discuss the special handling of a document in the 9/11 case but that he doesn't recall the specific details.

The weapons registry document never proved particularly significant in the 9/11 lawsuit, but the episode shows how the lawyers involved in the 9/11 case were initially willing to go along with Asimos and his strange relationship with the Pentagon.

After the Bush administration launched the invasion of Iraq in March 2003, Asimos informed his colleagues working on the *Burnett* case that the Pentagon was calling him back to duty. As always, he was suggestive but vague on what kind of work the Defense Department would have him doing.

Late one night, soon after the invasion, Asimos called Specter staffer Mark Heilbrun to ask for help, saying that "OSD" (the Office of the Secretary of Defense) secretly wanted him in Iraq but could not get him into the country through normal channels, Heilbrun said. According to Heilbrun, "[Asimos] said he was going to get a stash of documents. Somehow Wolfowitz wanted him to get documents from Iraq."

Asimos told Heilbrun that he needed Senator Specter's assistance to arrange his off-the-books mission, advising Heilbrun to confirm the arrangement with Bucci in Donald Rumsfeld's office. Asimos gave him Bucci's cell phone number, and Heilbrun called to ask if the Pentagon needed Specter's help in getting Asimos into Iraq. According to Heilbrun, Bucci said yes.

Heilbrun did not understand why the OSD could not get Asimos into the country via military transport. Nevertheless, he was willing to help, and arranged for Specter to call Deputy Secretary of State

Richard Armitage for assistance. Heilbrun said that Armitage told Specter (who died in 2012) that he should talk to Marc Grossman, then the U.S. ambassador to Turkey, who might be able to help Asimos cross the Turkish border into Iraq. Heilbrun said that he contacted Grossman. He, too, agreed to help.

In the end, Bucci says he is certain that his own, separate efforts helped Asimos to get into the country, because he ultimately made the arrangements to reserve his friend an open seat on a military flight into Kurdistan — an action that would later earn Bucci trouble back in Washington. He says that he has no recollection of Heilbrun's calling him about Asimos's traveling to Baghdad, but does remember Asimos's calling on his own behalf to ask for assistance. "Right after we did the invasion into Iraq, Mike called me and said, 'It would be very helpful to get into Kurdistan. . . . Is there any way you can help me do that?' I said, 'I don't know, I'll ask around and see.'"

Bucci did not seem to know with certainty what Asimos intended to do in Iraq but said, "I believed he was still working for [Motley Rice], but also believed he was providing useful info to our folks." So Bucci made his phone calls. As Bucci recounted in an interview, "I basically vouched for him — that he was doing legitimate stuff, that the information he was gathering had been of use to our intel people in the past and that he was a legitimate guy, and they put him on an airplane and got him into country."

After he arrived in Kurdish-controlled territory in northern Iraq in April 2003, Asimos contacted a small element of a ragtag force created by the Iraqi National Congress (INC), the Iraqi exile group headed by Ahmed Chalabi, the controversial Iraqi exile who many in Washington hoped would run a post-Saddam government in Iraq.

Chalabi sought to deploy the small force he had assembled to help him ride triumphantly into Baghdad. On the eve of the invasion, he gathered his force of about seven hundred in Kurdish-controlled territory in northern Iraq. But Chalabi lacked the formal backing of the

U.S. military, which meant his force did not have transportation or logistical support and could not get into the action. Through a secret process that caught most senior Bush administration officials by surprise, Chalabi managed to win the Pentagon's approval for an airlift of his force from Kurdistan to a captured airbase in southern Iraq, near Nasiriyah. He then drove with them to Baghdad and quickly set up shop at the Baghdad Hunting Club.

The airlift of Chalabi's force led to a bitter round of finger-pointing in Washington, where some senior officials saw it as a brazen attempt by the administration to quickly move Chalabi into a position of power. It was as if Wolfowitz — possibly working with Dick Cheney and a few other administration hardliners — was trying to launch a sudden coup, taking advantage of the chaos of war to make Chalabi the leader before anyone else could fill the vacuum.

As a result, Chalabi's actions were being closely scrutinized in Washington, which made the sudden appearance of Mike Asimos, a former army officer and supposedly an investigator for the Charleston law firm of Motley Rice, all the more mysterious.

While Chalabi and his main force were flown to Nasiriyah, he left about one third of his group behind in northern Iraq. Asimos managed to find them in Kurdistan. He introduced himself to Nabeel Musawi, an INC political officer who had been left in charge when Chalabi went ahead with the larger group. Asimos told Musawi that he had been sent by the Pentagon to help the INC, and Musawi said he was welcome to join them as they drove south to join Chalabi and the rest of the INC in Baghdad. They finally arrived in Baghdad in mid-April, just a day or two after Chalabi had arrived from the south.

When they showed up at the Baghdad Hunting Club, with Asimos riding shotgun in an INC truck, Chalabi's senior aides were immediately suspicious. Asimos appeared with long hair, a pistol strapped to his thigh, and the type of bulletproof vest worn by journalists in war zones. Zaab Sethna, one of Chalabi's key advisors, asked Musawi about the stranger. "He told me this is Mike, he's from the Pentagon, and he has been really helpful," Sethna recalled. Asimos introduced himself to Francis Brooke, an American who was a longtime spokesman for Chalabi, and told him that he was a former Special Forces of-

ficer who had been sent by the Office of the Secretary of Defense to
help the INC.

Brooke recalled that Asimos was carrying a lot of cash with
him — approximately $25,000 — and that he had what appeared to be
official travel orders from the Defense Department. "He said he was
from OSD, and was there to lend us a hand," said Brooke. "He said he
was a high-level emissary, but he was always vague. I wanted to throw
him out right away. He didn't smell right."

In an April 2003 e-mail he wrote from Iraq, Asimos told other investigators working with Motley Rice back in the United States that
he had identified "a couple of things here that would really benefit the
boyz back in CS [Charleston] but getting cut loose to pursue them has
been a challenge. Have some folks back in DC working to get me solo
so I can exploit." In the e-mail, he asked Patrick Jost, "if you are aware
of any specific things/records/dox/individuals i should be looking for
here pls advise."

Asimos indicated to Chalabi's aides that he was interested in gaining access to the documents that Chalabi's group had already started
to collect from Iraqi government ministries, particularly the headquarters of the Iraqi intelligence service. Chalabi had used his mili-
tia force to move more swiftly than the U.S. military or the CIA to
track down the files of Saddam Hussein's regime, and was starting to
build his own library of secret Iraqi intelligence files. "Asimos was interested in the documents, he wanted to see what we were getting,"
recalled Brooke.

While it is not clear what Asimos was looking for in the documents, neoconservatives in the Bush administration, including both
Cheney and Wolfowitz, were eager at the time to find evidence of a
purported connection between Saddam Hussein's regime and the
9/11 attacks. They had sought to justify the invasion of Iraq by suggesting such a connection, and so it is possible that they were eager to
gain access to Chalabi's cache of captured Iraqi documents to find evidence that would vindicate their decision to invade. Ultimately, such
evidence proved illusory.

But no one from the Pentagon had ever bothered to tell anyone at
the INC that Asimos was coming. In fact, the U.S. Central Command,

the military command in charge of the invasion of Iraq, already had a liaison officer assigned to the INC. Col. Ted Seel, an army officer who was the official liaison between Chalabi's group and the U.S. military in Iraq, was surprised and confused by Asimos's appearance as well. "He was very flamboyant, he was larger than life," recalled Seel. "He came across as very flashy, and like he was playing a role. He told me that he was there because OSD sent him," he added. "But he also said he was there representing the law firm, and that there were people he needed to interview in Baghdad for the lawsuit. He said he was there both for OSD and the law firm, so I wasn't sure who Asimos was really working for."

Seel reported Asimos's arrival at the INC's compound to his superiors at U.S. Central Command, and asked them if they could confirm that he had been sent by the Office of the Secretary of Defense. Seel says he does not recall what response, if any, he received.

Francis Brooke also decided he had to check out the mysterious man's story directly with Washington. Asimos had told Brooke that he could call Bucci in Rumsfeld's office to confirm that he was there on behalf of the OSD, Brooke recalled. But Brooke had his own contacts at the highest reaches of the Pentagon, and so he called a top aide to Paul Wolfowitz. "I said there's this guy who is here saying he is from DOD, and he claims that Steve Bucci is the guy to talk to about him," recalled Brooke. Wolfowitz's aide agreed to check into the story.

"I called back a day later, and Wolfowitz's staffer said to me nobody knows who he is. Nobody here knows him," Brooke remembers. "I tracked down Asimos and told him nobody at the Pentagon knows him," Brooke continued. "I confronted him and said, you don't work for OSD, get out. And he left in about five minutes."

Brooke said that Asimos walked out of Chalabi's compound without a car or even a ride; he said Asimos simply disappeared, and Brooke never heard from him again. The next day, Brooke says he got another call from Wolfowitz's aide, who said that the INC should detain Asimos. "We didn't have any way to arrest people," recalls Brooke. "Plus, Asimos was already gone." To Brooke and others in the INC, Asimos remained an enduring mystery. Brooke's phone call set off alarms with his Pentagon contact, who tracked Asimos's connection back to Bucci. Bucci says that he freely admitted to making arrangements for Asimos's trip into Iraq on a military flight. That earned Bucci a verbal reprimand and clear instructions never to do anything like that again.

After he was kicked out of the INC's compound in Baghdad, Asimos made his way back to northern Iraq, and from there contacted Motley Rice. In an April 25, 2003, e-mail to the other investigators working for Motley Rice, Asimos said that he had "made it to Bagdad for a couple of days with the INC, but got recalled to the north quickly again." He added that he hoped to be able to leave Iraq within the next two or three weeks, because "my role in the Iraqi reconstruction" is looking "less likely, as key guy who wanted me to work for him is no longer involved." He said that he now expected he could turn his attention to the 9/11 lawsuit. "I think that's what the people at OSD want."

Bucci insists that Asimos was not in Iraq on assignment from the OSD, and could not speak to what exactly Asimos was telling people or why. But Bucci said that if his friend was saying such things to keep himself safe, then that would be fine. "[Asimos] is very, very talented at trying to stay alive, and the environments he was operating in require some degree of verbal manipulation skills. I was an intel collector . . . and you get paid to tell people they're your friend . . . when you don't really care whether they're your friend or not. So in the intel gathering business, the fact that he is a good liar perhaps is not necessarily a character flaw. It's called a skill. I never got the impression that Mike ever lied to me about any of the things he was doing or had done. The fact that we're very good friends is unfailingly true. If people took that to mean that I was his handler, that wasn't true."

In June 2003, just a few weeks after Asimos returned from Iraq, Motley Rice and other lawyers involved in the 9/11 lawsuit backed the creation of a new company, Rosetta Research and Consulting LLC, to handle the investigative work for the 9/11 lawsuit. Joe Rice recalls that the company was Mike Asimos's idea. He told the Motley Rice lawyers that the Bush administration would not contract with them, so Asimos proposed the creation of a separate business that would be able to get contracts while also conducting the investigation for the lawsuit. Harry Huge was named chairman of Rosetta, but the partners who would run Rosetta would be Asimos and Patrick Jost, another Motley Rice investigator.

Creating a separate company to handle the investigation seemed to have several advantages in addition to the potential for government contracts. It could enable Motley Rice to attract outside investors to help finance the investigation, and also provide Motley Rice with an opportunity to capitalize on the massive database of information it had been collecting by selling it to commercial customers through Rosetta.

Most of the database was made up of documents from terrorism-related criminal investigations in Germany and Spain. Harry Huge had traveled to Germany and Spain to meet with prosecutors handling those cases, which were directly related to the 9/11 attacks. In Germany, Huge said he befriended Walter Hemberger, the chief prosecutor in the German criminal investigation into al Qaeda's Hamburg cell, which had included lead hijacker Mohamed Atta. Hemberger agreed to give Huge and Motley Rice all of the documents that the German police had obtained in the case. He even agreed to name Huge as a co-prosecutor, which gave Huge and Motley Rice access to any document or piece of evidence that the Germans had collected. In Spain, Huge struck a similar deal with Baltasar Garzón, the Spanish magistrate overseeing the trial of members of the Spanish al Qaeda cell accused of providing support for the 9/11 hijackers.

Motley Rice's headquarters was soon flooded with documents from Germany and Spain—material that the Germans and Spanish had refused to give to the U.S. government, at least partly out of anger with the Bush administration for its unilateral approach in the war on terror. The law firm began to construct a huge database, which would turn out to be the most valuable asset Motley Rice ever got out of the 9/11 case.

In reality, Motley Rice never provided much oversight of Rosetta, and it quickly became the vehicle through which Mike Asimos ran his operations, seemingly for both Motley Rice and the U.S. government. In a 2004 internal Rosetta memo, Asimos made it clear that at that time, he was doing much of his work for the government, even though investigative work for the 9/11 lawsuit was supposed to be Rosetta's primary mission. Asimos wrote that 65 percent of his time and effort was then being spent working for the government—even though Rosetta did not have any government contracts. He wrote that he was supporting "USG efforts to combat terrorism financing" while acquiring documents and recruiting key witnesses for the government.

Although Rosetta was not receiving any payment for the work it was doing for the government, and was surviving on funds from Motley Rice and other investors, the evidence suggests that it wasn't simply sharing information collected in the course of its investigations for the 9/11 lawsuit: in some instances U.S. officials appear to have played an active role in helping to define its collection objectives.

Asimos shared with other investigators what he called his "KIL list," or "key insider list," which was a catalog of purportedly high-value individuals that the group would seek to contact. By 2004, the list had about twenty-five names and was dominated by Afghans, including many suspected of having ties to the Taliban and the Afghan drug trade. In a series of interviews, Patrick Jost recounted attending small meetings in hotel rooms at the Sofitel Hotel in downtown Washington, where he said that Asimos met with Defense Department officials to discuss who should be placed on the list. (One of the Pentagon officials whom Jost said he saw in one of these meetings, Douglas Feith, denied ever having attended such a meeting.) One of the Afghans on the KIL list was Haji Bashir Noorzai, a drug trafficker who eventually became the focus of Rosetta's work.

Sometime in 2004, Mike Asimos's shadowy and mysterious relationship with the Defense Department appears to have begun to wane, at least temporarily. To be sure, Asimos seems to have continued to have connections with some Defense officials, especially at the Defense Intelligence Agency. But soon he found a new governmental minder and protector—at the Federal Bureau of Investigation.

Mike Dick looked like a cop. A stocky man with an open face and a short, square frame, he appeared to be the kind of guy who could have spent his career pulling drivers over on the New Jersey Turnpike. But Mike Dick was also ambitious, and so he made it to the FBI.

But in a series of interviews over several years (and underscored by a 2013 lawsuit he filed against the Justice Department and the FBI), it became clear that Mike Dick never felt appreciated by his superiors in the bureau. After joining the FBI in 1996, he took on dangerous assignments in Pakistan after 9/11, and says he was involved in the investigation of the murder of *Wall Street Journal* reporter Daniel Pearl. He was also a reserve army officer and had been detailed to Special Operations. Yet he never seemed to be the guy who got the recognition he thought he was due. He appeared frustrated that there didn't seem to be any way that he could break through the bureaucracy and become a star.

He hoped that would change when he was transferred to the bureau's Terrorist Financing Operations Section (TFOS) at FBI headquarters in Washington. TFOS was the geek squad of the FBI, the unit set up in the wake of the 9/11 attacks to track al Qaeda's money. In the frantic days after 9/11, Dennis Lormel, a quiet, even-tempered senior FBI agent and an expert in forensic financial investigations, had, almost as an afterthought, been put in charge of the financial side of PENTTBOM, the FBI's code name for the 9/11 investigation. His group immediately produced results. Top FBI officials were initially counting on the bureau's field offices, particularly in New York and Boston, to take charge, but Lormel's small financial crimes group quickly pieced together a mosaic of the hijackers' lives and started asking the field offices to follow up on its leads, rather than the other way around — much to the irritation of the special agents in charge of the field offices. Eventually, Lormel was able to piece together a comprehensive understanding of the plot told through the paper trail of the $400,000 that supported the nineteen hijackers.

Lormel's success convinced FBI top management to make his unit permanent, and so TFOS was created in April 2002 with Lormel as its first section chief. Just as Ron Motley was gearing up his massive lawsuit charging the Saudis with financing 9/11, Dennis Lormel was becoming the nation's top cop on terrorism finance.

Lormel retired from the FBI in 2003 and went into private business in the Washington area. He recalled that after he left the FBI, he was approached by Mike Asimos, who was beginning to hunt for new government mentors. Asimos was hoping that Lormel could open doors for him at TFOS, which seemed like the perfect home for Rosetta, now that the Pentagon's support and interest appeared to be fading.

Asimos told Lormel that Rosetta was using "special means" to acquire documents from all over the world, and that the company would like to sell the information to the FBI, Lormel recalled. Lormel was suspicious of what Asimos meant by "special means" and said later that he was also suspicious because he couldn't figure out who was really behind Rosetta. He said he told Asimos he couldn't help him.

Lormel thought that was the end of it. But Asimos made another run at the FBI, and eventually found a willing partner in Mike Dick.

Dick was friends with Brian Mallon, whom Dick had known when they both had worked in Newark. Dick was intrigued by Rosetta. Asimos made it clear to Dick that he was willing to share Rosetta's information with TFOS for free — and without a contract, at least at first. Asimos also seemed willing to conduct operations for the FBI, and Dick thought that was an offer too good to turn down.

With what he later claimed was the approval of his supervisors at TFOS, as well as the legal blessings of an FBI lawyer, Mike Dick launched a secret relationship with Rosetta. Without a contract and without a formal agreement with the FBI, Rosetta became, in effect, an investigative arm of the FBI. In a sworn affidavit in a later court case, Patrick Jost said that Mike Dick, Mike Asimos, and Brian Mallon had "all told me that Rosetta had been designated as an FBI undercover operation." In the process, Mike Dick became either Mike Asimos's handler — or his stooge.

By the spring of 2004, the FBI and Rosetta were working so closely that Mike Dick was given his own Rosetta e-mail address. He was regularly receiving information from Asimos and Mallon while tasking them to gather more data for the FBI. In his 2013 lawsuit against the Justice Department and the FBI, Mike Dick offers his own explanation about his involvement with Rosetta. His lawsuit states that Dick "was assigned to secure information from the Motley Rice Law Firm, which represented the families of the 9-11 victims, who were pursuing a civil law suit against high ranking Saudi Arabian officials and bankers. . . . Dick was to collect information from the Motley Firm, but was not to disclose any information from the Bureau. Dick scrupulously followed this policy. The flow of information was one way from the families' attorneys to the Bureau."

In his suit, Dick also explains the benefits to the FBI of using Rosetta. Motley Rice's private investigators, the suit says, "pursued investigative leads outside the United States, without being subject to the limitations" imposed on federal law enforcement or the military.

Many of Rosetta's internal reports written by Asimos and Mallon were addressed to Mike Dick, who went by the Rosetta code name of GM, or "Go Mike," according to internal Rosetta e-mails and other documents.

"Received the attached docs from S12," Asimos wrote (referring to a source's code name) in a September 17, 2004, e-mail to Mike Dick and others. "He obtained from ISI [Pakistan's spy agency, the Inter-Services Intelligence Directorate]. These docs contain photos/ID info of numerous terror financiers who worked for a fraudulent charity in Peshawar. ISI facilitated their departure from PAK [Peshawar] immediately after 9/11. You guys need to run these names. If not in any USG databases, they need to be added immed."

Soon an FBI analyst was involved in the Rosetta-FBI relationship as well, searching FBI databases, sometimes doing records checks on people that Asimos was meeting or trying to recruit as informants, according to Jost and Rosetta's internal documents. While Rosetta was being funded with millions of dollars by Motley Rice and other private investors, the evidence suggests that Rosetta was conducting some of its work on behalf of Mike Dick and the FBI, rather than just for the 9/11 lawsuit.

According to Jost, Asimos often sought to convince Ron Motley and the Motley Rice lawyers that the informants he was recruiting around the world would be of use to the *Burnett* lawsuit. But Jost said he believes that Asimos was often just trying to mollify Motley while he conducted operations that were primarily geared to the government.

Jost complained that Asimos was dismissive of investigations that would only be of benefit to Motley Rice and the 9/11 lawsuit. On one occasion Jost recounted, he had been offered an invitation to a wedding that was to be attended by Khalid bin Mahfouz, who was of great interest to the Motley Rice lawyers handling the 9/11 lawsuit. Jost had hoped that the social event would present an opportunity to talk with bin Mahfouz and perhaps network with some of his closest associates, but Asimos was unwilling to have Rosetta cover his expenses for the trip. Jost said he believes Asimos didn't want to pursue the lead because it held no interest for the government.

An Afghan official in London became one of Rosetta's most important sources. While he was serving at the Afghan embassy in London, the diplomat was given the Rosetta code name of "S-1" in many of Rosetta's internal documents. In a series of interviews, Jost said that Rosetta had paid the diplomat huge amounts on a regular basis for his information and assistance, including helping Asimos to obtain visas and other documents to get in and out of Afghanistan. In an affidavit Jost later gave a defense lawyer in a criminal case in New York (involving the Afghan drug lord brought to the United States by Rosetta), Jost said that he told the Justice Department's inspector general about the financial payments made by Rosetta to S-1, whom he described as "an Afghan diplomat serving in London." In addition, a source directly involved with Rosetta said that, in one instance, he personally delivered cash to the Afghan in London who was code-named S-1 by Rosetta.

★

While Asimos may have been operating under the direction of officials at the Pentagon and FBI, it does not appear that they provided any more supervision than did Motley Rice. With little direction, Rosetta seems to have cast a wide, haphazard, and sometimes costly net for sources of information. Inevitably, that sometimes led to dead ends and strange encounters.

Afghan exiles living in London who were friends of S-1 started working for Rosetta, earning code names of their own. In order to keep their primary source happy, Patrick Jost recalled, he was tasked with finding British lawyers to assist with the immigration problems of some of S-1's Afghan friends living in London. S-1 "often asked Rosetta to help Afghans in London — legal problems, asylum petitions, needing jobs, and so on," Jost later wrote in a memorandum. "Doing this was also always a priority, as he had to be kept happy."

Before long, word apparently circulated among exiles about the money that might be available from Rosetta. One Afghan living in Sweden who knew S-1 was "willing to cooperate with Rosetta for financial gain," according to a Rosetta memo from Mallon to Asimos and Dick. S-1 claimed the source had information about the potential sale of 5 kilograms of uranium in Kabul, and could also help Rosetta find Mullah Omar, the Taliban leader who had been in hiding in Pakistan since the U.S.-led invasion of Afghanistan. S-1 also claimed that the source had only recently immigrated to Sweden from Quetta, Pakistan. "S-1 stated that he recently met an Afghan in Sweden with valuable information," Mallon wrote in a May 2004 Rosetta report sent to both Asimos and Mike Dick. "According to S-1 this individual's family is in the immediate circle of MULLAH OMAR. S-1 believes that this individual could locate OMAR for the USA in exchange for the reward of $25,000,000. . . . S-1 stated that he has information regarding the potential sale of approximately 5 Kilograms of URANIUM in

Kabul." Yet after traveling to Gothenburg, Sweden, to interview the man, Mallon reported back that the new contact was a father of four and an unemployed Swedish citizen collecting government assistance who walked with the aid of crutches and who said he wanted to work with Rosetta to earn money for a back operation.

Another eager source was an Iranian living in Germany, going by the alias Hamid Reza Zakeri, who claimed that he had been a high-ranking Iranian intelligence official and that he had firsthand knowledge that Osama bin Laden and his deputy in al Qaeda, Ayman al-Zawahiri, had been living in Iran. The Iranian's information about the supposed sighting of Osama bin Laden in Iran was detailed and breathless in a Rosetta field report. "Both UBL and Dr. AZ were dressed as Iranian clerics with black turbans," the Iranian claimed, when he saw them exit a Toyota Land Cruiser and walk toward a compound in Najmabad, Iran.

Asimos and Mallon traveled to Berlin to interview Zakeri in a Marriott hotel. The Iranian engaged in a general discussion about Iran's security services before stopping to say he would require a contractual arrangement before sharing any further details. Asimos e-mailed Motley Rice lawyers recommending that a contract be drawn up immediately, with payments contingent on Zakeri's passing a polygraph.

The polygrapher hired to assess Zakeri declared the Iranian a "phony" and unsophisticated, with "poor knowledge of the proper tradecraft." Further, the polygrapher reported, Zakeri had previously attempted and failed to sell information to a number of intelligence services including American, French, German, and Swedish agencies. The polygrapher determined, after two days of interviews, that Zakeri had "failed all of the important questions" according to a March 2004 Rosetta report on the case. The polygrapher also reported that Zakeri called him at his Berlin hotel "and attempted to woo him with a business proposition."

In 2005, Zakeri went public in a book by Kenneth Timmerman. The book, *Countdown to Crisis,* reported that in July 2001, Zakeri had warned the CIA of the 9/11 attacks; the book also said that Zakeri had evidence indicating Iran's support for al Qaeda and the 9/11 attacks.

Timmerman said in an interview that Zakeri told him about the polygraph test that he took in Germany while meeting with Rosetta. "Zakeri was pissed off with that polygrapher," Timmerman recalled, "because he pretended he was working for the FBI, or was presented as if he was working for the FBI."

Eventually, Zakeri did provide information in another 9/11-related lawsuit that had remarkable and surprising success in Judge Daniels's court in New York. In December 2011, Daniels ruled in a case known as *Havlish et al. v. bin Laden et al.* — like *Burnett,* a lawsuit that had been consolidated into *In re Terrorist Attacks* — that Iran and Hezbollah supported al Qaeda in the 9/11 attacks. Zakeri provided an affidavit in the *Havlish* case, as did Timmerman.

There is strong evidence that one Rosetta contact, who is referred to in internal Rosetta documents by the code name S-2, was a journalist. Rosetta reports and internal communications do not say that the journalist received any payment. But the reports indicate that Rosetta considered the journalist to be at the very least a valuable contact — and perhaps a valuable intelligence asset. Some level of information trading is common practice in journalism, but the relationship between the journalist and Rosetta was unusual. According to internal Rosetta reports and communications, the journalist introduced Asimos and Mallon to sources who subsequently became Rosetta assets.

With Brian Mallon, the journalist participated in the 2004 surveillance of a suspected Islamic extremist in London, but the two were questioned about their surveillance activities by British authorities, according to Jost and an internal Rosetta report. Mallon denied this incident occurred, despite the Rosetta report that described it in detail. Mallon wrote in the report that while he and S-2 were trying to conduct their surveillance operations in May 2004, they were asked by a local police officer to accompany him to the Barking Police Station in London. About three hours later, two detectives from the antiterrorist branch of New Scotland Yard arrived at the station. "Neither was very friendly," Mallon wrote, and they "suggested" that Mallon abandon his efforts.

The journalist was even issued a Rosetta e-mail address, which records indicate the journalist did use. Internal Rosetta memos indicate that Asimos and Mallon sought to "task" the journalist with specific assignments.

It is unclear whether the U.S. officials on the receiving end of Rosetta reports were aware that they may have become complicit in the exploitation of a journalist as an asset for intelligence collection. The U.S. intelligence community bans American intelligence officers from posing as journalists overseas, and has tight restrictions on exploiting or manipulating the press, so the officials involved in the government's relationship with Rosetta may have been in violation of those rules.

It is certainly possible that the internal reports suggesting that the journalist was a source for Rosetta were exaggerated. The journalist denied having been a source for Rosetta. Mallon and Asimos both denied that the journalist was an intelligence asset.

Another journalist introduced Rosetta to one of England's most incorrigible con men, who claimed he had valuable intelligence to offer. Paul Blanchard had been jailed for fraud and drug trafficking in the past, but now claimed to have connections with radical Islamists that could be useful to Rosetta — as long as Rosetta could help protect him from British law enforcement. Mallon asked Mike Dick and the FBI analyst involved in the FBI-Rosetta relationship to run a check on Blanchard's name through government databases, and to recommend questions for the new source, according to Rosetta documents. Dick responded that the FBI analyst was "running some local checks for threat assessment," and the analyst replied with a list of specific queries.

British authorities later charged and convicted Blanchard of involvement in a 2003 scheme to steal £4.3 million from a tech company. Blanchard was also busted for his role in a separate conspiracy to launder £375,000 by falsifying sales records for a nonexistent yacht. A detective with the North Yorkshire Police who pursued Blanchard told a British newspaper that investigators had "found it extremely difficult to discover a single honest transaction which he has conducted."

Rosetta's internal communications also offer insight into the occasions when Asimos turned over sources to the FBI or Defense Department. One example was a source who had previously worked at the Islamic Development Bank (IDB), a Saudi-based international financial institution that serves as an Islamic version of the World Bank for Arab nations. Rosetta paid his expenses to travel from his home in Britain to the United States, where he was debriefed by both the FBI and the Defense Department, according to internal Rosetta documents. He also met with Motley Rice lawyers, but Mike Dick seemed more enthusiastic.

Dick praised Rosetta's work in bringing the source and his information on the Islamic Development Bank to the FBI, according to Rosetta's internal e-mails:

> Hey guys . . . Just got off the phone with you . . . fantastic work!!! The home run he gave us concerned details as to the IDB's Management team (unofficial IDB operations of course) that controlled/distributed Saudi money going to the "Al-Aqsa Fund." He gave us the full names of three Saudi nationals that the USG had no knowledge of. . . . He was also able to give us enough clues to locate these guys living inside Jordan . . . where two of them are currently . . . still passing money to Hamas and others. . . . I'm in the process of passing this via official USG channels to our Israeli friends.

In some cases, Asimos was open with Motley Rice about the degree to which he was cooperating with the government. In the case of the source with information about the Islamic Development Bank, Asimos sent an e-mail to Ron Motley and other lawyers involved in the *Burnett* case laying out the source's schedule with the government investigators: "He will fly into Dulles where he will be met by Federal Agents," Asimos wrote in 2004. "They will take him to the Doubletree Inn in Tyson's Corner." The source's "interactions with the USG will be COMPLETELY non-threatening. In fact, he will be treated like a valuable asset to the USG. I hope he conducts himself appropriately (i.e., doesn't get drunk before noon, doesn't whine and complain incessantly). He will be very busy for a week in DC, then come to Charleston. At that point, he's completely yours. . . . Rosetta is responsible for paying [the source's] travel, lodging, out-of-pockets, monthly stipend, etc. during his entire stay in the US."

★

In other instances, however, Asimos seemed to be working solely for the FBI. In November 2004, Mike Dick asked Rosetta for help in locating three United Nations personnel who had been taken hostage in Afghanistan. "Received a request from GM to query Rosetta sources regarding the recent hostage situation in Afghanistan (3 UN employees kidnapped)," Brian Mallon wrote in a November 2004 internal Rosetta report. Mallon contacted one of Rosetta's Afghan sources in London, tasking him to reach out to contacts in his native country and see if the hostages could be located. The source, referred to as S-12 in Mallon's report to Asimos, made a round of calls, reporting back the next day that a friend of a friend knew the kidnappers. Mallon requested that S-12 pinpoint the location of the hostages.

In this case, Rosetta was forced to halt its activities after the U.S. ambassador in Kabul queried FBI headquarters about the firm's involvement. The reaction at FBI headquarters was swift: Dick had recruited Rosetta for the mission without getting prior approval from his superiors. FBI management reined him in, and issued Dick a harsh verbal reprimand. "GM [Rosetta's code name for Dick] believed that Rosetta would be asked to assist SEAL Team 6 on the ground in Afghanistan to assist in locating the hostages," Mallon wrote in his internal Rosetta report. "GM stated that the USAMB [U.S. ambassador] in Kabul heard about the situation prior to FBI Executives and it was presently causing a problem. GM feared being pulled off the Rosetta Project. . . . GM suffered a severe verbal reprimand. . . . GM opined that the people in Afghanistan [U.S. officials in Kabul] were not familiar with Rosetta and didn't want to deal with a private outfit."

Dick told Mallon that he had been ordered to hand off the hostage operation to an agent from the FBI's military liaison unit. Yet even after that episode, Rosetta continued to serve the government, according to interviews as well as Rosetta's internal reports and other communications.

Soon, Asimos became fixated on recruiting one potential informant in particular — Afghan drug lord Haji Bashir Noorzai.

In 2000, Patrick Hamlette, a young agent in the New York office of the Drug Enforcement Administration (DEA), received an anonymous letter in the mail revealing the existence of a heroin trafficking network in the New York area that had its roots in Afghanistan. The letter triggered a five-year investigation that would eventually lead to the arrest of Haji Bashir Noorzai, the drug lord at the Afghan end of the network. Yet Hamlette's years of quiet legwork leading to the DEA's breakthrough in the case were overshadowed by the drama at the end, when Mike Asimos and Brian Mallon from Rosetta lured Noorzai to the United States in one of the most surreal operations in the DEA's history.

While Hamlette gradually built his case against Noorzai, there were plenty of other people throughout the U.S. government who were also interested in the Afghan, and not just because he was an infamous narcotics trafficker in opium-rich southern Afghanistan. Noorzai was a wealthy tribal leader from Kandahar Province, the same region that produced the Taliban. He had three wives and thirteen children and was living in Quetta, Pakistan, at the time of the 9/11 attacks. Under the Taliban regime, Noorzai had been a major figure in the Afghan heroin trade, controlling huge poppy fields while providing financial backing for the Taliban.

The U.S.-led invasion of Afghanistan that toppled the Taliban upended the Afghan drug business, and Noorzai was smart enough to realize that he had to try to reach some kind of arrangement with the country's new American occupiers. In the 1990s, he had agreed to try to help the CIA track down Stinger missiles that the Americans had originally provided to the Afghan resistance; after 9/11, he thought he could renew his relationship with the CIA.

In November 2001, he met with men he later described as American military officials at Spin Boldak, near the Afghan-Pakistani border. Noorzai was taken to Kandahar where he was detained and questioned for six days by the Americans about Taliban officials and operations. He agreed to work with the military and CIA, and was released. In January 2002, he handed over fifteen truckloads of weapons, including about four hundred antiaircraft missiles that had been hidden by the Taliban inside his tribe's territory.

Noorzai also offered to act as an intermediary between Taliban leaders and the Americans, and helped to persuade the Taliban's former foreign minister, Wakil Ahmad Mutawakil—the son of the mullah in Noorzai's hometown of Maiwand—to meet with the Americans.

But there was growing confusion within the U.S. government about what to do with Noorzai, confusion that would last right up until his 2005 arrest. Even as he was cutting deals with the U.S. military and CIA in Afghanistan, a counterterrorism team at CIA headquarters wanted to place him on a list to be targeted and captured or killed. The headquarters team was finally stopped from taking action against him because of his new relationship with CIA case officers on the ground.

Attitudes about Noorzai within the U.S. government kept shifting over the next few years as American priorities in Afghanistan kept changing. In the immediate aftermath of the invasion, the Bush administration ignored the Afghan drug trade, which flourished as U.S. military and intelligence officials dealt openly with drug traffickers who offered information about the Taliban or al Qaeda. At the time, Noorzai's value as an informant trumped other considerations.

Mike Asimos included Noorzai on his KIL list, and Patrick Jost said that he believed that Asimos was told to target Noorzai by the Defense Department or the FBI, who were mostly interested in his connections to Mullah Omar. But Mike Dick insisted in an interview that Asimos came up with the KIL list on his own. Mike Elsner, a Motley Rice lawyer assigned to the *Burnett* case, said that he thought Asimos was trying to bring Noorzai to the United States as a witness in the 9/11 case. Nonetheless, interviews with sources as well as Rosetta e-mails and documents indicate that the Noorzai operation was conducted in cooperation with and at the behest of U.S. government officials.

As Asimos developed his network of Afghan sources, built around S-1, the Afghan diplomat in London, he was introduced to a Major Babar, a well-connected former Pakistani ISI officer. Asimos told Major Babar that if he cooperated with Rosetta, he could be included in a significant business opportunity in the United States, according to Rosetta's audio recordings of their meetings. The audio recordings of the secret meetings in Pakistan among Asimos, Mallon, and Babar are revealing, showing the extent to which Rosetta depended on and perhaps manipulated Babar in order to deliver Noorzai. Babar's value as a source for Asimos and Rosetta was that he could communicate directly with Noorzai. The Afghan drug lord had gone into hiding from the Americans after one of his partners was killed in a raid, which made him suspect that he was being hunted. So Asimos relied on Babar to pass messages and arrange meetings with Noorzai.

Asimos had an initial phone conversation with Noorzai arranged by intermediaries in July 2004. In his summary of the conversation, Asimos reported back to colleagues, including Mike Dick, that he had informed Noorzai (referred to as HBN) that "Rosetta was potentially in a position to intermediate HBN's surrender to the USG, perhaps even brokering a deal if HBN would agree to cooperate with Rosetta's project and also agree to fully cooperate with USG officials." According to Asimos, "HBN reiterated . . . that he would hold Rosetta responsible for his security during any meetings and he expressed some concern that he not be arrested as part of any Rosetta meeting and interview." Asimos reassured Noorzai, telling him "that Rosetta was not interested in arresting HBN and that no such activity would occur as part of any HBN-Rosetta dialogue."

With Babar's help, Asimos and Mallon arranged a meeting in the fall with Noorzai in Dubai, where Noorzai felt safe. Mike Dick was scheduled to join them there and negotiate a deal in which Noorzai would become a full-fledged informant. Asimos and Dick planned to arrange for Noorzai to come to the United States for secret debriefings with analysts from the FBI and Pentagon.

For Mike Dick, getting directly involved in an off-the-books over-seas operation with Rosetta was worth the bureaucratic risk. In interviews, Dick said that Noorzai claimed to have current information about Mullah Omar's location.

Mike Dick and another FBI official were preparing to leave for Dubai in October 2004 when the CIA stepped in and blocked them. Officially, Michele Sison, the U.S. ambassador to the United Arab Emirates, denied the FBI agents "country clearance"—the ambassadorial permission that every U.S. government official is supposed to obtain from the local ambassador when traveling overseas. But in reality, she barred them at the request of CIA officials, who had, at the last minute, discovered what Rosetta was doing with Noorzai and were furious. While Noorzai was not a fully paid-up asset of the CIA, agency officials did not want Rosetta and the FBI getting in the middle of their Afghan operations.

But Asimos still needed Mike Dick's help. While in Dubai, Asimos had run up huge expenses to arrange the meeting with Noorzai, and he needed an immediate cash infusion. Mike Dick was unable to convince his supervisors at the FBI to cover Rosetta's Dubai bills; Rosetta didn't even have a contract with the bureau. So Dick withdrew approximately $10,000 from his personal savings and wired it to Asimos in Dubai. Asimos repaid him after he returned to the United States. "Mike and Brian were in Dubai, meeting Noorzai, and the FBI was supposed to send guys over there," Mike Dick recalled in an interview. "Motley was paying for it. And he cut them off, and decided it wasn't worth it to him anymore. And Mike said we need $30,000 for expenses and the whole Noorzai entourage and security. I couldn't get the FBI to agree to give them the money. The FBI said drop it. I got pissed. So I gave them $10,000 of my own money. They then paid me back."

The financial transactions between Mike Dick and Mike Asimos would later become the focus of an investigation by the Department of Justice's inspector general.

Mike Dick's derailed trip to Dubai and the intervention by the CIA seemed to shake FBI senior management, which apparently began to realize what a mistake they had made by failing to supervise Mike Dick's relationship with Rosetta. Dick had promised Asimos that Rosetta would eventually be awarded a contract with the FBI. But now top FBI officials wanted nothing more to do with the strange little company, and rejected the proposed contract. They also wanted nothing more to do with Rosetta's plan to recruit Haji Bashir Noorzai.

But Mike Asimos was not willing to give up on Noorzai. Neither was Mike Dick, who met with a friend in the DEA's Special Operations division about Noorzai. The DEA agreed to work with Rosetta. The Defense Intelligence Agency also got involved, assigning one of its top counternarcotics officials to work with Rosetta on the Noorzai case. What Asimos didn't yet know was just what the DEA wanted with Noorzai. Were they willing to deal with him as an informant or did they want to arrest him?

Asimos got his answer in January 2005, during a meeting with Boyd Johnson, a prosecutor from the U.S. Attorney's Office for the Southern District of New York, according to Patrick Jost, who said he also attended the meeting. Thanks to the evidence compiled from Patrick Hamlette's investigation, Asimos was told, there was already a sealed criminal indictment against Noorzai in federal court in New York. If Rosetta brought Noorzai to the United States, Noorzai would be arrested.

Asimos and Mallon had spent months cultivating Noorzai and trying to win his trust. They had told him that they were trying to arrange for him to come to the United States to finalize his new status as a high-level informant. Asimos had also assured Major Babar and other sources close to Noorzai of the same thing.

In a Rosetta audio recording of a July 2004 meeting with one source close to Noorzai, Asimos told the source, "We make this work and everyone will win. . . . We will have positive results for everyone — not just for the US, but for Afghanistan, for you, for Haji Bashar, for everyone." Asimos added, "Our job is not to capture Taliban. Our job is not to put people in jail. . . . Our job is to get people to cooperate. . . . That's our only job here."

As a show of good faith, Asimos had even promised to arrange for the son of one of Noorzai's closest friends to receive medical care in the United States, according to Jost.

During the meeting with the federal prosecutors, Asimos, Mallon, and Jost all protested the plan to arrest Noorzai, Jost said. They argued that he would be more valuable to the government as an informant rather than sitting in prison on drug charges. They gave the prosecutors a detailed written proposal for the operation, and warned that Noorzai's supporters would be holding hostages who would be killed if anything happened to the drug lord, according to Jost. But the prosecutors were unmoved.

Despite their disagreements, Asimos and Mallon went ahead with the operation. They sent a series of messages to Major Babar and Noorzai insisting that they had reached an agreement with the government to make Noorzai a valued informant. Noorzai was convinced that if he came to the United States, he would meet Defense Secretary Donald Rumsfeld. Asimos and Mallon made certain that Noorzai had no reason to suspect that his trip would end in his arrest. "We have it set up with the US government exactly as discussed with HBN in Dubai and Peshawar," Mallon wrote in an e-mail to Major Babar. "Tell HBN to be patient and he will not regret it."

After months of planning, in April 2005, Asimos traveled to Pakistan to meet Noorzai and then continued with him on a commercial flight to New York. Major Babar traveled with them as well. When they arrived at Kennedy Airport in New York, they were met by DEA agents who escorted Noorzai to a Manhattan hotel for a series of interviews.

Bush administration officials were so shocked that Asimos and Mallon had actually convinced the Afghan drug lord to come to the United States that top officials still weren't certain what to do with him. Officials from the CIA and Pentagon got involved and mounted a last-minute campaign to convince the Justice Department and DEA not to arrest Noorzai. The debate continued for two weeks while Noorzai sat in an Embassy Suites hotel room, answering questions from DEA agents.

Finally, at the end of a lengthy interview, the DEA arrested Noorzai and took him to jail. The next day, federal prosecutors and DEA officials held a press conference announcing that they had arrested a major Afghan heroin trafficker in New York—without explaining how it was that they had found him in the United States.

Major Babar was also briefly detained but then allowed to leave. When he returned to Pakistan, Babar was interrogated by the ISI about his involvement in the Noorzai case. According to Noorzai's American lawyer, Ivan Fisher, who interviewed Babar in Pakistan, Babar was tortured by the Pakistani intelligence agency. The fate of the hostages who Jost said were held while Noorzai traveled to the United States is unknown.

Just after hearing the news of Noorzai's arrest, Mike Elsner, the Motley Rice lawyer, sent an e-mail to Mike Asimos which showed that he and the other lawyers on the *Burnett* case had only a vague understanding of what Rosetta had been doing. "Ron just told me that he saw that Col. Norzi [*sic*] just got arrested trying to get into New York," Elsner wrote in an April 25, 2005, e-mail. "Any news on that? Can you confirm?" As Joe Rice recalls, "We thought Noorzai was going to come over and help us on our lawsuit."

The Noorzai operation was considered a triumph inside the DEA, yet there were still lots of nagging questions about the roles played by Mike Dick and Rosetta in the case.

Noorzai hired Fisher, a wily old New York defense lawyer, and through an interpreter, Noorzai told him the story of how he had been brought to New York by two men named Mike and Brian, who had promised him safe passage in order to become a secret informant for America. Fisher began to dig deeper, to try to determine whether Mike and Brian were government agents who had made an officially sanctioned promise to the Afghan that he could come to the United States safely.

Meanwhile, the Justice Department's inspector general was beginning to try to sort out the FBI's weird relationship with Rosetta, focusing on the cash transfers between Mike Dick and Mike Asimos. The Rosetta tale, however, was so strange and embarrassing that a lot of the people involved had an incentive to keep the whole thing quiet. But they didn't count on Patrick Jost's turning on Rosetta.

Investigators with the inspector general pressured Jost to talk, and forced him to provide documents under subpoena. He said in interviews that they threatened him with indictment for violating the Neutrality Act and the Foreign Corrupt Practices Act. But what they really wanted was evidence against Mike Dick, since the IG's mission was to investigate abuses inside the FBI and Justice Department. So, in order to get out from under the investigation, Jost agreed to make a taped phone call to Mike Dick to try to get him to admit that he had taken money from Rosetta.

During the recorded phone call, Mike Dick told Jost that he had loaned money to Rosetta while Asimos and Mallon were in Dubai, an answer that didn't satisfy the inspector general's staff, Jost stated in an affidavit in the Noorzai case. In an interview, Dick said that he was later informed that Jost had tape-recorded a phone call with him at the request of the inspector general.

In his 2013 lawsuit, Dick states that the inspector general's investigation continued through 2005 and 2006 but that he was informed by the inspector general in 2007 that he had been cleared of criminal misconduct. Yet, the lawsuit adds, the matter was then referred to the FBI's Office of Professional Responsibility, which in 2007 proposed Dick's dismissal. He then was forced to wage a prolonged legal battle in an effort to keep his job.

A spokesman for the Justice Department's inspector general said he could not comment on the investigation of Rosetta and its relationship with the FBI — and would not even confirm or deny that the investigation occurred or that there is any report about the inquiry's findings. Eventually, a federal judge in New York ruled that all evidence about Rosetta's involvement in the Noorzai operation was inadmissible, and so Rosetta's role was kept out of Noorzai's criminal trial. Convicted in 2008, Noorzai was sentenced to life in prison in 2009.

Finally, not long after the Noorzai operation, Ron Motley had had enough. He cut ties with Mike Asimos. Rosetta, burdened by huge unpaid bills for travel and payments to informants, collapsed. The company's private investors lost all of their money. The funds that the 9/11 lawyers had spent on Rosetta had produced no smoking gun for the lawsuit. "We never got anything useful from them, Rosetta," said Motley Rice lawyer Jodi Flowers. "It seemed like an unnecessary distraction from our case. They were going to help the investigation, going to be on the ground to be helpful for the investigation, and I can't point to anything that we didn't have to do ourselves." Added Motley Rice's Elsner, "When you have someone willing to go into a place like Afghanistan it has an appeal, but over time it wasn't useful. There were some useful things, but over time, it wasn't worth the money and effort."

In effect, Asimos had hijacked the Motley Rice investigation, some of his critics believe. While he was taking advantage of Motley Rice's resources, he was doing work for the Pentagon, the FBI, and the DEA — and the 9/11 lawsuit withered.

Joe Rice was furious that the government, by willingly exploiting Rosetta, had effectively commandeered Motley Rice's 9/11 lawsuit. "All we got were promises, and they got all our work product," he says. As Rice recounted with simmering resentment: "How much money are we out on the 9/11 lawsuit and Rosetta? A bunch. A whole bunch. It's a big number. It would be in your millions type number." (In 2005, Ron Motley told a reporter that he had already invested $18 million in investigations for the 9/11 lawsuit.)

The 9/11 lawsuit, *Burnett v. Al Baraka,* consolidated into *In re Terrorist Attacks,* was on life support. Some life was breathed back into the case in December 2013, when an appeals court ruled that the 9/11 families could pursue their case against the kingdom of Saudi Arabia, reversing an earlier ruling that dismissed the Saudi government because it had sovereign immunity under U.S. law. But the legal road ahead for *Burnett* was still long and winding.

★

The web of relationships that developed among Motley Rice, Mike Asimos, Rosetta, the Pentagon, the FBI, and the DEA operated completely outside the U.S. government's normal intelligence-gathering processes. The relationships were so dependent on personal connections that few people in the government have ever had the nerve to go back and try to unravel exactly what happened. It appears that the investigators for the Justice Department's inspector general, who conducted an inquiry into Rosetta's relationship with the FBI, were so confounded by the tale that they decided to focus simply on the question of whether a couple of FBI employees got too close to Rosetta.

Rosetta operated in the purgatory of the intelligence underworld. It was gathering intelligence for the U.S. government but didn't have a contract, and in fact, was being financed privately by a law firm seeking to gather evidence for a civil lawsuit. It was able to operate because no one in the government knew what to make of it. Since it didn't have a contract with either the Defense Department or the FBI, it may not have been strictly subject to all of the laws covering federal contractors.

Certainly, Motley Rice and the private investors in Rosetta were potentially victimized by the scheme, since their money was largely being used to finance Rosetta's operations. Haji Bashir Noorzai may also have been victimized, since his lawyers were never allowed to pursue his legal claim that he had been promised safe passage to the United States by government agents — Rosetta.

By working with Rosetta, the government put its imprimatur on foreign intelligence operations that it could not really control. The U.S. intelligence community helped create a rogue elephant.

While maneuvering around the inspector general's investigation and the Noorzai criminal trial, Asimos was rewarded by the government with more work in Pakistan and Afghanistan. But in 2006, he returned from Pakistan with a violent illness and was hospitalized with a severe stomach ailment. Asimos suspected that he had been poisoned in Pakistan, possibly by Noorzai's associates. He spent months recovering.

In 2013, Mike Dick found himself in more trouble with the FBI. The bureau briefly issued a bulletin to Washington-area law enforcement officials to be on the lookout for Dick, after he allegedly made threats over a dispute about a worker's compensation claim, according to a May 2013 report by FoxNews.com. The news site reported that officials said that Dick had threatened to come to FBI headquarters, even though he no longer had access to the building. The news site said that the FBI had later withdrawn the alert, which had apparently been made public by mistake. Dick's lawyer told FoxNews.com that Dick had been the victim of retaliation because he had complained about his treatment after he was injured at a shooting range. He told FoxNews.com that this was just the latest in a series of acts of retaliation that Dick had suffered over the years.

In his 2013 lawsuit, Dick accuses the FBI of violating his privacy by issuing an alert that contained false and defamatory statements about him, claiming that he was armed, dangerous, and had threatened FBI officials. The suit claims that the incident was just part of a broader pattern of harassment against him by FBI officials. "For several years now, the Bureau has engaged in a protracted effort to drive Plaintiff from its ranks," Dick's suit alleges. "Tools of harassment include a seemingly endless 'administrative investigation' of Special Agent Dick."

In 2013, Ron Motley died, his dream of holding Saudi Arabia accountable for 9/11 in an American court still unfulfilled.

The ultimate victims of the story of Rosetta were, of course, the 9/11 families. They had signed on to a lawsuit seeking justice against those who had helped murder their loved ones. That lawsuit went nowhere, while Rosetta engaged in its strange forays into the shadow world of intelligence.

5

ALARBUS

Charging into downtown Amman, Jordan, in a high-end Audi, I'm riding beside a smooth and elegant Palestinian with a keen eye for the creative movement of money. As he drives through a highway cloverleaf that would do Atlanta proud, blaring into the light of a former Middle Eastern backwater now under siege by bulldozers and five-story construction cranes, filled with half-naked, spherical-shaped gray stone-and-glass towers while small, whitewashed cement boxes line the brooding hills, he's talking in perfect English, underneath his expensive sunglasses and receding hairline, about the best ways to hide and move cash.

He advises that buying a resort hotel on the Dead Sea would be a great investment, because hotels are like cash machines. Tourists love the Dead Sea, the hotels have high occupancy rates, and they offer a good stream of revenue in which to hide other cash moving through the hotel's cash registers and bank accounts, he explains.

What could be more fitting, I think to myself as we steam through Amman, than to launder money of questionable Middle Eastern provenance by cleansing it through the pockets of a bunch of American tourists floating on their overfed stomachs on the Dead Sea, at the lowest point in the world?

"Maybe real estate is better." The Palestinian, thin yet with an air of toughness, is quickly reassessing the economics of hiding and moving money. He is an advocate of and a guide to the dark side of Middle Eastern finance. Flipping houses is a great way to move money, he suggests, particularly in Amman, where real estate is booming.

In fact, endless American wars have been good business for Amman and many of the Middle East's other newly gleaming cities. Money from taxpayers in Wichita and Denver and Phoenix gets routed through the Pentagon and CIA and then ends up here, or in Baghdad or Dubai, or Doha or Kabul or Beirut, in the hands of contractors, subcontractors, their local business partners, local sheikhs, local Mukhabarat officers, local oil smugglers, local drug dealers — money that funds construction and real estate speculation in a few choice luxury districts, buildings that go up thanks to the sweat of imported Filipino and Bangladeshi workers kept on the job by their Saudi and Emirati bosses who confiscate their passports. In Wichita, Denver, and Phoenix, meanwhile, McDonald's is hiring.

The Palestinian slows the Audi, quietly passing the lush, walled district reserved for the Jordanian royal family.

He looks through the windshield into the sunlight and says, in something close to a statement of principle, that life is really all about knowing the right people, and making sure you work with the right people who know the right people. The prime minister? Went to school with him, the Palestinian says. He's an old friend.

This is the easiest place in the world to launder money, he adds. Not just Jordan, but Jordan, Lebanon, Syria.

But you have to know people.

"I know the right people," he insists.

The Palestinian glides the Audi out of Amman, and the highway straightens and the tall towers fall into the rearview mirror. The desert reasserts itself on the road to Jerash, a city of ruins.

I know a lot of Americans, he adds, now, more cautiously. I work with a lot of Americans, and I have very good relationships with Americans.

The highway stretches into the country, and he pulls the Audi past low-slung, fading warehouses and storefronts, on the scuffed edge of the urban landscape.

"Are you interested in art?"

He has something to sell.

Another side business. "People I know have an ancient Torah scroll from Iraq that they want to move," he says.

He doesn't disclose how his friends came by this antiquity.

The Palestinian turns the Audi onto a narrow dirt road that winds into the rock-strewn hills. He climbs through gnarled olive groves and into the fresh, dry scent of high plains, toward his new weekend estate, still under construction.

He parks amid lush trees and walks the grounds, avoiding mud on his loafers or stains on his pressed slacks, urging on a dozen men as they scurry to finish installing the landscaping, the in-ground lighting, and of course the automatic sprinklers. The swimming pool is filled. Sparkling kitchen appliances have just come from their boxes. Finally, we sit for tea outside on his new patio, with a full view of the sweating, shirt-sleeved workers wrestling stone and, beyond, the brushed desert floor that falls away from the white-walled mansion.

The house could be in Scottsdale.

In a short profile that was on file with his American handlers, a secret Pentagon contractor, the Palestinian was described as "a well-known mafia figure" who has "excellent networks in Syria and Lebanon, as well as with underworld figures throughout the Middle East, Central Asia and Eastern Europe."

But most importantly, the Palestinian, Nazem Houchaimi, was an asset of a secret intelligence program for the U.S. Special Operations Command.

I was in Amman to meet with a Palestinian with a bent toward the creative movement of money because I had heard that some bizarre things were happening along the claustrophobic corridors of Washington's intelligence community. Houchaimi was right in the middle of what appeared to be a runaway covert action program that had triggered a top-secret criminal investigation by counterintelligence agents from the FBI, amid allegations of attempted money laundering, illicit arms dealing, and other questionable activities. The existence of the criminal investigation of one of the Pentagon's most sensitive intelligence operations was one of the most closely guarded secrets in the government. Above all, the tale of the secretive operation underscores how greed and the hunt for cash have all too often become the main objects of the war on terror.

The Pentagon has long been eager to expand its ability to conduct clandestine intelligence operations on its own, instead of relying on the CIA. In the early days of the Bush administration, the Defense Department moved aggressively to increase the intelligence-gathering role of U.S. Special Operations personnel, creating new, highly secretive teams that began to roam the globe seeking information far from any combat zone. The Pentagon's new network of spies conducted their intelligence operations with little coordination with the CIA, setting off a bitter turf war over which agency would be in charge of espionage in the post-9/11 world.

Despite resistance from the CIA, the Defense Department has continued to move more heavily into the spy business ever since. But big problems have come with the Pentagon's increased intelligence role. The Defense Department lacks the CIA's experience in handling sensitive intelligence operations, and its bloated bureaucracy makes it a poor master of the secret arts of espionage. Those problems became apparent when the U.S. Special Operations Command turned to Mike Asimos — following his experience with Rosetta Research and Motley Rice — to handle one of its most secretive attempts to get into the intelligence business. Rosetta eventually collapsed amid mountains of unpaid bills and unanswered questions about the exact nature of its relationship with the government — and in the midst of an investigation by the Justice Department's inspector general. But Rosetta's messy aftermath did not block Special Operations Command from making Mike Asimos one of its secret agents.

U.S. Special Operations Command, the military command involved in the raid to get Osama bin Laden, experienced rapid growth in power and status within the Pentagon after 9/11. The global war on terror has relied heavily on small-unit combat, air-to-ground coordination, liaison with foreign forces, and covert operations, all areas in which special operators excel. With an expanded global role, Special Operations Command began to think that it needed its own version of the CIA. One idea was to set up front companies through which to conduct intelligence operations.

So in 2007, Asimos and one of his West Point classmates, Frank Lacitignola, created Alarbus Transportation, a small company based in Tampa, near the headquarters of the U.S. Special Operations Command at MacDill Air Force Base. According to sources who were involved with the company, Alarbus received a secret, multimillion-dollar annual contract to conduct intelligence operations for Special Operations Command.

They then set up another company, Jerash Air Cargo (JACO), based in Amman, Jordan, as a front company through which they could conduct intelligence operations. On the surface, Jerash was an Amman-based air freight company, and Nazem Houchaimi was the head of the firm. But the business was really an intelligence front, and Houchaimi was working for Asimos, Alarbus, and U.S. Special Operations Command.

To help set up JACO, Asimos directed that $300,000 be transferred from Alarbus to Houchaimi in May 2008, according to an e-mail from Asimos. Alarbus account ledgers also show that an additional $300,000 was wired to Houchaimi for the same purpose the following September. Houchaimi in turn established JACO as a family enterprise, bringing in his father, Samir Houchaimi, as a paid intelligence asset, and his sister, Haifa, to manage the business.

Asimos was awarded a new contract with Special Operations Command in part because of the belief inside the Pentagon that Rosetta's operation to lure Afghan drug lord Haji Bashir Noorzai to the United States had been a remarkable success, according to sources involved with the operation. Officials at Special Operations Command either didn't know or didn't care that Rosetta had collapsed soon after the Noorzai operation.

By setting up corporate fronts, Special Operations Command was copying a longstanding practice of the CIA, which uses what it calls "proprietary" companies to conduct clandestine operations in a way that cannot be traced back to the CIA. Combined, Alarbus and Jerash Air Cargo represented one of four intelligence "platforms" that Special Operations Command was creating in its secret program to set up false front companies, according to sources involved with the operation. But Alarbus/JACO was the only platform that ever became operational, according to sources familiar with the program.

Two sources involved with Alarbus said that when the intelligence program first started, there was talk that it would be used to conduct assassinations of high-value terrorist suspects.

One source involved with the operation said that when he was first brought into the program, Asimos told him that there would be different levels of operations. The most basic would involve intelligence gathering for Special Operations Command, but the most sensitive cases would call for the Alarbus/JACO program to target and kill individuals.

The source said that he was skeptical but that he attended a meeting with Asimos and an official at a large defense and intelligence contractor during which Asimos asked whether the defense contractor could provide his operation with poisons. The official with the defense contractor said that such items could be obtained, but the source who attended the meeting does not know whether any poisons were ever procured.

Another source said that the group's main focus was providing detailed intelligence throughout the Middle East and in Afghanistan. There is some evidence that the group was capable of providing good intelligence early on in its operations. In one instance, some members of the group provided credible information to the *New York Times* in connection with the 2008 kidnapping of journalist David Rohde in Afghanistan. Rohde eventually escaped from his captors in 2009.

But a source involved with the operation said that the Alarbus/ Jerash Air Cargo program was ultimately hampered by the fact that Special Operations Command did not really know what to do with it once it was created. While Special Operations Command wanted to field its own intelligence operation, to free it from the frustrations of relying on the CIA, it had not yet developed the infrastructure needed to process and analyze the information once it began to come in.

The CIA had analysts who could take field reports and, in combination with information from other sources, synthesize them into finished intelligence that would be promptly distributed throughout the intelligence community. But unlike the CIA, Special Operations Command had not developed any real analytical capabilities, the source complained. Field reports, mostly from Afghanistan, would be sent in, but they would languish, the source said. One problem may have been that the intelligence was coming from sources with which U.S. military officers were not accustomed to dealing. Sources say that the group relied heavily on information from a small network of Afghan exiles living in the United Kingdom, who in turn provided contacts in Kabul and around Afghanistan.

But bigger problems soon developed with the operation, because there seemed to be little oversight from Special Operations Command. The lack of oversight was compounded by the secrecy that surrounded the operation, which meant that only a handful of officials knew about and understood the purpose of the program. That may have made it possible for the program's reputation to be hyped within the Pentagon.

One source involved with the program said, for example, that despite Asimos's assertions, Alarbus and Jerash Air Cargo never carried out assassinations. The source said that Asimos talked about a lot of grandiose plans that never came through.

Without adequate oversight and insulated by secrecy, some individuals involved in the covert program, or with some connections to the program, also began working on questionable side business deals. It is not clear whether any of these troubling side business deals were ever completed, but the fact that plans were being discussed and worked on by people involved with the covert program showed the degree to which the intelligence operation had lost its moorings. (There is no evidence that Mike Asimos or Frank Lacitignola, who jointly set up Alarbus, were involved in any of the questionable side deals or violated any laws.)

One business that Nazem Houchaimi and others with ties to Jerash Air Cargo attempted to enter was the international market for unmanned aerial vehicles — drones. Arab countries are tired of ceding control of their own skies to the Americans. Ever since the start of the global war on terror in 2001, when the Hellfire-laden Predator made its debut, the CIA and U.S. Air Force have held an enormous advantage over every potential adversary. They can launch high-flying pilotless planes that loiter over targets for hours at a time, taking photographs and video of people on the ground, eavesdropping on their conversations — and then killing them. And the United States can do it without sending any American personnel anywhere near the targets.

The drone is the ultimate imperial weapon, allowing a superpower almost unlimited reach while keeping its own soldiers far from battle. Drones provide remote-control combat, custom-designed for wars of choice, and they have become the signature weapons of the war on terror.

The Americans have tried to keep a virtual monopoly over this power for as long as possible, and have continually upgraded their drone technology, to the point where the CIA developed a stealth drone to fly high over Osama bin Laden's compound in Pakistan to spy on him. Just the threat of an Arab drone program, in fact, was enough to help scare Washington into war. During the run-up to the

2003 invasion of Iraq, one piece of intelligence that the Bush administration employed to justify the attack was evidence that Saddam was
developing unmanned aerial vehicles (UAVs) that he might use to deliver weapons of mass destruction—a claim that later proved to be
specious. In 2011, Iran was able to down an American stealth drone
flying over its territory, prompting U.S. officials to scramble to determine whether the Iranians had uncovered a weakness in the drone's
technology.

Every country in the Middle East, from the United Arab Emirates
to Pakistan, is searching for ways to buy or build their own versions
of the Predator. Even small Arab countries like Jordan have been eager to build up their UAV capability to liberate themselves from their
chafing tether to American power. Drone sales are fast becoming bar-
gaining chips in the international arms race; Israel sold advanced
UAVs to Russia, but only after Russia agreed to drop its sales of advanced fighter jets to Syria.

The Arab demand for drones presents an exciting business opportunity, and the defense industry has been gearing up to supply the
market, with companies in both the United States and Europe eagerly
shopping their wares to new customers in the Middle East. But there
are strict export controls and technology transfer limits that regulate
shipments of advanced Western weapons like unmanned vehicles.
Washington does not want the drones falling into the wrong hands.

Such legal limits and export restrictions create an opening for
politically well-connected middlemen and arms dealers, who might
want to take advantage of the potential premiums to be paid for creative deals that could get around American economic sanctions and
export license requirements. According to extensive interviews with
sources close to the program, Houchaimi and several individuals involved with or with close connections to Jerash Air Cargo considered
selling advanced American-built UAVs to Jordan, as well as to Lebanon and possibly Syria. The attempts to sell them in the Middle East
had nothing to do with the intelligence operation for Special Operations Command. It was purely a moneymaking proposition.

Proposals to sell drones to Lebanon or Syria raise even more serious concerns because of the likelihood that the sales would have

benefited terrorist organizations like Hezbollah. The Iranian-backed terrorist organization is based in Lebanon and now has a major role in the Lebanese government. In addition, it is supported by Syria. Hezbollah has been locked in a bitter war with Israel for a generation, and air power and superior intelligence have always been essential Israeli advantages. A drone program for Hezbollah could alter the military dynamics along the Israeli-Lebanese border. Hezbollah, or its Syrian and Iranian protectors, would almost certainly pay a handsome premium for highly advanced drone technology. The profit margins for middlemen capable of delivering them would be immense.

Hezbollah, with the backing of Iran's clerical state and its oil wealth, has already proven to be a willing customer. Hezbollah has launched small, unarmed UAVs over Israel, and then flown them back over the Lebanese border. These drones were said to be simple, Iranian-built models, hardly much more than a hobbyist's remote-controlled plane. They don't pose any real threat, except to embarrass the Israeli Air Force, frighten the Israeli citizenry, and perhaps serve notice that Israel's technological edge may not last forever.

It would be far more significant if Iran, Syria, or Hezbollah or Hamas — let alone the Taliban or al Qaeda — could gain access to advanced U.S.-designed drones, with sophisticated guidance and surveillance systems, and perhaps even the aerodynamics required to carry a large weapons payload. An advanced fleet of missile-carrying drones could, overnight, turn a group like Hezbollah into a legitimate military power.

In an interview, one source involved with Alarbus and Jerash said that he attended meetings with others who had ties to Jerash Air Cargo to discuss a complex smuggling operation with a plan to purchase advanced American-built drones, supposedly for sale and shipment to Jordan. Since Jordan is such a strong U.S. ally — Jordanian intelligence is the CIA's favorite and most reliable Arab partner — it might have been possible to obtain the necessary U.S. export licenses authorizing the drones' sale and shipment. But in addition to drone sales to Jordan, the group was also seeking to find a way to sell to Lebanon and Syria, according to the source. The source said that they discussed a scheme through which drones would be shipped to a company based in Cyprus, where documents would be forged to make it appear as if the unmanned vehicles were from China rather than the United States. They would then be shipped from Cyprus to Damascus as if they had just been transshipped from China, leaving no official record of any shipments of American-made drones to Syria. The unmanned vehicles could then be easily moved from Syria to Hezbollah in southern Lebanon, or even to Iran. The discussions about UAV sales in the Middle East apparently did not lead to any sales, although individuals with ties to JACO did meet with representatives of at least one drone manufacturer, according to people who attended the meeting.

Another questionable plan discussed by individuals involved with Jerash was for the purchase of chemicals from European suppliers that could be used to make certain types of high explosives preferred by terrorists, according to two sources who attended a meeting in Paris where the matter was discussed. They said there was discussion of a proposal to sell the chemicals to Turkish organized-crime figures.

One British business associate of several individuals involved with JACO said that he had attended the meeting but wasn't certain what the chemicals were to be used for. Still, he said that he was concerned about the discussion, enough to contact an official in the British Home Office to tell that person about the meeting. He said that the British government official told him that the chemicals they had discussed were often used in explosives, and that he should have nothing further to do with the group's plan. The proposed chemical sale raised red flags among intelligence officials in Britain, the business associate said.

Meanwhile, Nazem Houchaimi told others in the group about another side business deal: selling an ancient Jewish Torah written on parchment, one that had apparently been looted from Iraq. Houchaimi told colleagues involved with Jerash that he was working with associates in Amman who had custody of the Torah, and that they were willing to part with it for "several hundred thousand dollars." He told two Americans working on the Jerash Air Cargo intelligence program that the artifact included "several chapters" of a "Jewish Torah or Talmud," and that it was so old that it had been "written on deer skins," according to an internal memo written for Alarbus.

But that was just a sidelight. Houchaimi and at least some others involved with Jerash were more interested in money laundering. According to several sources with direct knowledge of the intelligence operation, they wanted to move vast sums.

Nazem Houchaimi proposed using Jerash for money laundering on a huge scale, according to two sources involved with the program. In separate conversations, he discussed with two Americans involved in the program plans to use the program to launder hundreds of millions of dollars. He approached one American about a scheme through which he would gain access to bank accounts controlled by the American covert action operation in order to launder about $300 million. His plan seemed designed to take advantage of the fact that the intelligence operation's bank accounts might not be monitored or investigated, and that no one in the U.S. government would suspect that a clandestine program run by the Defense Department had been turned into an international money laundering scheme. Houchaimi told at least one American involved with the operation about his plan, and proposed splitting the profits in order to gain access to the bank accounts in order to launder the cash.

Houchaimi said that he was working with three Jordanians, including one intelligence officer, who were in turn working with a group of money launderers based in Brussels, including a "sheikh." They were looking for "clean" bank accounts in Western Europe, Houchaimi told the American, and that if they were successful in moving the $300 million, they had more to launder beyond that. Houchaimi said they had "several lots" of additional funds to follow once the "beta test" was successful. He offered his American colleague a 35 percent cut—equal to $105 million, with about 10 percent of that lost for expenses—"ensuring the security, storage and movement" of the cash, according to an internal memo written for Alarbus.

The fact that Houchaimi was in business with Jordanian intelligence officers was not a surprise to others involved in the program. He was known to have strong connections to the General Intelligence

Directorate (GID), the Jordanian intelligence service that functions as the Praetorian guard for King Abdullah. Houchaimi claimed that he had two Jordanian intelligence officers on his payroll, although it was not clear whether they were currently serving or former officers. For a Palestinian, operating in an Arab monarchy where the royal family hates Palestinians (for trying to kill King Hussein in the 1970s), that was a remarkable achievement.

The American who was approached by Houchaimi about the possibility of using bank accounts controlled by the program for money laundering filed an internal Alarbus memo on his discussion with Houchaimi. "Disappointingly," he wrote, Houchaimi wasn't telling him about the money laundering scheme in order to have it reported to the authorities, or to somehow leverage it for intelligence purposes for Special Operations Command. Instead, Houchaimi approached him about it because he wanted him "to consider how our group/company might facilitate this requirement [for the bank account] and subsequently profit from participation in the money laundering."

The American said he gave the memo to Asimos, who was supposedly in charge of the intelligence operation, warning that Houchaimi's involvement in money laundering might mean he was also linked to terrorists. Houchaimi, the memo concluded, "is involved in several highly sensitive operations countering terrorism, and his identities and activities must be protected, but in (my) assessment, some of these activities have gotten out of hand and must be addressed. The possibility exists that [Houchaimi] may be privy to a significant money laundering scheme which involves currency from drugs which is funding Islamic terrorist operations."

But when Asimos was presented with the memo about Houchaimi, he downplayed the whole matter and claimed that the "client"—Special Operations Command—already knew all about Houchaimi's plans, according to the American who wrote it. Asimos acted as if everything Houchaimi was doing was approved by the Defense Department, the American said.

Houchaimi also approached another American involved in the program about a similar scheme. Soon after the Alarbus/JACO program began, key members of the intelligence operation held a meeting in

Amman. According to one American who attended, Houchaimi used the meeting of the Alarbus/JACO leadership to propose that Jerash's cargo planes be refueled in Damascus. Houchaimi said he could get a good deal on fuel if the aircraft were allowed to fly in and out of Syria. The American quickly objected to Houchaimi's proposal, because he believed that the Palestinian was proposing that the company violate U.S. sanctions.

Later, in another private discussion with the American who had earlier objected to flying into Damascus, Houchaimi proposed a money laundering scheme that the American believed made it clear why he really wanted to fly planes in and out of Syria. He told the American that he needed to move $300 million in currency out of Syria, the American recalled. Houchaimi said he wanted to launder the money, possibly through Russia, and hoped to take advantage of the American's contacts to arrange the transfer of the cash into Russian banks. Houchaimi claimed that this cash was actually counterfeit, almost certainly U.S. dollars printed to high specifications, possibly in Syria. Syria has in the past been accused of trafficking in counterfeit U.S. currency.

The two Americans Houchaimi approached about these deals said that they did not get involved in the schemes, and that they were uncertain whether they ever took place.

Nazem's father, Samir Houchaimi, also played a role in the Alarbus/ Jerash Air Cargo intelligence program, according to an official profile of him on file with Alarbus. His life helps explain the Houchaimi family's connections both to the U.S. government and to the dark side of the Middle East.

Samir Houchaimi, now in his seventies and originally from Jerusalem, has claimed that he was one of the early members of the Palestine Liberation Organization (PLO), according to a short profile of him written for Alarbus. He even has claimed that he was one of the founders of Black September, the radical PLO terrorist group responsible for the massacre of Israeli athletes at the 1972 Munich Olympics. Like many early PLO operatives, Houchaimi was jailed in Jordan in the 1970s for trying to overthrow Jordan's King Hussein.

By the 1980s, however, Samir Houchaimi had moved into the international drug trade. In late 1986 or early 1987, according to federal court documents, Houchaimi traveled to Karachi, Pakistan, and met Mushtaq Malik, a Pakistani narcotics trafficker who went by the nickname "the Black Prince." They eventually cut a deal to smuggle heroin into the United States. In September 1987, they agreed that Malik would deliver 8 kilograms of heroin to Cyprus, and Houchaimi would smuggle the drugs into the United States.

In January 1988, Houchaimi flew to the United States with 2.2 kilograms of heroin hidden in his luggage, court documents show. He made it through customs in New York and began looking for buyers. He eventually called someone he had met during an earlier stint in an American prison, and traveled to Springfield, Massachusetts, to close the sale. But when he arrived for the meeting he was arrested. He confessed and agreed to cooperate with the government against Malik.

Houchaimi agreed to call Malik and lure him into a meeting with an undercover Drug Enforcement Administration agent pretending to be a heroin buyer. Houchaimi reassured Malik that he had only been arrested on a minor immigration violation, but the suspicious Malik still refused to come to the United States. Instead, he agreed to meet the undercover DEA agent, who Houchaimi said was a contact named Costa, in Rio de Janeiro. In Rio, Malik told Costa and his bodyguard, another undercover DEA agent, that he was the Black Prince. He talked about heroin and his plans for future shipments. After their meeting, Brazilian police arrested Malik, and he was extradited to the United States, tried, and convicted.

That was apparently the start of Samir Houchaimi's long and profitable career as an informant and intelligence asset of the U.S. government.

★

There was only one member of the group involved with JACO who had any actual air cargo experience: Malcolm Bayes, a British expatriate living in a château in France. A former executive of a telecommunications company, he had become involved with a Johannesburg air cargo company run by a well-connected former African National Congress intelligence operative close to key South African military and intelligence officials. That air cargo company was eventually tied to a controversy in South Africa involving allegations of contracting "irregularities" at the South African defense ministry. (There is no evidence the air cargo company was found to have done anything improper.)

Later, Bayes created a joint venture between Jerash Air Cargo and another air cargo company that he ran, LSM-Star. But while he worked with Jerash, he continued to pursue other business opportunities including a highly questionable deal involving the movement of a large amount of cash on behalf of his unidentified clients. One source involved in the Alarbus/JACO program said that Bayes discussed with him a plan in which Bayes would fly $1 billion in cash on behalf of clients from an African country through the Dubai airport to be laundered. The source allowed me to listen in to a telephone conversation in which Bayes discussed his plans on how he would transport the cash through the airport, and then move it into either real estate or the banking systems in the United Arab Emirates and Saudi Arabia. It is unclear whether he ever followed through with the plan.

The biggest mystery surrounding Jerash is how the group managed to operate a top-secret program for the Special Operations Command while attempting to do so many questionable side deals. The FBI secretly struggled for years to answer that question.

Stunned by the questionable activities they saw being conducted with the protection of the Pentagon, at least two Americans affiliated with the Alarbus/Jerash intelligence operation went to the FBI. They said they provided FBI agents with internal documents and statements detailing how Special Operation Command's intelligence platform had been compromised by attempts at money laundering, arms dealing, and sanctions busting.

FBI counterintelligence agents began a secret criminal investigation of the Special Operations Command program. The agents even considered conducting an undercover sting of Alarbus/JACO, setting up FBI agents as arms dealers or money launderers in order to uncover the full extent of the potential criminal activities under way, according to one of the Americans involved in Alarbus who met with the FBI. The FBI agents hoped that the sting operation would catch members of the Alarbus/Jerash crew in one of their illegal side deals, according to the American.

Over the course of two or three years, FBI agents repeatedly told the informants from within Alarbus that they were conducting a highly sensitive investigation of how Special Operations Command's intelligence operation had gone so far off the rails. The FBI agents vowed that the investigation would go "up the chain of command," and that they would make presentations to the senior leaders at Special Operations Command that would "have their complete attention by the second slide," recalled one of the Americans involved in Alarbus who met with the FBI.

And yet, in the end, the FBI did not move aggressively, apparently reluctant to delve too deeply into the secret world of Special Operations Command. Sources say that the investigation was stymied and eventually put on hold. It is possible that the FBI could never find enough evidence to corroborate what the informants and others had revealed about Alarbus and Jerash. It is also possible that the case was so complicated, so difficult to untangle, and so potentially embarrassing for the government that the FBI decided not to proceed with its investigation.

The FBI did not conduct a sting operation, sources said, in part because it would have required a lengthy and costly undercover operation overseas. Instead, they relied on informants. But that left their informants vulnerable, with little protection if something went wrong. Eventually, the FBI seemed to be searching for ways to conduct a narrower inquiry. Frustrated by the slow pace of the FBI's inquiry, sources involved in the program began to talk to me about the case, hoping that the public disclosure of the activities of the contractors would force the FBI or Pentagon to take action to clean up the mess. Those sources provided documents and a detailed understanding of the program and the side businesses of those connected to it. They also introduced me to some of the key figures involved in the operation, including Nazem Houchaimi and Malcolm Bayes. In an effort to get Houchaimi and Bayes to talk with me, I did not identify myself as a journalist or author; instead, I simply told them I was an investor interested in what they were doing. My sources vouched for me, and that allowed me to get them to open up and discuss their business dealings. They talked far more openly than I had expected. When I subsequently e-mailed them and explained that I was a reporter writing this book, Houchaimi and Bayes did not respond to requests for comment.

Eventually, I had so much information about the operation that I approached the FBI to ask about its own investigation. I told the FBI's press office the details of what I was working on, and within days an FBI spokesman said that agents from the bureau's counterintelligence division wanted to meet with me. The press officer said that the agents might be willing to corroborate some of the things I had already uncovered.

I went to FBI headquarters in Washington for the meeting. I was ushered into a windowless conference room where seven FBI agents were waiting. None of them would give me their names. I told them what I had learned, providing names and details, hoping that they would in turn also provide confirmation that they were looking into the same things. After finishing, I looked up and asked for a response to what I had learned about the program. The seven FBI agents just sat and stared at me, not saying a word, refusing to comment or answer any questions. In a follow-up meeting, another counterintelligence agent also refused to say anything when I told him what I was reporting. But a senior official subsequently confirmed the existence of the FBI investigation.

The Americans who had become informants for the FBI said that they believed that the Pentagon may have intervened with the FBI to try to convince the bureau to drop its investigation while the Defense Department conducted its own internal examination of the program. The sources said that it appeared that Special Operations Command finally was forced to drop its secret contract with Alarbus and Jerash Air Cargo. Corporate records show that Alarbus Transportation was dissolved in 2012.

For its part, Special Operations Command acts as if it has never heard of Alarbus or Jerash. Press officers for Special Operations Command say that they do not know of any contracts with Alarbus or Jerash Air Cargo, and add that they cannot find anyone at Special Operations Command who says they have ever heard of either company. But when given the name of Special Operation Command's first program manager for the Alarbus operation, a spokesman for the command told me that Special Operations Command had nothing more to say. One Pentagon official contacted me while I was doing reporting on Alarbus/JACO and confided that my reporting was "making people at SOCOM nervous."

Asimos declined to discuss the operation other than to warn that writing about him would put him and his family at risk. His New York lawyer, Kelly Moore, also declined repeated requests to respond to questions.

6

TOO BIG TO FAIL

Far more than any other conflict in American history, the global war on terror has been waged along free-market principles. In Iraq and Afghanistan, American soldiers actually on the payroll of the U.S. Army were outnumbered by independent contractors working for private companies hired to provide services from meals to base security. From Pakistan to Yemen to Somalia, American counterterror operations have relied heavily on outside contractors to provide intelligence and logistics. As a result, the tenets of twenty-first-century American capitalism have become the bywords of twenty-first-century American combat. That includes the most infamous catch phrase of the global financial crisis—"too big to fail."

When applied to banks, "too big to fail" referred to financial institutions that were so large and critical to the economy that they had to be bailed out by the government, no matter how execrable their past behavior or how badly they had been mismanaged. Letting them fail, refusing to bail them out, would only sink the American economy.

In the global war on terror as well, Washington has treated some of its biggest military and intelligence contractors as if they are too big to fail. The American enterprise in the Middle East has been so heavily outsourced, and the Pentagon, CIA, and other agencies have become so dependent on a handful of large corporations, that the government has been reluctant to ever hold those firms accountable for their actions.

And if any one contractor has attained the status of "too big to fail" in the war on terror, it is KBR.

KBR, a Houston-based firm that has been the military's largest single contractor for war-zone services, has helped to define the post-9/11 age. KBR and Blackwater became the two iconic corporate names of the war in Iraq. Both gained riches and infamy. Blackwater followed a more violent path in Iraq. But KBR was much larger and generated far more money.

KBR was the company that allowed America to go to war without a draft. The United States did not have to send tens of thousands of soldiers to Iraq or Afghanistan to perform the traditional supply and rear echelon work of an army, like building bases, cooking food, or finding clean water. KBR contractors did all of that instead. Napoleon famously said that an army travels on its stomach. Well, then, the American army traveled on KBR. It was the company that made it possible to prosecute wars of choice.

It was so big and so influential — so necessary to the Iraq enterprise — that KBR was repeatedly able to survive controversies and investigations and a lengthy series of allegations of wrongdoing in its operations in Iraq. (Its standing as a central player in the war on terror even survived a bribery scandal that ultimately led to a former KBR chief executive being jailed for his part in a plot to bribe Nigerian officials.)

Blackwater was eventually humbled, especially after the infamous 2007 shooting incident in Baghdad's Nisour Square that left at least seventeen Iraqis dead. But KBR was in Iraq until the end — even though a Pentagon auditor said that the company had been connected to the "vast majority" of war-zone fraud cases referred to investigators, according to the *Washington Post*. (A KBR spokesman disputed the auditor's assertions.)

It flourished under George Bush, and then it flourished under Barack Obama. Near the Iraq war's close, the chairman of the largely toothless commission that was supposed to investigate wartime contracting threw up his hands and wondered aloud whether KBR was "too big to fail" in Iraq.

KBR won its coveted role in Iraq while it was a subsidiary of Halliburton, the company Vice President Dick Cheney ran before the 2000 presidential campaign. KBR was later spun off from Halliburton, but by then, it was well entrenched with a virtual monopoly over basic services for American troops in Iraq. At the height of the war, KBR had more than fifty thousand personnel and subcontractors working for it in Iraq, making the company's presence in Iraq larger than that of the British Army.

After KBR lost Cheney's protection, it still had strong bureaucratic insulation. Every general in the military hoped to cash out by going to work for a major defense contractor as soon as he or she retired from active duty. Many feared that if they took any actions against those contractors while they were still in the military, their postretirement employment prospects would dim. It was much more rewarding to give the contractors what they wanted. KBR's dominant position in Iraq — its money, its power, and its close ties to the Pentagon and the White House — meant that KBR was hard to stop.

Indeed, fighting KBR was an uphill struggle. In 2014, Harry Barko, a former KBR employee, filed a complaint with the Justice Department and the Securities and Exchange Commission that claimed to reveal the lengths to which KBR has gone to try to suppress whistleblowers. Barko charged that KBR forces its employees to sign a confidentiality agreement that restricts their ability to report fraud at the company — even to government investigators or prosecutors. KBR "has engaged in a systemic tactic of instructing employees to keep information they possess regarding fraud 'confidential' and to withhold disclosure of this information to anyone without the prior consent of KBR general counsel," stated a letter from Barko's attorney to Attorney General Eric Holder and Mary Jo White, the chairman of the Securities and Exchange Commission. (A KBR spokesman denied that the confidentiality agreements were designed to block employees from reporting fraud.)

But some people have tried to fight back. When the health and safety of American troops and veterans were threatened or taxpayer money was at stake, a few Americans took a stand. They fought back against KBR and the government bureaucrats who directly or indirectly protected it. They often lost. But they kept trying, and in the process transformed themselves.

★

After the U.S. invasion of Iraq in 2003, Joint Base Balad became one of the largest American military facilities in the country and one of the busiest airports operated by the U.S. Air Force anywhere in the world. At its peak in the midst of the war, Balad was staffed by a combined total of approximately 36,000 troops and contractors. It was home to F-16 fighters, Predator drones, and other aircraft, as well as the largest U.S. military hospital in Iraq.

Balad also hosted the largest burn pit in Iraq, a 10-acre open-air waste site. Operated by KBR, the Balad pit burned as much as 250 tons of waste a day from 2003 until 2009.

At Balad, KBR burned everything, from plastic bottles and food trash to computers, ammunition, oil, paint, medical waste, solvents, dead animals, batteries, appliances, and reportedly even amputated human body parts — all consumed with heavy doses of jet fuel. Thick plumes of black smoke rose from the pit each day, casting a pall filled with a toxic brew of particulates over the base.

The Balad burn pit was just the largest of hundreds of such pits used at American bases throughout Iraq and Afghanistan during the two wars, exposing hundreds of thousands of American troops to their smoke. KBR operated the burn pits for years — despite Pentagon requirements that they were only to be used in short-term, emergency situations. They were supposed to eventually be replaced by incinerators or other more environmentally sound waste management practices, but the Defense Department provided virtually no oversight. Living under the haze of smoke from burn pits became a fact of life for American soldiers.

In 2008, Steven Coughlin, an epidemiologist at the Centers for Disease Control in Atlanta, was recruited by the Department of Veterans Affairs (VA) to help run the largest health survey of veterans of Iraq and Afghanistan ever conducted. He jumped at the chance to shape what he hoped would be a comprehensive inquiry into the health effects of modern war. In 2009, the VA's National Health Study for a New Generation of U.S. Veterans was launched with an effort to contact sixty thousand recent veterans. Eventually, more than twenty thousand responded to the survey.

In 2012, while he was reviewing the questions and answers in the data, Coughlin discovered a clear correlation between veterans who said they had been exposed to burn pits in Iraq or Afghanistan and those who said they had recently been to a doctor or medical clinic because of asthma or bronchitis.

The evidence seemed to support a growing belief, among both veterans and health professionals who had studied the issue, that the KBR burn pits had damaged the lungs of American soldiers. Several studies had already revealed that veterans returning from Iraq and Afghanistan had higher rates of asthma and bronchitis than other soldiers who had not served in the war zones, and some health experts saw a link between burn-pit exposure and the higher rates of respiratory diseases. Dr. Anthony Szema, a researcher at Stony Brook University's medical school, found in one study that 6.6 percent of veterans from Long Island who served in Iraq between 2004 and 2007 had contracted new cases of asthma, compared with just 4.4 percent among soldiers who had remained in the United States. "Deployment to Iraq and Afghanistan is associated with new-onset asthma," his study concluded. In addition, he said that his and other studies found that about 14 percent of veterans who had served in Iraq complained of shortness of breath. Separately, Dr. Robert Miller of Vanderbilt University treated soldiers from Fort Campbell, Kentucky, home of the 101st Airborne Division, and discovered a high rate of constrictive bronchiolitis among troops who had deployed to Iraq. Those findings followed a 2006 internal air force memo, later made public, that concluded that the burn pit at Balad represented "an acute health hazard" for personnel stationed there.

There was also mounting anecdotal evidence that, in addition to the inhalation diseases, alarming numbers of previously healthy veterans were coming home from Iraq with unusual yet dangerous medical conditions. For example, Szema discovered titanium and unusual biomasses in the lungs of several veterans of Iraq who had reported trouble breathing. "My patients shouldn't have lots of metal in their lungs," said Szema. "They didn't have it when they left for Iraq, but they have it now." Medical experts began to describe a new disease unique to veterans from Iraq and Afghanistan —"war lung injury."

Among veterans, war lung injury soon began to take its place alongside post-traumatic stress disorder and traumatic brain injury as one of the signature medical problems of the global war on terror. Independent veterans' groups fielded worried calls from returning soldiers, and, beginning in 2008 and 2009, hundreds of veterans around the United States filed lawsuits against KBR seeking damages for their exposure to the burn pits in Iraq.

But the medical establishment at the Department of Defense and the VA were not yet willing to draw a connection between war lung injury and the KBR burn pits. A 2008 Pentagon study found no significant health risks tied to the burn pits in Iraq, and a 2011 study by the independent nonprofit Institute of Medicine conducted for the VA was inconclusive. Outside medical experts following the issue began to suspect that the medical establishments at the Defense Department and the VA were downplaying the possible connection between burn pits and war lung injury.

Meanwhile, KBR was aggressively fighting back in the courts against the veterans' lawsuits. So by 2012, when Steven Coughlin discovered the connection in the survey data between burn-pit exposure and reports of asthma and bronchitis, the battle lines on the issue were already clearly drawn.

Officially, the Department of Veterans Affairs did not acknowledge any conclusive evidence of a connection, but Coughlin saw that the initial tables prepared by statisticians working on the VA's New Generation survey included data showing a strong correlation. According to Coughlin, that initial analysis was later discarded by VA officials in favor of more general — and much more vague — data. "The tabulated findings obscure rather than highlight important associations," Coughlin later complained to Congress. He said that his supervisor "told me not to look at data regarding hospitalizations and doctors' visits."

Coughlin was furious. With a doctorate from Johns Hopkins and a long career in epidemiology, he was professionally offended. But more importantly, he believed that his superiors at the VA were purposely trying to hide the evidence of the link to burn pits, just as hundreds, if not thousands, of veterans were coming home and reporting that they were getting sick. "It downplayed any connection," he said. "It was very obvious."

To Coughlin, it seemed to be a replay of the way in which an earlier generation of bureaucrats had turned a blind eye to the evidence of the health effects of Agent Orange among veterans returning from the Vietnam War. And it also appeared to be similar to the way the Pentagon's medical establishment had initially expressed skepticism that Gulf War syndrome was a legitimate medical condition, not just some sort of mental-health mirage. In fact, Szema, Coughlin, and other experts were beginning to view war lung injury as the Iraq war's equivalent of Gulf War syndrome—but the VA and the Pentagon didn't want to admit it.

Coughlin came to believe that the Department of Veterans Affairs had an inherent conflict of interest that hobbled its ability to conduct honest research. The VA was charged not only with conducting research on medical conditions afflicting veterans but also with paying the benefits to veterans who suffered from those conditions. Whenever VA researchers discovered a new health problem, the VA had to pay out more money. The VA thus had an incentive not to discover new illnesses among veterans.

For Coughlin, the VA's suppression of the evidence on burn pits came after he had already been engaged in a running battle with his supervisors over survey data related to suicides among veterans. In addition to his role on the survey of Iraq and Afghanistan veterans, Coughlin had also been assigned to a 2012 follow-up health survey of Gulf War veterans. The VA was trying to track the health of a large group of Gulf War veterans over long periods of time, and since the veterans had not been surveyed since 2004, Coughlin decided to check the VA's rolls to see how many from the group had died since they were last contacted.

What he found was disturbing: Many of the veterans who had said in the 2004 survey that they had been thinking of killing themselves were now dead. The VA had not conducted any follow-up with the veterans who had expressed suicidal thoughts in 2004, and had not referred them to mental health professionals. The VA had simply taken their responses and filed them away.

Coughlin told his supervisors at the VA what he had found. He said that he wanted to report his findings from the 2004 survey and include new procedures for follow-up interviews by mental health professionals with any veterans who expressed suicidal thoughts in the New Generation survey and in the 2012 follow-up of the Gulf War survey. He was told to drop the matter, not to report it. His supervisor also initially refused to include mental health follow-up calls in the new surveys. Coughlin contacted the VA's inspector general to complain. That action forced his superiors to agree to the change, but it also meant that his relationship with them became turbulent. And that was before he discovered that the data on burn pits was being suppressed.

A series of e-mails and internal memos provided by Coughlin document Coughlin's deteriorating relationship with his supervisors in the VA's office of postdeployment health, including a formal written reprimand for insubordination. Coughlin was under so much stress that he began to grind his teeth intensely and eventually shattered one. Finally, Coughlin had had enough. He decided to resign from the VA in December 2012.

In January 2013, under pressure from veterans' groups, President Obama signed legislation requiring the VA to create a burn-pit registry to help track military personnel and veterans who were exposed to the pits while they were deployed. It remains unclear how the VA will use the registry, and whether the department will be forced to alter its skeptical position. Coughlin said that his superiors inside the

VA were privately opposed to the creation of the registry because they did not believe it was necessary.

Just as the burn-pit data was being suppressed in the New Generation survey, KBR was winning its own counterattack against veterans who claimed that they had gotten sick because of the company's burn pits. In February 2013, a federal judge in Maryland dismissed a consolidated class-action lawsuit brought by veterans against KBR. The judge ruled that since KBR was working on behalf of the government, it could not be held liable for the effects of its war-zone operations. Whether the survey data suppressed by the VA could have helped the veterans in their case against KBR is uncertain. But it seems possible that if the Department of Veterans Affairs had issued a report officially identifying a connection between KBR's burn pits and the mounting illnesses among veterans, it could have had a powerful legal impact.

On March 13, 2013, Coughlin went public and testified to Congress. He told the House Veterans' Affairs Subcommittee on Oversight and Investigations that the VA's Office of Public Health had repeatedly engaged in unethical research practices. "On the rare occasions when embarrassing study results are released, data are manipulated to make them unintelligible," he testified. Coughlin's congressional testimony finally forced the issue out into the open, prompting the VA to launch its own internal investigation into his allegations of data suppression. The VA, Coughlin says, is reluctant "to release information that veterans, outside researchers, and policymakers need to know."

On March 16, three days after Coughlin's testimony, Timothy Lowery, fifty-one, who had been healthy before spending three years in Iraq working as a plumber for KBR, died of amyotrophic lateral sclerosis, also known as Lou Gehrig's disease. His son, Dylan Lowery, said that before he died, his father told him he believed that he had been poisoned by working in Iraq.

(In 2014, House staffers said that they had been told by VA officials that their internal review had confirmed some of Coughlin's allegations, including the fact that VA personnel failed to follow up on some veterans who had admitted to suicidal thoughts during a study of Gulf War veterans, and that there was retaliation against Coughlin for attempting to address problems with several VA studies.)

Burn pits were just one of many problems that plagued KBR as a result of its work in Iraq and Afghanistan.

On the night of January 2, 2008, Cheryl Harris answered the door of her home in suburban Pittsburgh and saw an army chaplain accompanied by two noncommissioned officers. She trembled. Her twin sons were both serving in Iraq, and she knew this visit meant grim news. It turned out that one of her sons, Army Staff Sgt. Ryan Maseth, a Green Beret, had died in Iraq that day.

But Harris could not get straight answers about what exactly had happened to her son. Many grieving parents in her situation would defer to the military, but Harris wasn't satisfied. She kept asking questions and kept digging, refusing to be ignored by the Pentagon bureaucracy. Her persistence eventually helped to uncover one of the biggest safety hazards American troops faced in the Iraq war.

Ryan Maseth was electrocuted while taking a shower in his quarters in Baghdad. The army wanted to treat it as a random and unavoidable accident in the midst of a combat zone, and at first, army officials gave Cheryl Harris a version of events that suggested that her son was to blame for his own death. They told her that Maseth had taken an electric appliance into the shower with him and had been electrocuted as a result. Later, they changed the story and said that loose electrical wiring hanging down around the shower killed him.

In fact, neither story was true. Cheryl Harris kept digging. Eventually, the trail led to KBR, the defense contractor responsible for maintenance and repair at the building where Maseth had been housed. There was evidence that KBR had failed to adequately update and ground the electrical wiring in the facility, work that it had been contracted to perform. Thanks to Cheryl Harris's digging, the army finally launched a probe into her son's death, and an army criminal special agent handling the investigation in Iraq later told her that Maseth's official cause of death was being listed as negligent homicide, rather than accidental. The army special agent told Harris that investigators had received credible information that the negligence of KBR and two of its supervisors had led to Maseth's death. An army criminal investigator also told Harris that on the night after Maseth's death, officials from both KBR and the Defense Contract Management Agency, the Pentagon unit responsible for supervising contractors in Iraq, were in Maseth's bathroom arguing and blaming each other for Maseth's death.

In a December 16, 2008, e-mail to Harris, Amber Wojnar, the army special agent, told Harris that she had just sent in a report "titling two KBR supervisors and KBR itself for the offense of negligent homicide. . . . I believe there is credible information that their negligence led to Ryan's death. I believe they failed to ensure that work was being done by qualified electricians and plumbers, and to inspect the work that was being conducted."

But the army never pressed criminal charges against KBR or any of its supervisors. The idea of charging the Iraq war's largest contractor with negligent homicide evidently did not get very far once the army investigative report made its way to Washington. In 2009, more than a year after Maseth's death, officials from the army's Criminal Investigations Command met with Harris in Pittsburgh and told her that Maseth's cause of death was being changed back from negligent homicide to accidental death. As she was leaving the meeting, one of the army officials told Harris that, "if she wanted justice, she would have to go to court" herself, Harris recalled.

In an e-mail to one of the army investigators who met with her in Pittsburgh to tell her about the reversal, Harris vented her anger. "After Ryan died . . . I was told by a military person [name withheld] that 'KBR runs Iraq.' Every ounce of my being didn't want to believe that statement was true. Today, the CID confirmed that statement and I have an in-depth understanding of how KBR does run Iraq, and in a sense controls the U.S. Army CID [U.S. Army Criminal Investigation Command]."

The meeting failed to deter Harris. She went after KBR on her own. She kept gathering information from army investigators and other government officials, she buttonholed members of Congress, she talked to reporters, and she filed a wrongful death lawsuit against the company in federal court in Pittsburgh for its negligence. She kept the issue alive.

She wasn't afraid to berate colonels, generals — anyone and everyone in the army chain of command who refused to provide adequate answers or make the changes needed to protect more soldiers from electrocution. "I have no words to express my disappointment with the U.S. Army Corps of Engineers lack of interest in doing what's best for our soldiers," Harris wrote in a 2009 e-mail to one general. "While you are dragging your feet in conducting the legal review of my son's case, the U.S. Army Corps of Engineers continues to award KBR contracts worth millions of dollars," she wrote to a senior army lawyer. "I'm NOT a mother that will sit for years without answers. I want closure on my son's case and I also want to ensure the safety of our troops. Is there anyone on this email distribution list that is willing to step up and provide me with answers?"

"The generals all wanted to protect KBR because that's where the money is," says Harris today.

Her digging also revealed that her son's death was far from an isolated incident. The Pentagon was eventually forced to acknowledge that at least eighteen American military personnel were electrocuted during the war in Iraq. In fact, army experts had warned about the safety threat posed by shoddy electrical work on bases in Iraq as early as 2004, but virtually nothing had been done about it. Worse, it turned out that another soldier had previously been shocked in the same shower in the Radwaniyah Palace complex in which Maseth died. The soldier had asked for the shower to be repaired, but no repairs were made until after Maseth's death.

The Maseth case finally forced Gen. David Petraeus, then the overall American military commander in Iraq, to order a broad review of electrical work on American bases throughout Iraq in 2008. The case also prompted KBR electricians to come forward to say they had been warning KBR managers and military officials for years about the shoddy electrical work on the bases in Iraq—work that was often performed by low-paid and poorly trained workers from other Third World nations.

One of the hidden problems in the Iraq war was that the Defense Department's auditors and contract managers were simply overwhelmed by the scale of outsourcing to private contractors. There were far too few of them to perform any significant oversight of a war-zone behemoth like KBR. The Pentagon also lacked enough experts in specific trades like electrical work or plumbing who could understand and adequately review KBR's work. At the height of the war, KBR was responsible for the maintenance on 4,000 buildings and 35,000 container housing units spread around Iraq, and it was impossible for military contract officers to supervise and keep up with work on so many facilities. All the auditors could really do was review contract paperwork, which meant that KBR and other contractors were, in effect, operating in an oversight-free zone.

Only after Ryan Maseth's death and Cheryl Harris's digging did the Defense Contract Management Agency conclude that KBR had been guilty of "serious contractual noncompliance" in its handling of electrical work. Harris, a grieving mother from Pennsylvania, shook up the Pentagon establishment and put a scare into KBR. Her actions undoubtedly saved the lives of American troops who might otherwise have suffered the same fate as her son.

"All of your efforts and your tenacity in bringing this issue to light has radically changed Iraq," one army CID agent told Harris in an e-mail. "I saw it as I left Iraq and saw many facilities being upgraded to U.S. safety standards. Many Soldiers in Iraq, including all the Soldiers on Camp Slayer, where I was, can now safely use water without any harm to their well-being. Although there is no way to measure how many lives were saved and will be saved as a result of your fight on behalf of your son and all military service members in Iraq and Afghanistan, I wanted you know how much change you affected and how much gratitude I feel that you fought an issue that I and many Army leaders should have seen and fought."

Unfortunately, she has struggled to defeat KBR in a court of law. In 2012, her wrongful death lawsuit against KBR was dismissed by a federal judge. But Harris doesn't like to take no for an answer. Long after the last American troops were withdrawn from Iraq, she vowed to fight on. In 2013, Cheryl Harris's case was revived when an appeals court reversed the dismissal of the case by the judge in the lower court, prompting KBR in early 2014 to ask the U.S. Supreme Court to hear the case.

Charles Smith was a plainspoken army contracting specialist not looking to rock the boat. He spent his career working at the historic Rock Island Arsenal and living a quiet life with his family in nearby Davenport, Iowa. His ambitions were modest. He just wanted to support the troops in Iraq and climb one or two more rungs on the ladder of the army hierarchy before he retired.

But his showdown with KBR changed all that. Smith came closer than anyone else to blocking the massive waste that highlighted the Iraq war. But when he got close to achieving his objective, the largest contractor in the Iraq war struck back with all of its force.

Born in Louisville, Smith graduated from Washington and Lee University in Virginia and went to graduate school in philosophy at Vanderbilt before marriage and a family prompted him to find steady work as a civil servant. He got a job in army procurement at Rock Island in 1976. In 1999, his supply operation there was put in charge of army field support, which meant handling the army's contracts with outside companies that would provide basic services for troops who were deployed on missions overseas. During peacetime, that assignment was a sleepy backwater.

During 2000 and 2001, Smith focused on a lengthy bidding process among three companies to take over a contract called LOG-CAP — the army's main field support program. The final award for the bidding came in December 2001, just after 9/11, when KBR defeated two other major defense contractors, Raytheon and Dyncorp, with an extremely low-cost bid. At the time, KBR had a lot going for it. The military, particularly the army Corps of Engineers, liked the work the company had done for U.S. troops in the Balkans in the 1990s. But more importantly, KBR was then a subsidiary of Halliburton, the Texas-based oil services company run by Dick Cheney before the 2000 presidential campaign.

Under the terms of the LOGCAP contract, KBR would be reimbursed for all of its costs associated with performing the work required by the contract — as long as the costs were approved and allowed by the army. On top of that, the contract called for bonus payments, called award fees, which would be determined by panels set up by the army.

When KBR won the bidding, the LOGCAP program was still in peacetime mode and no one gave much thought to those contract specifications. Before long, however, they would turn KBR into the biggest money machine of the Iraq war.

The U.S. invasion of Iraq came just over a year after KBR won the LOGCAP bidding, making the company the army's prime contractor for all field services for troops in Iraq, Kuwait, and even Afghanistan. KBR was now asked by the army to handle all of the basic services, including food, housing, water, and sanitation, for hundreds of thousands of American troops throughout the Middle East. It was a contracting bonanza on an unprecedented scale. It was as if a single company had been awarded a contract to provide every service needed by every citizen of a small state. The company's virtual monopoly over basic services for American troops gave KBR enormous influence and inevitably helped to shape the course of the war. As the U.S. military established bases scattered around Iraq, KBR was responsible for supplying them, and soon KBR's long truck convoys became favorite targets of insurgent attacks. The army, in turn, had to divert troops to escort the convoys, and ambushes and IEDs hitting convoys led to mounting casualties.

The chaos in Iraq in the early days after the U.S. invasion posed an enormous challenge for KBR as it sought to keep up with the growing American presence. Overall, the army was generally pleased with how rapidly KBR was able to provide good food and decent housing on forward bases. KBR managers made it a top priority to keep American officers in Iraq pleased by ensuring that the services that affected them the most were up to their standards.

But soon, Charles Smith, now running LOGCAP and overseeing KBR, began to see looming financial problems. In 2003, in the months after the U.S. invasion, the army started demanding that camps and bases be built overnight throughout Iraq. Smith's office would write huge orders for KBR to spend billions of dollars to build the bases and provide services. Because of the army's need to get the work done as quickly as possible, Smith would allow KBR to do the work and submit the paperwork and billing records later. The army often changed its mind about where to build the bases, adding an extra layer of confusion for Smith and KBR to sort out.

Faced with so much upheaval and uncertainty, Smith gave KBR the benefit of the doubt on its paperwork throughout 2003. But by 2004, as the invasion turned into a prolonged American occupation and KBR's role in Iraq became more stable, Smith began to demand answers.

KBR stalled. It would not give Smith auditable proposals to cover its cost estimates. It would not explain how it had been spending money in Iraq. Over time, Smith grew angry and frustrated over what he believed was KBR's refusal to cooperate with his efforts to piece together the bottom line for the costs KBR had actually incurred in Iraq.

As he dug, Smith began to conclude that KBR had been effectively taking full advantage of the open-ended nature of its deal with the army. Since KBR had never had to provide the army with an original cost estimate for its work in Iraq in the rush to invade, there were few limits on how much money KBR could claim it was owed by the army—with extra profits and bonus payments added on for good measure. And by claiming that Iraq was still too chaotic for KBR to provide adequate records, KBR could come up with its own figures for how much it was owed. There was no way for the army to double-check KBR's numbers. It was as if it had a blank check.

The only obstacle in KBR's way was Charles Smith.

In 2004, Smith told KBR that he would not give his approval to their requests for their bills to be paid by the army until they began updating their paperwork and providing clear records to prove what they had really spent in Iraq. Pentagon auditors told Smith that as of the end of 2003, about $1 billion in KBR's supposed costs in Iraq were not credible and should be thrown out. Armed with that information, Smith became more insistent that KBR provide the records and paperwork due for the billions of dollars in costs that it had been billing the army. Smith told KBR officials that he would block reimbursements for their bills, prevent them from getting contract bonuses, and slash 15 percent of their payments for future work if they did not get him the documentation to back up their bills to the army.

Now, he had KBR's attention. But not in the way he was hoping.

Smith's tough stance with KBR was initially backed by his boss, Maj. Gen. Wade McManus, even in the face of mounting concerns over the worsening confrontation with KBR from the Pentagon. But after McManus retired later in 2004, Smith no longer had a protector. In June 2004, Smith went to a meeting at KBR's office in suburban Virginia, outside Washington. There, Brig. Gen. Jerome Johnson, McManus's successor, argued with Smith in front of a roomful of KBR officials. Smith interpreted Johnson's decision to dress him down during a meeting with KBR as sending "a message to KBR that my influence on the program wasn't going to be there much longer."

With Johnson now in charge, Smith began to lose his leverage with KBR. Johnson and top civilian officials at the Pentagon now seemed to be in "let's take care of KBR mode," recalled Smith.

In August 2004, after months of back-and-forth with KBR, Smith told one of his deputies to give a letter to a KBR official that said that Smith was about to unilaterally impose penalties on KBR because the company had not come through with the records he had been demanding. But when his aide hand-delivered the letter, the KBR official said that the decision was "going to get turned around." Just as the KBR official predicted, Smith got a call the next morning from Johnson, who told Smith to rescind the letter.

Then Smith was ambushed. He went to a scheduled meeting at

Rock Island with KBR officials and discovered that another army official was there in his place. That was how Smith learned that he had lost his job and that his replacement had already taken over. Smith was sidelined and later retired. Soon, the aide who had hand-delivered his ultimatum to KBR was moved out as well. The calculated move against Smith sent a clear message to other officials: don't mess with KBR.

In addition, the army arranged for an outside contractor to review KBR's costs, replacing the role previously played by army auditors at the Defense Contract Audit Agency, who had provided Smith with the data showing that KBR's bills weren't credible.

With Smith and the army auditors out of the way, KBR began to get what it wanted. Its bills were approved and its bonuses were awarded. The threat of penalties on its future work evaporated. Instead, KBR's dominant role in Iraq was extended throughout the rest of the war. The Obama administration cut a secret deal to allow KBR to keep its monopoly over basic services for American soldiers in Iraq until the end of the war. That decision reversed a plan, originally conceived by Smith and his team, to open up the Iraq work to other companies and force KBR to compete for the work. That secret decision meant billions in additional revenue for KBR.

KBR went on to become far and away the largest single Pentagon contractor of the entire war, receiving a combined total of *$39.5 billion* in contracts, according to calculations by the *Financial Times* in 2013.

Charles Smith (who died in 2014) didn't stop KBR. Neither did Cheryl Harris. Steve Coughlin struggled to get the VA to deal more openly with the aftereffects of KBR's burn pits. But all of them stood and fought.

PART III

ENDLESS WAR

7

THE WAR ON DECENCY

Damien Corsetti can't really talk unless he smokes dope. Marijuana is his medicine now. A bong or a pipe has to be at hand in order for Corsetti to revisit his past. He smokes in the morning, in the afternoon, and at night. He doesn't really get high. He has smoked so much that it doesn't have much of an effect anymore. It helps him relax and lowers the guardrails in his head. Only then can he begin to talk about his life.

He has told his doctors at the Veterans Administration that dope helps him, and he has pleaded with them to give him a medical marijuana prescription. But the VA doctors have fended off his requests and repeatedly told him that they are forbidden from prescribing marijuana, even though it is now approved for medical use in many states. So Corsetti is forced to medicate himself, and that means he has to scrounge for his medicine out on the streets of Savannah, Georgia, his latest sanctuary from his past.

He grew up in the suburbs of Washington, D.C., and his family still lives there. But since coming back from war, Corsetti has bounced between Washington and the South. He finally landed in Savannah in 2011—seven years after he returned from Iraq—because he was fearfully convinced that there were too many Arabs on the streets of Washington and northern Virginia. He was seeing Arabs everywhere, he believed, and felt constantly under siege. His past as an infamous screener and interrogator at American prisons in Afghanistan and Iraq made him fear that retribution might come from any street corner.

His time as an interrogator, first at Bagram Prison in Afghanistan and later and even more painfully at Abu Ghraib — the closest place to hell on earth that Damien Corsetti has ever been — killed something inside him. "Abu Ghraib, if an evil place ever existed that was it. It was all just death, and fucking death. That single place changed everyone who was there.

"A cancerous growth went on there."

His nineteen months deployed, mostly at the two war-zone prisons, left him an emotional cripple. The VA has granted him 100 percent disability status based on the post-traumatic stress he suffered as an army interrogator in Afghanistan and Iraq.

As an interrogator, he was meting out the abuse, not suffering from it, but today Corsetti is still a victim of the American torture regime. He has hurricane-force post-traumatic stress disorder not because of combat but because he followed orders and abused prisoners. He is one of the first veterans known to have been given full disability based on PTSD suffered while conducting harsh interrogations in the war on terror.

When he smokes and talks, Corsetti is surprisingly candid in admitting that what he did was wrong. Yet he also expresses anger and frustration at the army and government that first ordered him to abuse prisoners, then turned on him, charged him, and put him on trial for doing it.

"Yes, I think I did some very bad things," Corsetti says. "And I think I was a bad person at that time. But fuck anybody else who tells me that. Self-righteous motherfuckers."

He is just one of many American interrogators who now find that they are suffering, long after leaving the interrogation booth. Corsetti says that virtually every interrogator he served with in Iraq and Afghanistan now suffers from some form of PTSD, mostly in silence. One of Corsetti's friends, a former interrogator from Texas who served with Corsetti at Abu Ghraib, tried to kill himself in 2011 by picking a fight with a Texas Ranger. (He asked that his friend not be named because he remains deeply troubled.) Others, like Corsetti, are burdened by chronic drug and alcohol problems, sleeplessness, failed marriages, joblessness, and poverty.

The United States is now relearning an ancient lesson, dating back to the Roman Empire. Brutalizing an enemy only serves to brutalize the army ordered to do it. Torture corrodes the mind of the torturer.

Damien Corsetti provides an unflinching glimpse into the nightmare world that now consumes those ordered to take America to the dark side.

"I didn't like it," Corsetti recalls, of his initial attitude toward the interrogation methods the Americans used on prisoners in Afghanistan and Iraq. "But I remember when it went from me having to mentally prepare myself to go do this, to go in and throw chairs against the walls, and break tables, and sit there and leave a guy on his knees for two hours, to having to mentally prep myself to do that—to the point where I enjoyed doing it. Fuck yeah, I got to the point where I enjoyed doing it."

The people now suffering from PTSD are not the politicians who sat above it all, back in Washington, and secretly approved the faraway use of torture. They are not the well-credentialed lawyers who provided abstract legal justifications. They are certainly not the psychologists awarded millions of dollars in contracts in exchange for dreaming up scientific-sounding rationales.

Instead they are the people who actually held the collar and the leash. The United States has been running a decade-long experiment on the lives of Damien Corsetti and the other men and women who physically lowered themselves into cramped, secret dungeons, looked into the eyes of other human beings, and then, with their own hands, tortured them. It happened in Afghanistan and Iraq, Thailand and Lithuania, and at other secret locations. They followed orders. They were given interrogation protocols with Orwellian names like "fear-up harsh." They used "enhanced interrogation techniques."

★

The results of this experiment are in, and we now know how average Americans — mostly low-ranking military personnel and outside contractors — respond to the experience of inflicting torture. They have come home shell-shocked, dehumanized. They are covered in shame and guilt, not the glory of the returning war hero. They are suffering moral injury.

"Every day I lost a little bit of who I was," says Corsetti. "I was becoming this other person, and it was like Mr. Hyde was taking over. Fucking more sleeping pills, more anti-depressants, more sleeping pills, more anti-depressants."

President Barack Obama famously said that America needs to "look forward," not back. There would be no Truth Commission, no aggressive investigations by Congress or the Department of Justice of those who authorized or enabled torture, or got rich off torture. A decade after 9/11, those who launched the torture regime have made millions from book deals, the lecture circuit, and contracts and research grants with the CIA, FBI, Pentagon, and Homeland Security. Spared prosecution, spared even investigation, they now live in splendor.

The only people who have been held to account are those who were at the very bottom of the chain of command, the enlisted personnel and low-level contractors who conducted interrogations for a government that told them that the old rules didn't apply and that the gloves had to come off. A handful, like Damien Corsetti, faced prosecution for their actions. The rest are dealing with post-traumatic stress disorder and will most likely be suffering for the rest of their lives.

★

Corsetti was a private in the U.S. Army's 519th Military Intelligence Battalion, a military counterintelligence specialist with no training in interrogations when the war on terror began. He says that in

2002, when he first arrived at the "Bagram Collection Point," the official name for the main U.S. prison in Afghanistan in the early days of the war, he was not given any clear rules on how to handle prisoners. His commanders simply told him to watch how interrogations were being conducted by the first group of interrogators assigned to the prison, a mixed batch of National Guard troops and other military personnel who had been thrown into Bagram with virtually no preparation, after the fall of the Taliban in 2001. They were preparing to leave as Corsetti's unit was arriving, so Corsetti and other members of his unit sat and watched their final interrogations before taking over. They were openly abusing prisoners, and Corsetti's commander did not tell his unit to refrain from the harsh tactics already in use; instead, he ordered them not to question or criticize the previous interrogators. The message was clear — Corsetti and his unit were to apply the same tactics.

Corsetti now knows that he should have refused to go along and should have followed the example of the only man from his unit who did resist. "You ultimately have a choice. You have to do what you know is right. There was one guy, a really solid dude, who saw what was going on the first day, and said I can't do it. I can't do this. So they put him in charge of computers, doing the database. He was the only guy over there who stood up, and said, I can't fucking do this. People made fun of him, called him a pussy. But he stood by it."

The other early guidance Corsetti says he received from his commanders was that the detainees were not to be considered prisoners of war but rather enemy combatants, and so did not have the same rights under the Geneva Conventions or the laws of war. That policy decision, handed down by President George W. Bush in February 2002, was, the White House insisted at the time, carefully crafted and narrowly constructed to deal with the capture and interrogation of the terrorists responsible for 9/11.

Out in the field, however, it meant that the rule book had been thrown out the window. No distinctions were made by interrogators between suspected al Qaeda terrorists and poor, illiterate Afghans captured on the battlefield after fighting for the Taliban-controlled government. The Afghan and Pakistani farmers rounded up by mistake, or turned over to the Americans by rivals eager to settle scores or for the cash bonuses the United States began to pay, were treated as if they were al Qaeda masterminds. They were all "Bobs"— the nickname the American interrogators gave them because of the uniforms the prisoners had to wear, which were made by the Bob Barker Company, a North Carolina prison supply company.

Before the war on terror, the U.S. military had a well-earned reputation for the humane treatment of prisoners of war. In the closing days of World War II, German soldiers flocked west in order to be captured by the Americans rather than the feared Russians closing in from the east. During the postwar years, the United States was a driving force behind the 1949 Geneva Conventions, codifying the rights of prisoners in armed conflict. During the first Gulf War, Iraqi troops surrendered en masse knowing that they would be well treated by the advancing U.S. Army.

Bush's decision to abandon the Geneva Conventions changed everything. And it changed Damien Corsetti's life forever. "When you compromise your morals, and do things you know are wrong, maybe not legally, but you know are morally wrong, then yeah, you've done something wrong. And I did a few of those things."

★

After he returned to the United States, after Bagram and then Abu Ghraib, and finally after he was tried in a military court and then acquitted of charges of prisoner abuse, Corsetti's mind and body shut down. Paranoia gained hold. He decided he had to find a city with as few Arab Americans as possible, at least someplace where his fevered imagination wouldn't conjure them in his head. Savannah's beauty and orderliness settled him. Its lush historic squares, lined with the elegant town homes that were the real stars in *Midnight in the Garden of Good and Evil,* and which still draw thousands of tourists to the city, provided a calming, organizing effect on his mind.

Savannah is also closer to Florida, where Corsetti's wife had fled with their son after he started beating and abusing her, after she took out a restraining order against him. As time has passed, she has finally agreed to let him occasionally see his son, and he eagerly makes the drive from Savannah to Florida. And so he now lives quietly and reclusively in Savannah, along with his girlfriend and their young daughter.

Still, Savannah wouldn't be calming enough for Damien Corsetti without the marijuana. Nothing else has worked. Certainly not the Seroquel, which, along with other antipsychotics and antidepressants he was prescribed by army doctors for his PTSD, gave him nightmares and prompted him to gain more than 100 pounds.

The officially prescribed drugs, which he took in his first years back from Iraq, turned him into a bloated caricature. The images from those days haunt Corsetti, particularly since that is what he looked like when he appeared in the film *Taxi to the Dark Side,* the 2007 documentary about torture. He is most famous as an obese and villainous figure. Now that he is off the antipsychotics, Corsetti has shed the weight and looks trim, tall, and muscular, much as he did when he first went to Afghanistan in 2002. Apart from his shaved head, he would be unrecognizable to anyone who saw him in the film during those grim days. He looks deceptively healthy.

He wasn't obese when he was deployed. The pounds came after he returned from Iraq to the United States in 2004, while he was stationed at Fort Bragg in North Carolina, waiting to face charges in connection with a wide-ranging investigation of prisoner abuse in Afghanistan. When he came back to the United States and was jarred with a welcome home consisting of arrest and prosecution for his actions overseas, Corsetti was already burdened with fully formed PTSD. He spiraled into depression. He became addicted to heroin, which he found easy to buy around Fort Bragg.

By that time, he was no stranger to doing drugs on duty. He had smoked hash in Afghanistan, which he readily bought from Afghan locals, and he says that he and other American soldiers were able to find remote places around Bagram, including the roofs of buildings, where they could smoke in peace. He says that he conducted interrogations at Bagram while high on hash, and that he even smoked hash with prisoners he was supposed to interrogate.

He says he got high when he was ordered to repeatedly question Afghans who obviously knew nothing more than they had already said in countless previous sessions. "You'd have to talk and talk, and you would take the job as a joke after a while," says Corsetti. "You'd think, my job is fucking meaningless today. I'm going to go in there and fucking get stoned. And that's how your day goes. Hey, I even smoked hash with a few fucking prisoners."

But once he was back at Fort Bragg, he switched to heroin and quickly became hooked. Since he was still in the military—the army wouldn't let him out while they prosecuted him—he became adept at shooting heroin into parts of his body where the needle marks wouldn't show. He tried other hard drugs, too, including PCP, but they didn't help to control the demons building inside him.

The heroin could dull the pain, but it could not control his rage. Once, when he was stuck in traffic in Fayetteville, the hometown of Fort Bragg, Corsetti became so angry that he got out of his car, ran up to the car in front of him, and pulled the driver out and started beating him. Corsetti said he sped away before any police arrived on the scene. With PTSD, "you feel like God's administrator of fucking karma in the universe," says Corsetti. "You feel the need to personally exact fucking vengeance on people for karma. And you have no problems doing it."

There were other episodes in which he lost control and angrily took out his rage in public. "It's not that I say and do these horrible things, it's that I take so much pleasure in it, now that is what fucks with me." Invariably when he was confronted by the local police, they showed extraordinary patience, realizing that he was a soldier just back from Iraq. They would give him time to calm down and then quietly drive him home. It was the Fayetteville police department's informal method of dealing with PTSD.

The police could not save Corsetti's marriage, however. He met and married his wife while he was in the army. But after returning from Afghanistan and Iraq, he beat and abused her so badly that she took his son and left him. He and his wife, as his parents wrote in a

2009 letter to the Veterans Administration, "could not be in the same room. This has led to a total separation and the wife has a restraining order against him."

By the end of his time in the army, Corsetti weighed over 300 pounds and truly looked like a monster, which was horribly ironic because his nickname was "the Monster." Oddly, he didn't earn it in the military; it was jokingly applied by a teenage friend long before he joined up and long before he became obese. Before he enlisted, Corsetti liked the nickname so much that he got a tattoo that read "il Mostro," Italian for "the Monster," inked across his stomach.

The nickname fit him perfectly in Afghanistan and Iraq, where the drifting boy from Fairfax, Virginia, was transformed into a fearsome figure along the dim corridors of Bagram and Abu Ghraib. Corsetti was often the first person detainees would meet once they were brought into Bagram. Corsetti's job as the "screener" was to provide an initial traumatic experience for the prisoner, a shock to their system to ensure compliance. He was also supposed to help decide which detainees were likely to require extra measures later.

Corsetti was willing and able to quickly become an angry pit bull in the faces of the newly arrived prisoners. He was also often asked by other interrogators to act as the bad cop during their sessions with detainees, and so Corsetti became infamous at Bagram as the crazy one, willing to explode into interrogation sessions, throwing chairs and screaming and threatening detainees. He earned another nickname, given him by a sergeant who served with him at Bagram: "the King of Torture."

He became so enthusiastic about finding ways to break and abuse prisoners that Corsetti began experimenting with new types of stress positions:

I used a combination of shit that I had seen during the handoff from the group of interrogators that had been there before, and some that I came up with. Like putting a guy at a 45 degree angle with your body straight and your head against the wall, I came up with that. I sat down and was like, the knees [another stress position] aren't doing it enough for me anymore. It's not quick enough.

What can make them feel that fucking 20 minute knee pain in about two minutes? And I figured that out, I sat there in the interrogation booth, and put myself in different positions, and I did this and it was like, oh, this one fucking sucks. So then you go and share it with other people, and you go, hey guys, I just discovered this, it's great. It's like prison experiments, what's tolerable to you over time becomes more tolerable, and limits get pushed further. You don't even think about it.

But Corsetti also saw firsthand evidence that his unit was not employing the most extreme methods then in use by other American personnel. He said that he witnessed U.S. Special Operations personnel waterboard an Afghan prisoner at Bagram. For years, the U.S. government has insisted that only three detainees — all high-level al Qaeda prisoners at CIA secret prisons — were ever subjected to waterboarding during the war on terror. But Corsetti, who at the time was eager to join either the CIA or U.S. Special Operations, said that he watched as Special Operations personnel brought an Afghan prisoner in to Bagram and waterboarded him. There is no evidence that U.S. Special Operations forces have ever been investigated for the use of waterboarding, a torture tactic that was never approved for use by the U.S. military, only by the CIA. But the fact that the Special Operations personnel allowed Corsetti to watch as they waterboarded their prisoner suggests that their use of the tactic was not unusual or something they felt they needed to hide.

Corsetti's account of witnessing the waterboarding of a detainee at Bagram is not the only evidence that the use of waterboarding by U.S. personnel was more widespread than the government has ever acknowledged. In 2012, Human Rights Watch reported that two Libyans who had been held by the CIA were also waterboarded; the two are not among the three detainees that the CIA has officially acknowledged as having been subjected to waterboarding.

After the prisoner abuse scandal at Abu Ghraib exploded in 2004 and the military finally began to investigate cases of torture, Damien Corsetti's nickname brought him plenty of unwanted attention. He became one of the poster boys for the scandal. After his stint at Bagram, Corsetti and his unit were assigned to Iraq in 2003, and were the first interrogators to help open Abu Ghraib for use by the U.S. military. He returned to the United States in February 2004, just two months before the public disclosure of horrific, graphic photographs of the torture and humiliation of Iraqi prisoners at Abu Ghraib.

The global release of the photographs did what nothing else could — bring sudden and intense pressure on the White House, Pentagon, and CIA for an accounting of how the United States had been treating prisoners captured in the global war on terror. Congress and the press began to investigate, forcing the U.S. military and the Justice Department to pursue the evidence of prisoner abuse and torture more aggressively than ever before. Of course, the Bush administration knew how the abuse had started: the president had declared that the Geneva Conventions did not apply in the war on terror; the Justice Department had given legal opinions to the CIA authorizing the use of "enhanced" interrogation tactics; Defense Secretary Donald Rumsfeld had approved the use of harsh tactics at the U.S. prison at Guantánamo Bay, Cuba; and no guidelines had been put into place to prevent the spread of those abusive practices at other U.S. prisons in Afghanistan and Iraq. And it was no secret within the government that the abusive interrogation techniques had spread far beyond the CIA black sites and Guantánamo Bay. In fact, a January 2003 memorandum by the chief military lawyer at Bagram spelled out how interrogators there were using the same kind of tactics that Rumsfeld had authorized for use at Guantánamo, the *New York Times* later reported.

But stating the obvious — that torture was the direct result of official American policy — was an uncomfortable truth, one that could lead to war crimes trials for top government officials. And so it was not long before the calls for justice led the White House, Pentagon, and CIA to search for scapegoats. After Abu Ghraib, the army suddenly took renewed interest in the deaths of two detainees at Bagram in December 2002, while Corsetti and the 519th Military Intelligence

Battalion had been assigned to the prison. The two detainees, Dilawar and Habibullah, were found dead in their cells after being manacled in stress positions and beaten for days on end. The case of Dilawar, a young Afghan taxi driver who had simply been in the wrong place at the wrong time, ultimately became the basis for *Taxi to the Dark Side*, the documentary in which Corsetti made his first public appearance.

The probes of the two deaths eventually led to a wider investigation of prisoner abuse at Bagram and finally to charges against Corsetti. He had not been directly involved with the two prisoners when they died, and he was not charged in connection with their deaths. But statements from other interrogators about Corsetti's actions, as well as from another detainee who had been interrogated by Corsetti at Bagram, led military prosecutors to target him. In 2005, Corsetti was hit with a long series of charges related to specific acts he allegedly did to prisoners. He was charged with maltreating prisoners by sitting on them, striking them, throwing garbage on them, putting cigarette ashes on them, pulling on their beards, forcing them to be exposed in front of women interrogators, and, most embarrassing of all for Corsetti, pulling out his penis, putting it up to a detainee's face, and then telling him, "This is your God." To top it off, he was also charged with alcohol and drug use.

While Corsetti and other enlisted personnel from his unit faced courts-martial, no senior army officers or other senior government officials were held to account for what happened at Bagram or later at Abu Ghraib. (Capt. Carolyn Wood, who was in command of Corsetti's interrogation unit at both Bagram and Abu Ghraib, was investigated but not charged, and remained in the army.)

But the fact that the Bagram investigation targeted a group of enlisted personnel, just like the investigation of Abu Ghraib, backfired on the army when Corsetti's case went to trial before a military jury at Fort Bliss, Texas, in 2006. After deliberating for less than half an hour, the jury acquitted Corsetti on all charges, even on those for drinking and drug use. The jury was clearly sending a message to the army that it should stop the scapegoating.

But while the scandal slowly faded from the headlines, Corsetti's life spun out of control, clouded by his raging PTSD and worsening drug problem. An outpatient drug rehab program finally helped him to shake off heroin, but getting help for his PTSD was much more difficult. While he was facing prosecution, he was afraid to open up to army psychologists and psychiatrists because he knew they could be subpoenaed to testify against him in his court-martial. After he left the army, he was admitted to a VA hospital in West Virginia with an in-patient PTSD treatment center. He said that the program was divided between older Vietnam veterans and younger veterans of Iraq and Afghanistan, and that at night, after the clinic staff went home, arguments and battles broke out between the two sides — different generations, different wars. Nothing much helped Corsetti, and after three months he left and began drifting again.

The letter his parents sent to the VA in 2009, pleading for help for their son, describes in sorrowful detail how deeply Corsetti had sunk in the years after he left the army. Corsetti lost his house and car because he was unable to hold a job, his parents wrote.

At the time, Corsetti was living with his parents, and so they saw his behavior on a daily basis. "On numerous occasions, he has called us both at work, in a panicked state and totally out of control. There have been many times he has stated he cannot take it anymore. We immediately leave our offices and come home to take him to the VA hospital. Of course halfway there he asks, why are you taking me to the hospital, what is wrong?"

They added that "he has panic attacks a couple of times a week that prohibit him from taking public transportation and dealing with crowds. . . . In the TV room he insists on keeping all the shutters closed for fear that someone is looking in on him. The room is kept dark, no lights are ever on and when we let some light in he either has a panic attack or gets totally abusive. . . . He has attempted to take his life on multiple occasions. Fortunately he has not succeeded, however we are in constant fear of what we will find when we get home every day."

Corsetti and his parents had to wage a prolonged battle with the VA to win full disability benefits for his PTSD, but there is no doubt that he was completely disabled by the trauma and ghosts that still haunt him. He has made some progress, in part by trying to come to terms with what he did and finding ways to make amends. One opportunity came in 2010, when he testified for the defense of Omar Khadr, a fifteen-year-old Canadian captured in Afghanistan, interrogated at Bagram, and then sent to Guantánamo Bay.

Corsetti finally had the chance to testify about the constant pressure for new intelligence that was placed on his unit while assigned to Bagram. The pressure came from the top, he said, from the secretary of defense, and worked its way down until it created an environment in Bagram in which the demands for intelligence reports outweighed the need to treat prisoners in a humane way. The pressure led directly to the abuse of prisoners.

But even though Corsetti can now talk about what he did and what he witnessed in both Afghanistan and Iraq, and can also discuss in excruciating detail the symptoms and consequences of his PTSD, he does not believe that he will ever be free of his illness. He simply understands his plight better. He thinks that he will never be able to hold a job again. On his worst days, he doesn't try to leave his apartment; he now can tell when he is liable to launch into an angry confrontation with a store clerk or another driver. He has been left handicapped by the war on terror, just as surely as if he had been blasted by an IED.

The American archipelago of torture in which Damien Corsetti was trapped was built on a myth. It was a myth built despite strong evidence to the contrary. It was a myth enabled by a community of supposed experts, many of whom now admit they knew better. It was a powerful myth that gained traction as it became clear that careers and riches could be had by those who endorsed it, and as a result, many who knew it was fiction from the first went along with it. Like many myths throughout history, its real resonance came from the fact that it helped powerful men justify what they wanted to do.

The myth was the assertion that the government could reverse-engineer the U.S. military's survival program to create "enhanced interrogation techniques" that would allow the United States to get prisoners to provide accurate information without torturing them.

The military's SERE program (Survival, Evasion, Resistance, and Escape) was originally designed to give American pilots and other personnel a taste of what it might be like to be captured and become prisoners of war. One part of the SERE training program included the simulated use of torture techniques that had been inflicted on American soldiers captured by North Korea and China during the Korean War in the 1950s, when American POWs were tortured, broken, and then paraded before television cameras to spout anti-American propaganda.

After 9/11, James Mitchell and Bruce Jessen, psychologists who had been trainers in the air force's version of SERE, worked as outside contractors to the CIA to help the agency turn the simulated torture tactics into offensive weapons — enhanced interrogation techniques — for use in obtaining intelligence from detainees held by the CIA. Mitchell and Jessen claimed that their interrogation meth ods would get recalcitrant prisoners to talk but would not be legally considered torture, because the U.S. military already used the same techniques in training its own soldiers.

Mitchell and Jessen were advocating torture tactics that had been originally designed to break men and force them to spout lies and propaganda, but they claimed that these techniques were not torture, and that they would elicit the truth, not lies and propaganda. In the upside-down world of the global war on terror, their explanations were widely accepted.

They not only received millions of dollars in classified CIA contracts through their Spokane, Washington, firm, Mitchell, Jessen & Associates, but they also gained power and status in the U.S. intelligence community as the architects of the CIA's torture program.

They were successful because they had lots of help. Some SERE experts knew the truth. And yet they remained silent during the crucial years when the CIA, led by Mitchell and Jessen, engaged in what is now widely acknowledged to have been torture. In fact, some SERE experts joined in.

America's psychologists, who also knew the truth, also remained silent. Psychologists knew there was a broad consensus in behavioral science research that showed that torture did not work. And yet they didn't complain. Worse, they participated, and quietly changed their profession's ethics code to allow torture to continue. In return, the psychologists were showered with government money and benefits.

Because the SERE experts and psychologists remained silent, Mitchell and Jessen were able to make bold claims about the enhanced interrogation program, and have them accepted by the Bush administration, the press, Hollywood, and the public.

The fact that there was a broad consensus among the professionals who knew best, who knew that SERE was torture and that it could not be used to gather accurate intelligence, has never before been fully explained.

Mitchell and Jessen's great achievement was to bend the accepted narrative of how SERE affects the mind and body. They made two important and related claims — that SERE could force prisoners to tell the truth, and that SERE did not constitute torture.

The CIA, based in part on the notion that SERE was safe, told the Justice Department that the enhanced interrogation techniques were safe. Based on those assurances, in turn, the Justice Department provided the intelligence community with secret legal opinions stating that the techniques did not constitute torture and were legal.

America's psychologists and behavioral scientists quickly accommodated themselves to this new reality. The e-mail archives of one researcher with ties to the CIA, who died on the cusp of becoming a whistleblower, provide a revealing glimpse into the tight network of psychologists and other behavioral scientists so eager for CIA and Pentagon contracts that they showed few qualms about helping to develop and later protect the interrogation infrastructure. The e-mails show the secret, close relationships among some of the nation's leading psychologists and officials at the CIA and Pentagon. And the e-mails reveal how the American Psychological Association (APA), the nation's largest professional group for psychologists, put its seal of approval on those close ties — and thus indirectly on torture.

The SERE community — the instructors and staff at the survival schools, and the psychologists and behavioral scientists who support them — is a tight-knit subculture within the U.S. military. Within that community, there was no question that the most severe of the SERE torture techniques were torture. There was also widespread agreement that the techniques could not be used to obtain accurate intelligence from prisoners. The tactics, even when originally used by the North Koreans, Chinese, and Soviets, had never been designed to collect intelligence.

They had been designed to break men. They had been used to silence dissidents, to force false confessions out of political rivals and prisoners of war. There was no basis to believe that these methods could be used to get prisoners to tell the truth. When tortured, prisoners will say anything to make the pain stop. What's more, the intense trauma of enduring abusive tactics damages the memory and leads to even more false statements.

Perhaps no one knows more about SERE tactics and their impact on the human brain than Yale psychologist Charles "Andy" Morgan. For years, Morgan has been given unique access by the military to study the psychological and biochemical effects of SERE's simulated torture program on military personnel as they go through the program. As part of his studies, he has been allowed to question the trainees immediately after they have been subjected to harsh tactics, and has been able to collect blood and saliva samples in order to study their biochemical reactions to the use of the tactics. He has regularly presented his findings at conferences of SERE psychologists, and his studies are widely recognized as providing the most conclusive findings on SERE yet written.

Yet Morgan and his research work were ignored while the CIA and Mitchell and Jessen were creating their torture program, and his research has been ignored ever since by current and former government officials who have sought to defend the use of the SERE tactics in the enhanced interrogation program. Morgan's studies show that the use of the SERE simulated torture techniques impairs memory and prompts inaccurate answers from those subjected to the tactics. Mitchell and Jessen's methods, Morgan said, create a mental state that makes it difficult to remember information accurately — making the credibility of all statements suspect.

"By making people fearful and stressed, they were getting worse information," Morgan said of Mitchell and Jessen's techniques. "If you can make me anxious, fearful and alarmed, I am more likely to give you what you want. I will give you a false confession. High stress doesn't seem good for good data retrieval."

"Torture works at some things," Morgan added. "It's good for silencing opponents."

Morgan also stated that it was long-established conventional wisdom within the SERE community that the simulated torture could not be used to collect accurate information. That simply wasn't the point of SERE. "The research was well established," Morgan noted. "The psychologists in the SERE program were all aware of the false memory findings."

In fact, Morgan recalls discussing his research on how the SERE tactics prompted false memory with Mitchell. "I bumped into Jim Mitchell once at a SERE conference, and I mentioned my false memory study, and he said, yes, I know about it," recalled Morgan.

In response to a request for comment about Morgan's research and whether it was well known within the SERE community that SERE techniques could not be used in interrogations to elicit accurate intelligence, James Mitchell initially asked to see the written formal results of Morgan's studies. I replied that I was basing my reporting on interviews with Morgan and others psychologists and former SERE personnel. Mitchell did not respond further.

"What I couldn't get my head around is how they thought this would work," Morgan observed. "It makes no sense." (Morgan said that he worked for a time for the CIA, in the agency's unit that conducted medical intelligence, analyzing the medical and mental health conditions of foreign leaders and other prominent foreign figures, but was not involved in interrogations. He said that the CIA behavioral science officials who brought him into the agency misled him about their involvement in the interrogation program, and when he discovered their involvement, he quit.)

Still, there were plenty of people who agreed both that what Mitchell and Jessen were advocating was torture, and also that it would not work. Shane O'Mara, a professor at Trinity College's Institute of Neuroscience in Dublin, published a report that corroborated Morgan's findings. In a 2009 article in the journal *Trends in Cognitive Science,* O'Mara concluded that there was no scientific basis for the American use of the harsh interrogation techniques based on the SERE program, and that the shock and trauma of being subjected to the tactics harm memory.

A long-delayed yet detailed report by the Senate Select Committee on Intelligence confirmed such findings, concluding that "enhanced interrogation techniques" did not produce useful counterterrorism intelligence and did not help the United States find Osama bin Laden. In fact, the Senate report shows that the CIA had to deceive the nation about the effectiveness of its torture program in order to keep it going, and also had to mislead the nation about the full extent of its brutality to make sure that no one from the CIA was ever held accountable for engaging in torture.

The Senate report concluded that the CIA gave inaccurate information to the Justice Department about its torture program in order to win its stamp of legal approval; misled the White House, Congress, and even the CIA's own inspector general about the effectiveness of the program; and hid the true brutality of the torture techniques it employed. The Senate report's main findings, first disclosed by McClatchy Newspapers, also concluded that the agency never conducted a thorough accounting of the people it was holding and torturing, and manipulated the press with calculated leaks designed to make the torture program look good. The report also confirmed that two "contract psychologists" developed the interrogation program and were key to its operations, according to the findings disclosed by McClatchy.

The Senate report was so damning that it was bitterly contested by the CIA, triggering a feud between the agency and the Senate Intelligence Committee, and leading to accusations by committee chairwoman Sen. Dianne Feinstein that the CIA had spied on committee staffers working on the report. Many of the Senate report's conclusions echoed Morgan's research, as well as the broad consensus among behavioral scientists that torture doesn't work.

"Absolutely, there is a consensus in the psychological profession that this was no way to gather accurate information," agreed Saul Kassin, a psychology professor at the John Jay College of Criminal Justice in New York. "There is certainly no scientific basis for believing it."

"It was right out of *Clockwork Orange*," added Philip Zimbardo, a professor emeritus at Stanford University. Zimbardo is a legend among American psychologists. He developed a worldwide reputation with the so-called Stanford prison experiment, in which students were assigned to be either guards or prisoners in a mock prison set up at Stanford in the 1970s. The experiment had to be ended abruptly after it became clear that the role-playing led the students pretending to be guards to quickly become abusive. No one has a more authoritative voice on issues related to the psychology of detention and interrogation than Zimbardo.

Zimbardo has no use for Mitchell and Jessen. In his view, "They are a big disgrace." He continued, "There never was any evidence that this would work." (In 2010, critics filed a formal complaint against Mitchell with the Texas State Board of Psychologists, seeking to have his license to practice psychology revoked because of his role in developing the CIA's interrogation program. The complaint was unsuccessful.)

In her groundbreaking 2007 *Vanity Fair* article on Mitchell and Jessen, journalist Katherine Eban found that a myth of success was built up around the pair following the capture and interrogation of Abu Zubaydah, the first major al Qaeda figure to be captured after 9/11. FBI agents questioned him first and began to get him to provide information using traditional rapport-building techniques used by U.S. law enforcement. The CIA then sent Mitchell and its own team to take over. They started using the harsh techniques that later became infamous. Mitchell was trying to break Zubaydah and put him in a state of helplessness, which, Mitchell argued, would then force him to confess in order to regain his humanity.

That failed to produce breakthroughs, but the facts surrounding the Zubaydah case, hidden behind walls of secrecy, quickly became blurred. As news of the case spread in Washington, the fact that he had provided information to the FBI and the fact that he had later been the first prisoner subjected to harsh interrogation techniques became interconnected in the collective consciousness of the American national security community. Mitchell and Jessen's approach was credited with a great success. Thus, the enhanced interrogation techniques spread and began to be applied as other high-value detainees were captured by both the CIA and the military. Compartmentalization and secrecy helped to spread the harsh techniques. Since their use was initially so secret, it was hard for critics to discover what was going on and try to stop it. The compartmentalization also convinced others that there must be secret information to prove that the tactics worked, and that they just didn't have access to that information.

Those were some of the same problems that plagued the intelligence community in its assessments of Iraq's supposed weapons of mass destruction in the run-up to the 2003 invasion. Then, many in the government assumed that there was top-secret information to corroborate the public assertions of the president, the CIA director, and others on the Bush team about Iraq's supposed weapons of mass destruction—and that those outside the inner circle simply didn't have access to it.

Perhaps the most important reason that the use of abusive tactics spread was because it fit perfectly with how the Bush White House wanted to prosecute the new "global war on terror." From the outset, President Bush and Vice President Cheney saw the fight against al Qaeda as a national security issue rather than a criminal problem to be dealt with by law enforcement. For Bush, that decision allowed him to disassociate himself from his Democratic predecessor, Bill Clinton. But Cheney had even deeper motivations; he wanted to roll back the reforms imposed on the executive branch in the 1970s, when he served in the White House under President Gerald Ford. Although torture had never been condoned in the United States, Cheney wanted to demonstrate that there were virtually no limitations on presidential power in a time of war.

In the end, Mitchell and Jessen got their way because too few either knew the full story or objected. Many in the government went along because they were following orders, or because participation meant the chance for promotion or wealth, or it meant the excitement of being an insider in the war on terror.

Zimbardo believes that once Mitchell and Jessen's theories became accepted wisdom within the CIA and Pentagon, "they sucked in" other psychologists, especially in the military. "They got these psychologists to identify the vulnerabilities of high-value detainees, who had phobias of snakes or dogs. I know some of these [psychologists], and they are not experts. They know something about people's vulnerabilities, but nothing about interrogation."

"You can be seduced to do this," Zimbardo added. "It's easy for people to delude themselves into thinking that they will be the ones who will do it the right way. Self-delusion is a powerful force for evil."

Malcolm Nance, a former navy senior chief petty officer and Arabic speaker who spent much of his career in intelligence, was the director of training at the U.S. Navy's SERE program at Coronado Naval Station in San Diego in the years just before 9/11. Nance said that SERE trainers knew that the SERE tactics could not be used to collect accurate intelligence. "You are bringing them to a state of compliance, not a state where they will give you intelligence," Nance said. He said that at the navy SERE program, a PowerPoint presentation given during each training session to the students makes it clear that the torture techniques they endure in SERE school are terrible for finding out the truth.

The navy SERE PowerPoint presentation could not have been clearer:

Why is torture the worst interrogation method?
Produces unreliable information
Negative world opinion
Subject to war crimes trials
Used as a tool for compliance

"The first slide we teach is that none of these techniques work," said Nance. Exposure to the simulated torture at SERE makes trainers and other personnel involved with the program "100% diametrically opposed to this use of torture," continued Nance. "You can't go through SERE and not become a human rights advocate. You don't want any part of it. This is a lethal virus."

But after 9/11, after Mitchell and Jessen won over the Bush administration and were given multimillion-dollar contracts with the CIA, the attitude within SERE changed, Nance said. SERE trainers who knew that the tactics would not elicit accurate information agreed to get involved in the new American torture regime. Nance, who had already left by then, said he "started hearing from my guys at SERE that they were reorienting things to be more offensive." Nance said that a friend of his who was at the navy SERE school at the time told him that in 2003, officials from the Joint Prisoner Recovery Agency, the Pentagon unit that is an umbrella organization overseeing all SERE programs, came to the navy SERE school in Coronado to obtain the navy SERE "Red Books"—the program's manuals.

The navy program—conducted at Coronado and North Island near San Diego, and Brunswick, Maine—was known within the military for being far more intense and brutal than the SERE programs in any other service, and so Mitchell and Jessen convinced the CIA to use the navy tactics as the basis for their enhanced interrogation techniques. The navy's "Red Books" had a guide on how to conduct waterboarding, walling, facial and abdominal slaps, and other techniques that have now become infamous. "The Red Books were how-to guides to do everything bad," recalled Nance. The visiting officials even measured the waterboard at the navy SERE facility at North Island, which was modeled after the waterboard used against American POWs by the North Vietnamese. The navy had built it at North Island to the exact measurements vividly recalled by former American POWs. (The CIA eventually used a gurney instead at its black-site prisons.)

Nance was especially bothered by one of the tactics the visiting officials took from navy SERE: talking about the rape of a child, then forcing the prisoner to listen to an endless tape of a baby crying and screaming. "I thought that was the worst," said Nance. "It's hard for the staff to go through. We put in earplugs." Nance said all of the tactics that eventually formed the basis for the enhanced interrogation program came directly from the navy's version of SERE; it was the only service that used them all.

Nance said that the navy SERE program was under such tight controls and monitored so closely by top navy officials that the decision to allow the direct transfer of its methodology for use in abusive interrogations had to have been known at the highest levels of the naval service, and approved by the chief of naval operations (CNO). "SERE is very carefully controlled. The CNO's office had to know what was going on," said Nance.

Few if any people inside SERE objected, largely because they believed that this was an exciting opportunity to be at the cutting edge of the war on terror, rubbing shoulders with what insiders call "Tier One operators"—CIA case officers and U.S. Special Operations personnel. "They had an advisor from SERE at Gitmo," said Nance. "I think you would find there have been SERE instructors all over the world advising the processing of prisoners."

In fact, in late December 2002, two instructors from the navy SERE school arrived at Guantánamo and began training interrogators there on how to administer the SERE tactics, according to a Senate Armed Services Committee report on detainee abuse.

"They threw everything they knew out the window," Nance added. "They were all gung ho to get in to the Tier One world."

Both Andy Morgan and Malcolm Nance said that the statements included in the Justice Department's legal opinions, which claimed that the tactics could not be considered torture because thousands of American service personnel had been subjected to them without any permanent damage, were false.

In a footnote to a 2005 Justice Department legal opinion, since declassified, Steven Bradbury, then the head of the Justice Department's Office of Legal Counsel, wrote that the tactics had been used safely on SERE students for years. The opinion, written by Bradbury in the form of a memo to John Rizzo, then the senior deputy general counsel of the CIA, states in the footnote that Rizzo had told Bradbury that at least two former SERE trainers—whose names are redacted—had assured him that SERE training had never inflicted any significant physical or psychological damage on trainees.

"Through your consultation with individuals responsible for such training, you have learned facts relating to experience with them, which you have reported to us," Bradbury wrote in the footnote. "You have advised us that these techniques have been used as a part of a course of training without any reported incidents of prolonged mental harm or of any reported severe physical pain, injury or suffering. With respect to the psychological impact, [redacted] of the SERE school advised that during his three and a half years in that position, he trained 10,000 students, only two of whom dropped out following use of the techniques. . . . [Redacted] who has had over ten years' experience with SERE training, told you that he was not aware of any individual who completed the program suffering from any adverse mental health effects."

The assertions that SERE tactics were safe provided a critical underpinning to the Justice Department's legal opinions. In order to authorize the enhanced interrogation techniques, the Justice Department's lawyers were trying to skirt U.S. and international laws banning torture. To do so, they had to be able to define the techniques as something other than torture.

Morgan said that he believes the assertions from the former SERE trainers described in the Office of Legal Counsel memo, particularly on the potential for psychological damage from SERE training, were false, designed to gain the government's approval of the use of enhanced interrogation tactics. "They would have had to know at the time they wrote that memo that the central assertions were not true." Whoever provided Bradbury with that information made inaccurate assertions "when they said that the SERE tactics couldn't lead to damage," he added. "That was well known in the psychological field at the time."

Among other things, Morgan noted that only a small number of military personnel who go through SERE training are subjected to waterboarding, one of the harshest SERE techniques reverse-engineered by the CIA. In SERE school, waterboarding is reserved for those very few students who attempt to "John Wayne" their way through the course, by trying to refuse all cooperation with their interrogators, which is not the approach SERE seeks to teach. Frequently those students are navy SEALs or other Special Operations soldiers trying to prove how macho they can be, and they are waterboarded only to demonstrate that anyone can be broken. "When they say that thousands of people going through SERE have been waterboarded, that is not true," said Morgan. What's more, the waterboarding and other tactics used at SERE are part of a highly controlled simulation — most crucially, the students know that the trainers are only pretending to be interrogators. (A Senate Armed Services Committee report released in late 2008 agreed with Morgan's assessment, concluding that the use of SERE techniques for interrogating detainees was "inconsistent with the goal of collecting accurate intelligence information." The techniques, the report added, were "based, in part, on Chinese Communist techniques used during the Korean War to elicit false confessions.")

After the Office of Legal Counsel memos became public, Morgan said that he tried to convince SERE psychologists to join him in speaking out by calling out the claims in the memos. "My biggest disappointment with the community of DOD psychologists was that there could have been a rebuttal," Morgan said. "But they were afraid to speak out, because they would lose their positions. They all feel that it would be disloyal to make a statement. I spoke at one of the conferences of SERE psychologists about it, but they didn't want to speak out."

Not long after the Abu Ghraib scandal led to a firestorm of protest over the Bush administration's use of the tactics, Morgan learned firsthand why so many people in the system were frightened to speak out. The White House was watching SERE very closely.

Morgan said he received a message through a colleague that Samantha Ravich, an aide to Dick Cheney (the same aide who met with Dennis Montgomery), wanted access to his confidential medical and psychological research data on the effects of waterboarding on SERE students. Morgan said he concluded that Cheney's office was only looking for information that it could use to publicly defend the use of waterboarding, so he refused to respond to the request.

He said he has always refused to publish any of his data specifically on waterboarding because it is badly skewed by the bias of who is selected for waterboarding at SERE — a small handful of navy SEALs "who are being blockheads" and purposely seeking a confrontation with their SERE instructors. "The data showed that the SEALs were found to rebound from waterboarding, and I won't publish that because it is biased by who is involved and the situation they are in," said Morgan. "It is not scientific data that is interesting, because it is so biased. I realized that publishing that would be like lighting a match. I don't know how Ravich found out that I had it, but I didn't want to give it to Cheney's office." Probably, some SERE officials, eager to cooperate with the enhanced interrogation program, told the White House about Morgan's unpublished research.

Many in the SERE community, especially SERE psychologists, recognized that participation in the Bush administration's interrogation regime was the path to wealth and power. The fact that so many within the SERE community were so willing to participate in the torture program deeply disturbs Nance, because they knew better than anyone else what they were doing was wrong and that it wouldn't work. He now believes that his former colleagues at SERE who participated were complicit in war crimes. "We teach that these are war crimes," said Nance. "We teach about Pinochet in Chile. We were using tactics that the Israeli Supreme Court had ruled to be torture."

At the time of his death in 2008, Scott Gerwehr was an enigma. He was a secretive man living a highly compartmentalized life, and no one fully knew him, perhaps not even himself. When he slid his motorcycle underneath a truck on Sunset Boulevard in Los Angeles and died at the age of forty, he was mourned widely and sorrowfully because he was many things to many people. He was the gregarious center of gravity of a tight-knit group of longtime friends in Santa Monica, the Peter Pan character in a crowd reminiscent of the cast of *Friends,* a short, stocky, and bald-headed slacker and computer geek who loved to work from home on his laptop, a gamer addicted to World of Warcraft, a liberal who expressed distaste for George Bush during long talks around the UCLA campus or in coffee shops near the ocean.

But he was also a behavioral science researcher who had cultivated close ties to the CIA and Pentagon while working as an analyst at the RAND Corporation and later at the Defense Group, a defense and intelligence contracting firm. He had a Top Secret/Sensitive Compartmented Information clearance, and his research focused on finding new ways of determining when someone was lying—"deception detection" research. He would regularly disappear from his Santa Monica apartment to fly to Washington for meetings with officials from the CIA, Pentagon, Department of Homeland Security, and National Security Agency. He sought meetings with top aides to Defense Secretary Donald Rumsfeld. He participated in an exclusive, CIA-backed workshop with Samantha Ravich, Cheney's aide. He was a protégé of one of the CIA's top psychologists, who quietly talked to him about moving to Langley. He considered taking a job with Mitchell and Jessen but decided against it because he didn't want to move to Spokane.

But the last twist in Gerwehr's life, not long before he died, was that he took tentative steps toward becoming a whistleblower. He started talking to an investigator for a human rights organization as well as to a journalist about what he knew about Mitchell and Jessen and the broader behavioral science infrastructure that enabled and supported the Bush administration in the development and use of its enhanced interrogation methods. He was cautious and hesitant, never fulfilling the tantalizing promise of a full-blown whistleblower. Even today, the extent of his knowledge of the CIA's detention and interrogation programs remains unclear, and it is also not certain that he would ever have been willing to reveal everything he knew to human rights organizations or to the press. Kirk Hubbard, a former senior behavioral scientist for the CIA who was close to Gerwehr, said that Gerwehr was not involved in the CIA's interrogation program and had no operational background. "Having said that, I don't know what he may have been doing for anyone else," Hubbard said.

It is possible Gerwehr was simply jealous of the success of other outside contractors, like Mitchell and Jessen, who were getting bigger contracts and becoming even more deeply enmeshed in the secret side of the war on terror. But it is also possible that the disconnect between his dual lives, one in Santa Monica and another in Washington, had become too much to bear as he approached his forties. He privately told a psychologist that he had innovative ideas for the protection of detainees, that he had proposed putting video cameras in interrogations at Guantánamo as a form of verification that they were not being tortured, but that his ideas had been rejected. Despite his misgivings, Gerwehr was "manic with ideas," recalled Brad Olson, a psychologist at National Louis University in Chicago and a critic of the Bush interrogation tactics. Olson had talked to Gerwehr and then put him in contact with a human rights organization. He said Gerwehr had told him he was eager to do research on detainees and interrogations. "He wasn't talking to me out of guilt, he was talking to me out of optimism about the potential for the work. He seemed optimistic about the possibilities of testing out psychological theories on interrogation issues. He never said exactly who he was working for, but at one point, he said, oh, they are doing it all wrong, they have to do it like this, but he never gave me any specifics."

Gerwehr's interest in videotaping interrogations would have run into a brick wall at the CIA, which was then secretly in turmoil over the earlier videotaping of the interrogations of at least three high-value detainees in the agency's secret prisons. Those tapes had been secretly destroyed in 2005; after the tape destruction was revealed by the *New York Times* in 2007, the Justice Department appointed a special prosecutor to investigate whether any laws had been broken.

★

Several years after his death, I obtained a copy of Gerwehr's personal computer files, including an archive of his personal e-mails. The Gerwehr computer files do not include any explosive bombshells that suggest that he was on the verge of making major revelations about the Bush administration or the CIA at the time of his death. His e-mails and other documents reveal that he was on the outer edges of the intelligence community and the war on terror. His deception detection research was abstract and had a number of potential uses, for the government as well as for corporate customers. For a time, the primary focus of his research was not interrogations at all but the study of how to apply deception detection methods to protecting computer systems from sophisticated cyberattacks.

Yet the computer files show that he knew the right people. He was part of a wide network of psychologists, academic researchers, contractors, think tank analysts, and intelligence and Pentagon officials who formed the behavioral science infrastructure that grew up suddenly after 9/11 to support the Bush administration's war on terror.

The significance of the Gerwehr files is not in what they say about him or in what he was doing. Rather, it is in what they help reveal about the tight network of behavioral scientists so eager for CIA and Pentagon contracts that they showed few qualms about getting involved with institutions that were using pseudo behavioral science to brutalize prisoners. They help reveal the close relationships between behavioral scientists and the government that made it easier for the CIA and Pentagon to develop such a large detention and interrogation infrastructure so quickly.

What is most striking about many of the e-mails is their utter banality, showing the connections between the intelligence community and the behavioral science profession in big ways and small.

For example, Dr. Martin Seligman, a former president of the American Psychological Association and an expert on the concept of "learned helplessness," which is at the core of the doctrine behind the CIA's enhanced interrogation program, is shown in an e-mail in the Gerwehr files to have had a professional relationship with Kirk Hubbard, the senior CIA behavioral scientist who was close to Gerwehr. Hubbard wrote to Gerwehr and others on March 30, 2004, to complain: "My office director would not even reimburse me for circa $100 bucks for CIA logo t-shirts and ball caps for Marty Seligman's five kids! He's helped out a lot over the past four years so I thought that was the least I could do. But no, has to come out of my own pocket! And people wonder why I am so cynical!"

In December 2001, Seligman held a meeting at his home outside Philadelphia with a group of academics and national security officials, including James Mitchell and Hubbard, to discuss ways to address Muslim extremism, according to the *New York Times*. Seligman told the *Times* that Mitchell introduced himself during the meeting and said that he admired Seligman's writings on learned helplessness. Seligman said that he was later horrified to discover that his work on learned helplessness had been used as the doctrinal basis for the interrogation program. In 2002, Seligman and Hubbard met again, this time at a SERE conference in San Diego where they had lunch, according to both men.

Seligman said that he never got the hats or T-shirts for his children, "nor any other token of gratitude from the CIA," and also said that he never worked for the CIA. Hubbard confirmed that Seligman did not work for the CIA and said that he ended up not buying the hats and T-shirts.

After 9/11, Scott Gerwehr began to make his mark in the burgeoning field of deception detection. In 2003, he was deeply involved with a conference on the topic that brought together leading experts from RAND, the American Psychological Association, and the CIA. The conference, funded by the CIA, marked Gerwehr's acceptance into a tight-knit network of behavioral science experts all playing roles in the war on terror. Mitchell and Jessen, who were then at the height of their influence within the CIA, attended the conference, along with Hubbard.

Hubbard sent Gerwehr an e-mail about the CIA's participation in the detection deception conference, which was revealing for the secretive way in which he identified CIA psychologists as well as Mitchell and Jessen. Hubbard wrote that CIA operational psychologists, whom he identified only as "Herb, Alisa, John and Dave," would be coming, along with "contractors to CIA" identified only as "Jim" and "Bruce."

Gerwehr began to ingratiate himself with a small clique of national security psychologists who had influence behind the scenes at key institutions throughout Washington. Among Gerwehr's closest contacts were Hubbard, who was chief of the CIA's Behavioral Sciences Staff; Susan Brandon, a psychologist who worked at the Bush White House as a behavioral science expert in the Office of Science Policy, and then bounced through other key positions in national security psychology; Geoffrey Mumford, director of science policy at the American Psychological Association; and Kirk Kennedy, the chief of the Center for National Security Psychology for the Counterintelligence Field Activity, a Pentagon unit that was later abolished after disclosures of its involvement in domestic spying. In a 2003 e-mail, Brandon, Hubbard, Mumford, and Gerwehr were identified as the "organizing committee" of the CIA-backed deception detection conference attended by Mitchell and Jessen.

Despite the professional consensus among psychologists that torture was counterproductive, the American Psychological Association, the largest professional organization for psychologists, worked assiduously to protect the psychologists who did get involved in the torture program.

In 2002, the APA issued subtle changes to its ethics rules that, in effect, gave greater professional cover for psychologists who had been helping to monitor and oversee harsh interrogations. Perhaps the most important change was a new ethics guideline: if a psychologist faced a conflict between the APA's ethics code and a lawful order or regulation, the psychologist could follow the law or "governing legal authority." In other words, a psychologist could engage in activities that the U.S. government said were legal—such as harsh interrogations—even if they violated the APA's ethical standards. This change introduced the Nuremberg defense into American psychology—following lawful orders was an acceptable reason to violate professional ethics. The change in the APA's ethics code was essential to the Bush administration's ability to use enhanced interrogation techniques on detainees.

Without the changes to the APA's ethics code, more psychologists would likely have taken the view that they were prevented by their own professional standards from involvement, and that would have made it far more difficult for the Justice Department to craft opinions that provided the legal approvals needed for the CIA to go ahead with the interrogation tactics. The involvement of psychologists in the interrogations helped the lawyers in the Justice Department to argue that the enhanced interrogation program was legal because health professionals were monitoring the interrogations to make sure they stayed within the limits established by the Bush administration.

If the American Psychological Association and its member psychologists had not gone along with the Bush administration, it is unclear that any other health professionals would have taken their place. In fact, in a 2006 Pentagon conference call with reporters, Dr. William Winkenwerder, then the assistant secretary of defense for health affairs, made it clear that the Defense Department had come to rely far more heavily on psychologists at Guantánamo than psychiatrists. "Psychologists and psychiatrists can do at times similar things," said Winkenwerder, according to a transcript provided by the Defense Department. "As we looked at the role of the behavioral science consultant first, it seemed to us that—and in fact it has been the practice for most of the history of Guantánamo Bay that it has been psychologists who have been in that role. . . . Our policy doesn't preclude a psychiatrist from performing the task. It recognizes that it typically would be performed by a psychologist."

"There is a second issue that did to some extent influence our thinking, and that is as we spoke to the American Psychiatric Association and the American Psychological Association—the American Psychological Association was—clearly supports the role of psychologists in interrogations in a way our behavioral science consultants operate," Winkenwerder added. "The American Psychiatric Association, on the other hand, I think had a great deal of debate about that and there were some who were less comfortable with that. I don't—I can't describe for you where they came out exactly on the policy with regards as to psychiatrists participating in interrogations. But . . . we try to be sensitive to the respective roles of—as they are viewed in their professions."

The APA cooperated not just because a few psychologists like Mitchell and Jessen were involved (Mitchell and Jessen were not APA members). Instead, critics say the psychological profession cooperated because it had so much at stake in its relationship with the government's national security apparatus. For America's psychologists, cooperation with interrogations was all about money and status, many critics argue.

The U.S. military had helped to foster the growth of the psychological profession throughout the twentieth century, dating back to its early involvement in the aptitude testing of soldiers in World War I and World War II. The Defense Department and the Veterans Administration eventually became two of the largest employers of psychologists in the nation, and both provide outside contracts to psychologists as well.

Many psychologists have long been deeply insecure about their status compared to psychiatrists, who are medical doctors and thus can prescribe medicine for their patients. Prescription-writing privileges have given psychiatrists a huge competitive advantage over psychologists at a time when the market for psychiatric drugs—from antidepressants like Zoloft and Prozac to antipsychotics like Thorazine—has exploded.

Here, too, the Pentagon has come to the rescue; the Defense Department has begun to grant prescription-writing privileges to some psychologists treating patients at military hospitals, an important professional breakthrough at a time when psychiatric drugs represent a huge growth industry. What the psychological profession wanted, in Zimbardo's view, "was prescription privileges." Turning against the interrogation program would have put the psychological profession's entire relationship with the CIA and Pentagon at risk.

After the Abu Ghraib scandal broke in 2004 and the public first learned about prisoner abuse by both the CIA and military, the APA was forced to respond to evidence of involvement by psychologists and other behavioral scientists. The APA created a committee to study the matter, which issued a report in 2005 that provided professional cover for the psychologists who had been involved with the interrogation program. The APA's Presidential Task Force on Psychological Ethics and National Security (PENS) concluded that it was appropriate and ethical for psychologists to be involved with interrogations, in order to ensure that they remained safe, legal, ethical, and effective — phrasing that was almost identical to the language used by the military's Behavioral Science Consultation Teams at Guantánamo.

The APA provided the Bush administration its needed cover

Gerwehr's e-mails show for the first time the degree to which behavioral science experts from within the government's national security apparatus played roles in shaping the PENS task force. They show that APA officials were secretly working behind the scenes with CIA and Pentagon officials to discuss how to shape the organization's position to be supportive of psychologists involved in interrogations — long before the task force was even formed.

In July 2004, just months after the graphic photos of abuse at Abu Ghraib were publicly disclosed, APA officials convened a private meeting of psychologists working at the CIA, Pentagon, and other national security agencies to provide input on how the APA should deal with the growing furor, Gerwehr's e-mails show. Among those receiving private invitations to the brainstorming session were Kirk Hubbard from the CIA and Kirk Kennedy of the Pentagon. Scott Gerwehr also received an invitation through an e-mail from Stephen Behnke, the director of the APA's ethics office.

The APA's ethics office and its science directorate, the invitation stated, were holding a private lunch meeting for psychologists involved in the government's national security apparatus to discuss the "unique ethical issues" that had been raised for psychologists in the wake of the Abu Ghraib disclosures. Behnke wrote:

> The purpose of the meeting is to bring together people with an interest in the ethical aspects of national security–related investigations, to identify the important questions, and to discuss how we as a national organization can better assist psychologists and other mental health professionals sort out appropriate from inappropriate uses of psychology. We want to ask individuals involved in the work what the salient issues are, whether more or better guidance is needed, and how best to provide guidance. . . . I would like to emphasize that we will not advertise the meeting other than this letter to the individual invitees, that we will not publish or otherwise make public the names of attendees or the substance of our discussions, and that in the meeting we will neither assess nor investigate the behavior of any specific individual or group.

Behnke offered sympathetically that the APA wanted to take a "positive approach, in which we convey a sensitivity to and appreciation of the important work mental health professionals are doing in the national security arena."

Psychologists and behavioral science experts in the national security community were happy to take advantage of the APA's offer of early involvement in the organization's process of dealing with the interrogation issue.

Kirk Hubbard of the CIA replied to Behnke by saying that he would be in charge of representing both the CIA's and the Pentagon's interests at the meeting. "I just spoke with Kirk Kennedy," Hubbard wrote in an e-mail on which Gerwehr was copied. "All the DOD shrinks will be tied up. . . . He and I decided that rather than delay the initial meet-ing, we should just go ahead. He and I will consult on the issues that concern CIA and DOD and I will represent both of us on July 20. I'll then brief him."

The invitation to the lunch meeting showed that the APA was opening the door to psychologists and other behavioral science ex-perts inside the government's national security apparatus to provide advice and guidance about how to address the furor over the role of psychologists in torture before the APA went to its own membership. The insiders were being given a chance to influence the APA's stance before anyone else.

In fact, this secret meeting of top government psychologists was held months before the APA finally began a public process among its members to address the controversy surrounding the involvement of psychologists in the enhanced interrogation program. On Janu-ary 3, 2005, Gerwehr and others who had been invited to the meet-ing in July 2004 received an e-mail including a draft proposal for an APA task force to deal with the role of psychologists in interrogations. They were receiving the draft proposal more than a month before it was made public to APA members.

Jean Maria Arrigo, an independent social psychologist who was a member of the PENS task force, said that the first she heard about the APA's plans to deal with the interrogation issue was in February 2005, when the APA issued a public notice of its plans for a task force. Arrigo now believes she was placed on the PENS task force to give the CIA- and Pentagon-backed psychologists the cover they needed to make it appear legitimate. "I was there as a dupe, purposefully," she said.

In fact, the deck appears to have been stacked on the task force. Of the ten psychologists appointed to it, six had connections with the defense or intelligence communities; one member was the chief psychologist for U.S. Special Forces. In addition, a senior APA official who attended meetings of the task force was married to a psycholo-gist assigned to one of the military's Behavioral Science Consultation Teams — military units involved in interrogations.

Arrigo said that Russ Newman, then the head of APA's practice directorate and one of the most powerful officials in the organization, attended the task force sessions as an observer, but she later came to believe that he was actually helping to set the task force's agenda. He told the group that "we have to put out the fires of controversy, and we have to do it fast," Arrigo recalled. She only learned much later about Newman's wife's involvement with the military. Newman was married to Lt. Col. Debra Dunivin, a member of the Guantánamo Behavioral Science Consultation Team. "A year after the task force, I talked to a couple of counterintelligence people I knew, who told me that this was a social legitimization process," she added. "This was an effort by the Bush administration to gain legitimacy through the APA."

After succeeding in getting the PENS task force to endorse the continued involvement of psychologists in the interrogation program, congratulations were in order among the small number of behavioral scientists with connections to the national security community who had been part of the effort. In a July 2005 e-mail to Hubbard from Geoffrey Mumford (on which Gerwehr was copied), Mumford thanked Hubbard for helping to influence the outcome of the task force. "I also wanted to semi-publicly acknowledge your personal contribution . . . in getting this effort off the ground," Mumford wrote. "Your views were well represented by very carefully selected task force members." Mumford also noted that Susan Brandon had served as an "observer" at the PENS task force meetings and "helped craft some language related to research" for the task force report.

At the time of the release of the task force report, Hubbard had just retired from the CIA to begin consulting for Mitchell and Jessen. "Now I do some consulting work for Mitchell and Jessen Associates," Hubbard wrote in a mass e-mail to many of his friends and colleagues in June 2005.

Hubbard tried to recruit Gerwehr to join him. In a May 2006 e-mail to Gerwehr, Hubbard told him there was an opening for a psychologist at Mitchell and Jessen's firm, and that he would be the ideal candidate. "I have attached a position description in the event you know of someone who might fit the bill," Hubbard wrote. "You would be perfect, but you probably wouldn't want to relocate to Spokane! Obviously candidates cannot be extreme liberals as some psychologists seem to be."

Gerwehr was intrigued, even though he knew full well by then what the firm did. He responded that "I must say that does sound like a dream job that was tailor made for me! I would be very interested in discussing it, though the Spokane thing is probably a non-starter. If they'd let me stay in LA though . . . !"

But by late 2006, Gerwehr was talking to Katherine Eban for her *Vanity Fair* article about the role of psychologists in interrogations, particularly Mitchell and Jessen. And there was one final twist for Gerwehr: Geoffrey Mumford and Susan Brandon were desperately trying to conduct spin control on Eban's story, and consulted with Gerwehr about how best to answer her questions. In an e-mail, Gerwehr disarmed Mumford and Brandon by blithely responding that he had already talked to Eban. "While there is always the chance that reporters will take quotes out of context, or arrange facts in a way that is sensationalist or suggestive of something sinister, I have nothing to hide here and feel transparency on this topic is a good thing."

8

THE WAR ON NORMALCY

The Haskell Free Library and Opera House was built more than a century ago to stand as a monument to the enduring friendship between the United States and Canada. The late-Victorian-era building, with a two-tone façade of gray granite and brown brick, was purposely constructed so that it literally straddles the international border, with the front door in the United States and the library's circulation desk and the opera house's stage in Canada. It was meant to encourage people from both countries to read books and enjoy musical performances side by side.

The Haskell is the best-known landmark in the small, adjoining towns of Derby Line, Vermont, and Stanstead, Quebec, and its quirky status — a black line marking the border runs along the floor through the library — has for generations lent the twin communities their special charm. The Haskell's staff comes from both countries. The collection has books in English and French. The building has official addresses in both the United States and Canada, on the streets that intersect beside the library — Caswell Avenue in Derby Line and Church Street (or Rue Church) in Stanstead.

Indeed, the Haskell's historic role as a symbol of openness and shared democratic values along the world's longest undefended border was the root cause of the 2010 Battle of Derby Line. The battle was an American classic — a little guy taking on cold and powerful interests. It galvanized an entire town and started a local grassroots rebellion against the excesses of the war on terror and the nation's post-9/11 fear-driven obsession with security.

A decade of fear-mongering has brought power and wealth to those who have been the most skillful at hyping the terrorist threat. Fear sells. Fear has convinced the White House and Congress to pour hundreds of billions of dollars — more money than anyone knows what to do with — into counterterrorism and homeland security programs, often with little management or oversight, and often to the detriment of the Americans they are supposed to protect. Fear is hard to question. It is central to the financial well-being of countless federal bureaucrats, contractors, subcontractors, consultants, analysts, and pundits. Fear generates funds.

One of the most baleful consequences of the toxic combination of fear and money in the post-9/11 era has been the constriction of the physical landscape of the United States. Freedom of movement — one of the greatest attributes of life in the expanse of the United States — has been curtailed. Money has flowed from Washington and corporate America to finance security guards, security gates, metal detectors, and Jersey barriers; bit by bit, the United States has become a nation whose watchwords are now "authorized access only."

It is enough to make a lot of Americans claustrophobic and angry. Including Buzz Roy of Derby Line, Vermont.

Buzz Roy is an institution in Derby Line. Born in 1942, he has lived virtually his entire life in the village, with the exception of his five years as a student at the Massachusetts College of Pharmacy. Since 1964, he has been the owner of Brown's Drug Store, which his father owned before him. He can still be found each day personally filling prescriptions at the store's counter, coming to work dressed in a dignified button-down oxford shirt and tie, looking trim and much younger than his age. He has long been an active community leader, serving as both a member of Derby Line's elected board of village trustees and a trustee of the Haskell Library.

Growing up in Derby Line in the mid-twentieth century meant that Roy was used to crossing the U.S. border whenever he pleased. The border between the United States and Canada was nothing more than a line on a map, two blocks down Main Street from the drug store. Americans crossed it to shop for groceries or to go to the barbershop or beauty salon; Canadians crossed to buy cheaper gas and milk. There was a lightly manned U.S. Customs office on Main Street in Derby Line, just one block from Brown's, but Derby Line and Stanstead really were one community. "Before 9/11 it was very open, it was just a wave and a hi at the customs officer," recalls Roy.

But the 9/11 terrorist attacks changed everything. To the new bureaucratic behemoth in Washington, the Department of Homeland Security, America's 5,500-mile-long border with Canada was a vulnerability that had to be sealed. It didn't matter that there was no evidence that the Canadian border had become a real threat; Homeland Security could find statistics to prove that it had. What's more, Homeland Security was flush with cash, and it was searching for ways to spend it.

Meanwhile, counterterrorism experts, many with lucrative government contracts or consulting deals with television news networks—in short, with an incentive to generate public fear and foreboding—had joined forces with zealous anti-immigration advocates to warn that the Canadian border was a dangerously unsecured back door. Members of the Minutemen, the anti-immigration organization that usually focuses on the Mexican border, even showed up in Derby Line. "They were not well received," says Buzz Roy.

Political pressure mounted. Homeland Security began to zero in on the Canadian border. The border crossing at Derby Line had to get with the times and follow new rules. Canadians and Americans who had been living and working side by side for generations had to be treated the same as suspected al Qaeda terrorists. Homeland Security moved in and began to physically break apart Derby Line and Stanstead for the first time in over a century.

Officials demanded that the streets connecting Derby Line and Stanstead be closed down. New border gates were constructed. Additional customs and border patrol agents flooded into town. Just to run errands, townspeople now had to show their passports — many locals had to apply for passports for the first time — and submit to lengthy questioning.

Buzz Roy is a traditional Vermonter, a native of what locals call the Northeast Kingdom. Like most of his kind, he has no use for bureaucrats. And so when Homeland Security officials began to demand changes in Derby Line, Roy began to push back. Along with a few other local leaders, he fought the street closings. Eventually, the local leaders worked out what they thought was a compromise with Homeland Security: two of the three streets connecting Derby Line and Stanstead would be closed. New border patrol gates would be built on those streets to control access across the border. But the third — Church Street, which passed right by the Haskell Free Library as it crossed the border — would remain open, without a security gate. People walking or driving up Church Street would simply have to follow the traditional procedure of checking in later at the local customs office. The open road would mean continued access for both Americans and Canadians to the Haskell Library, and would recognize the landmark's historic importance to both Derby Line and Stanstead.

Roy didn't really like the compromise, since it meant that a new border gate would be built on Main Street, less than two blocks from Brown's Drug Store. But at least Derby Line had won a small concession from Homeland Security.

And then it got worse.

Homeland Security had to find ways to spend the billions of dollars Congress was providing for counterterrorism and border security, and one idea that the Obama administration came up with was called Operation Stonegarden. Homeland Security would give large grants to local law enforcement agencies in states along the northern and southern borders. In exchange, local police, sheriff's deputies, and other officers would help to patrol the border along with customs and border patrol agents. In June 2009, Homeland Security announced it was giving grants of $60 million for fiscal 2009 to thirteen border states, including Vermont, and to Puerto Rico. Homeland Security Secretary Janet Napolitano said that Operation Stonegarden would help ensure that "our first responders are equipped with the resources they need to confront the complex and dynamic challenges that exist along our borders."

For police departments in Vermont and other states, the Operation Stonegarden grants were hard to refuse. For police chiefs, it was almost free money. All they had to do was send an officer up to the border for a while and the federal government would write a badly needed check. Vermont accepted $501,079 in Operation Stonegarden grants in fiscal 2009.

One of Operation Stonegarden's early targets was Derby Line, Vermont. Before long, law enforcement officers from all over the state — everyone from police from Vermont's larger cities to fish and wildlife agents — began to crowd into Derby Line. Unsmiling strangers with shaved heads and sunglasses were suddenly everywhere. It was as if the federal government had decided to conduct an experiment in Derby Line on how to create a mini–police state.

The Homeland Security surge into Derby Line had predictable and disastrous results. Dozens of out-of-town police officers, with no experience or training in how to work along the border, jammed into a village of eight hundred people. They had to find something to do and someone to arrest. It wasn't long before they were harassing Derby Line residents with nearly constant traffic stops and tickets for the most trivial violations. "They were enforcing all kinds of rules, they were stopping people for not having mud flaps on their trucks, for having rosary beads on their mirrors, all kinds of things," said Karen Jenne, Derby Line's town treasurer. "People were just not coming to Derby Line anymore because there were so many police here."

The police lurked on the village's downtown streets, barking at residents who wandered too close to the border. They barged into the Haskell Library, hunting for Canadians to arrest who had dared to park in front of the building—in the United States—rather than on the side safely in Quebec. At the new border gates, the out-of-town agents were rude to Canadians and Americans alike, demanding that locals submit to lengthy questioning when they were just going to the local mini-mart to buy gas and milk.

"They were trolling the line and waiting to see if they could get you," said Kim Prangley, a Stanstead native who had run the Haskell Library for twenty-four years. "People were not very happy with Stonegarden," added Florence Joyal, the feisty longtime cashier at Brown's Drug Store. "But they didn't scare me."

Things finally came to a head because Buzz Roy was hungry for pizza.

On a Saturday night in February 2010, Roy decided to order smoked meat pizza from Pizzeria Steve 2002, one of his favorite pizza places. It happened to be on Boul Notre Dame in Stanstead, two blocks into Canada.

Roy walked over to the pizzeria to pick up his pizza. When he started back home, he decided to walk up Church Street, the sole ungated road in the village. But just as he passed the Haskell Library, a Vermont state trooper, detailed to the border patrol under Operation Stonegarden, pulled up behind Roy in his cruiser, lights flashing, and ordered Roy to stop. The state trooper got out of his car and demanded to see Roy's identification. The trooper told him that it was illegal to use Church Street to enter the United States.

Roy knew that wasn't true—keeping Church Street open had been part of Derby Line's compromise with Homeland Security. But the trooper ignored his protests and insisted on seeing his identification. Standing in the cold Vermont night holding his pizza, Roy asked the trooper to hold the pizza box while he reached for his wallet. The trooper refused. Roy laid his pizza on the cruiser and finally found his ID.

Roy eventually made his way home, but as he sat eating his pizza, he grew increasingly angry. With each bite he thought about the indignity he had just suffered from a stranger in his own village. Like everyone else in Derby Line, he was fed up with Operation Stonegarden and the petty violations of the village's way of life. About half-way through his dinner, Roy decided to get up and do something about it.

He walked back to where he had been stopped on Church Street earlier that evening, and walked down the street across the border again. And then he walked up and down the street and crossed the border one more time for good measure. Finally, a sheriff's deputy pulled up and stopped him, and told him that he was breaking the law. Through gritted teeth, Roy said that it was his right as a U.S. citizen, that he had lived there all his life, and that Church Street had been kept open under Derby Line's deal with the federal government. The deputy pointed to a new sign that said it was illegal to cross Church Street. Roy, who had never seen the sign before, grew even angrier. Homeland Security had not talked to the village about closing off Church Street; they had just done it and then put up a sign without telling anyone. Roy told the sheriff that Derby Line had never agreed to it. As they were talking, a flock of border patrol agents descended on Church Street, gathered around him, handcuffed him, arrested him, and stuffed him in the back of a cruiser.

Roy's longtime partner, Sandra, watched the episode unfold with binoculars through the window of their home, and then listened on a police scanner as Roy was taken away.

"I was arrested for entering the United States at a nondesignated spot," recalls Roy. "It was ridiculous."

He was driven to a border patrol detention facility down Interstate 91 and placed in a holding cell for three hours. Finally, one longtime border patrol agent who had been stationed in the area for years and knew Roy discovered what was going on and drove him home.

News of the arrest spread like wildfire, and overnight, Buzz Roy became the hero of Derby Line. The quiet village, which had put up with so much from Homeland Security and Operation Stonegarden, was outraged and rallied to Roy's defense. At least two hundred people from Derby Line, along with some Canadians from Stanstead, held a rally at the border at Church Street to protest his arrest. They then marched through the village to a local park, many wearing masks with his picture plastered on them along with buttons that said "Free Buzzy" (many people in Derby Line call him Buzzy, even though he goes by Buzz).

Daria MonDesire, a local woman, then performed a song she had quickly written about Buzz: "The Feds say Derby Line's a big ole danger . . . / 'Give up your freedom for security,' well Buzzy wouldn't do it."

The Derby Line protest made the television news across Vermont, and Roy's case became a cause célèbre throughout the state. People from all over the state started sending Roy money to pay his $500 fine and help fight the government. He sent the money back, which only served to enhance his stature. Roy was now better known in Vermont than most local politicians, and Homeland Security and the border patrol were cast as the villains of the Northeast Kingdom.

Homeland Security officials tried to act like nothing had happened, but they could not ignore the fact that Roy had been turned into a martyr. Without any public announcement, a top regional manager for the border patrol was moved out of his job and replaced. The new manager called Derby Line officials to apologize. "A new guy came and said we're sorry, we won't do that again," recalls Karen Jenne. Operation Stonegarden came to an abrupt end in Derby Line, and Homeland Security transferred the project to other towns along the border. The customs and border patrol agents who remained toned things down and dropped some of their arrogant ways. "They aren't hassling people as much anymore," said Jenne. "I think Buzzy's protest really had an effect."

But Derby Line still cannot return to the old ways — Homeland Security won't allow it. Crossing the border on Church Street continues to be prohibited. After the Buzz Roy protest, a border patrol agent was assigned to sit in a cruiser, all day and all night, on Church Street just outside the Haskell Library to stop anyone from following in Roy's footsteps. Border patrol agents still yell at locals who don't immediately check in at customs after passing through a border gate. The unsmiling men with shaved heads and sunglasses haven't all left town. Crossing the border still means demands for passports and secondary questioning and even searches, and many on both sides have decided to avoid it as much as possible. "They don't treat locals any better than anybody else," said an exasperated Karen Jenne.

In an ironic twist, Canadian officials moved in late 2012 to close off the Canadian side of Church Street to stop people from illegally entering Canada from America. The Royal Canadian Mounted Police installed a row of flowerpots across the road, because illegal immigrants in the United States were seeking refuge in Canada, which has easier rules for obtaining political asylum.

The fortress-like mentality damaged businesses on both sides of the border. Fewer Canadians are willing to cross to shop in downtown Derby Line, and fewer Americans run errands in Stanstead. "Our business from the American side has gone down drastically," said Amber Stremmelaar, the daughter of the owner of Pizzeria Steve 2002. "It's a hassle for Americans to come over. If you have leftovers they won't let you bring them home with you across the border."

Fewer Canadians come to shop at Brown's Drug Store as well. Buzz Roy believes that Homeland Security is slowly killing his village, all in the name of an absurd concept of perfect security. "There's no negotiating with these people," says Roy. "It's totally senseless. There is no thought put into it. Al Qaeda has won. They have changed our lives."

For decades, the wooded campus of the National Institutes of Health (NIH) in Bethesda, Maryland, was a quiet, public oasis near one of the busiest suburban commercial districts in the Washington, D.C., area. Its 300 acres were open to all, and its long, narrow, winding streets, where researchers walked from one red-brick science building to the

next, gave NIH the feel of a sprawling state university. A subway station built nearby gave people from all over Washington easy access
to the campus. The academic atmosphere at NIH made it both an intellectual magnet for world-class scientists as well as a welcoming,
cultural jewel for the entire community, with outdoor film festivals,
picnics, and theater and orchestral performances that drew enthusiastic audiences from the surrounding neighborhoods.

For Gary Daum, a computer science and music teacher at a nearby
prep school, NIH gave him the opportunity to fulfill his dream of conducting an orchestra. In the late 1990s, Daum, whose wife worked at
NIH, helped found the NIH Community Orchestra, which was open
to any and all amateur musicians, both employees and nonemploy-
ees alike. The orchestra rehearsed and performed on the NIH campus, and its concerts quickly became a fixture on the NIH cultural
calendar. The highlight of the year came each December when the
orchestra, along with an NIH community choral group, performed
Handel's *Messiah,* including the Hallelujah Chorus, in NIH's Masur
Auditorium, attracting large, joyous audiences including top NIH officials.

The events of September 11, 2001, abruptly and permanently al-
tered life at NIH. Its traditional culture of openness was suddenly
ended. Newly empowered security officials dictated that the campus
be closed off from the public. Very quickly, new rules were interpreted
to mean that outside organizations like the community orchestra
were no longer welcome on the NIH campus. With its tight new security procedures, NIH would not allow outsiders — like nonemployee
amateur musicians — access to the campus in the evenings or on
weekends. And it would not open itself up to the crowds of nonem-
ployees who would come to listen to the concerts at the auditorium.
NIH was assuming a fortress mentality, just like Homeland Security
had done in Derby Line, Vermont, and the unintended consequences
were piling up.

"We were told that the Masur Auditorium was closed to outside
groups," recalls Daum. "We had no choice. We couldn't perform the
Messiah in December."

There was no chance for Daum to question or debate the decision. The NIH officials who banished the orchestra did not even consider that the orchestra's performances had always been well attended by the patients undergoing treatment at the NIH clinical center on campus.

Over time, NIH completely walled itself off from the surrounding neighborhoods, constructing 10-foot-high steel fences around its entire perimeter. It built security gates at each entrance, where guards stopped and often searched and swabbed down cars for bombs. Now, residents in the surrounding neighborhoods could no longer walk through the campus, and security officials threw up gates and blockades to make certain that no one exiting the NIH subway station could actually get into NIH without authorization. Even visiting foreign scientists were treated with suspicion.

Inevitably, working in such an isolated bubble threatened the very purpose of NIH, which was to bring together the world's greatest minds to foster cutting-edge medical research. Treating the NIH campus like the headquarters of the CIA meant that medical researchers could no longer benefit from the kind of intellectual spontaneity that so often leads to innovative ideas.

The scientific community began to chafe at the excessive security. To many, it seemed as if the security managers — often drawn from the same kind of people who had been high school hall monitors — were now taking control to transform the nature of the campus. The "paranoid security obsessiveness" at NIH, complained science blogger Mark Hoofnagle, was "unnecessary and counterproductive to the free exchange of ideas science needs in order to be open, international and collaborative."

Banning the orchestra, as well as a theater group that had performed on the campus for years, only served to make the isolation of NIH even worse. The new security regime at NIH left the sixty-piece orchestra without a place to practice or perform, and in the immediate aftermath of the 9/11 attacks, Gary Daum wasn't certain he could keep the group alive. He canceled rehearsals in September and October 2001.

But like Buzz Roy in Derby Line, Daum decided to fight back. He refused to let the orchestra become a victim of post-9/11 hysteria. He was determined that the orchestra would hold its Christmas concert, and perform Handel's *Messiah* and the Hallelujah Chorus one more time. "It was something we needed," said Harold Seifried, an NIH scientist and now the orchestra's president.

Daum cobbled together rehearsal spaces in church basements and high schools around Washington's Maryland suburbs. By November 2001, the orchestra was able to hold a series of intense practice sessions, making up for the lost time after the attacks. Finally, Daum found a stage at a high school in Rockville, Maryland, where the orchestra could perform during the holidays, and he put out the word that the orchestra's *Messiah* would go on as scheduled.

The December 2001 concert attracted a large crowd of people from around the Washington area who, just months after 9/11, were eager for some holiday cheer and seemed deeply moved by the Hallelujah Chorus. "It was very powerful for me," recalls Daum of that night's *Messiah*. "Because I thought these would be the last notes to be performed by the orchestra. We had no plans on what we were going to do next."

In the summer of 2002, a committee of orchestra members held a series of meetings to decide whether the group could continue. They decided to keep going, despite the fact that they were still unable to persuade NIH security officials to allow the orchestra back onto the NIH campus. Daum kept scrambling just fast enough to find churches and high schools that would take them, and the orchestra barely stayed afloat. That fall, a year after the attacks, the group performed a somber choral and orchestral piece that Daum had written, entitled *Psalm 9-11*, in yet another high school auditorium. Eventually, Georgetown Prep, the private school where Daum taught, agreed to host the group's performances, and did so for several years. The orchestra survived.

But while it is still called the NIH Community Orchestra, more than a decade after 9/11 the group has never been allowed back to rehearse or perform on the NIH campus. As a result, its ties to NIH have gradually diminished. Now, only about 25 percent of the group's musicians work at NIH, and most of its newest members are young musicians with no ties to NIH who joined simply for the chance to perform with a group of talented amateurs. They know little about its long-lost connections to NIH or about the fight to keep the orchestra alive in the days after 9/11.

But Gary Daum is still angry that NIH bureaucrats have been so willing to abandon their ties to the community — and to isolate themselves in the process — all in the name of security. "I ask every year whether we can go back and perform at Masur Auditorium," said Daum. "And every year, all they say is, we are working on it."

The rush to transform the United States from an open society to a walled fortress, prompted by the 9/11 attacks and propelled by billions of dollars spent on homeland security, has not been curbed by the killing of Osama bin Laden. The death of the nation's main adversary has done surprisingly little to change the debate over how best to balance security, civil liberties, and freedom of movement. It is no longer much of a debate — security always wins. Only a few Americans, like Buzz Roy and Gary Daum, have been willing to fight back against the forces compelling us to accept smaller lives.

Jeremy Németh, a planning and design expert at the University of Colorado at Denver, has begun to quantify how much space Americans have been willing to abandon. He found that more than 35 percent of the civic center district of New York City — the area around Foley Square and the downtown federal buildings and courthouses — is now inside a security zone, and thus open only to those with authorized access. In Los Angeles, 23 acres of land in the city is inside a security zone. Németh describes these new security enclaves in America's biggest cities as the result of "the architecture of fear."

"The security apparatus has kind of taken over," Németh says. "The security experts have begun to take over city planning and design." Indeed, the architectural profession has been forced — by clients, lawyers, insurance companies, and government regulators — to make security, rather than design elegance, a top priority. Now, there are even design firms, like Rock Twelve in New York, that specialize in security architecture, developing new types of car and truck barriers.

Airports, of course, are a lost cause; they have been the biggest victims of this security fetish and now feel more like temporary detention centers than gateways to the world. But American landmarks have also borne the brunt, turning from symbols of freedom and courage into signs of national paranoia and government control. At the U.S. Capitol, for example, lawmakers have insulated themselves from spontaneous contact with voters through the construction of a TSA-style "visitor center" that sharply limits and controls public access to the Capitol.

Across the street at the Supreme Court, the court's tall and majestic front doors, traditionally thrown open to allow Americans to hear judicial arguments, have been permanently closed. The decision, "like so many mindless decisions attributed to security concerns, is a grand affront — architecturally, symbolically, politically," wrote *Washington Post* architecture critic Philip Kennicott. "The decision will enforce new and unwanted meanings on one of the city's most dramatic and successful public buildings."

The exemplar of the new security obsession is, of course, the successor to the twin towers in New York, One World Trade Center. The tower's first 200 feet off the ground will be a solid pedestal built to be impervious to truck bombs. Yet that hardened design was not enough for the New York Police Department, which refused to give its approval to the design until even more security measures were added and the building's base was set farther back from sidewalks and the street. The *New York Times* reported that the building will come equipped with $20 million in electronic security, including chemical, biological, and radiation detection, and "video analytics" that use computers to continuously scan video feeds from the building's cameras to alert human guards if a nearby car is lingering too long or a person is walking too fast. One World Trade Center will be the tallest castle in America.

Outside the country, U.S. embassies, America's symbolic outreach to other nations, are now among the most forbidding buildings on the planet. Collectively they send a message that foreigners are no longer welcome. The U.S. embassy in Britain, located in London's Grosvenor Square, is being replaced with a new terrorist-proof building across town that has drawn withering English criticism. Warren Ellis, a British graphic novelist, was particularly scathing. The new embassy, he wrote on his blog, is "a 12-story cube clad in a blastproof glass and plastic façade surrounded by a 30-meter blast zone. . . . It looks not unlike a high-end bunker that has been simply dropped from space on London, an impregnable and isolated chunk of America. And while security is an obvious and present concern, I think perhaps this building says a little more than it was intended to. In fact, let's admit it. IT'S A FORTRESS WITH A FUCKING MOAT. It doesn't say, welcome to a little piece of America, one of the best ideas the world ever had and a country that welcomes the tired and poor and afraid. It says, if you even look at us funny we'll pour boiling oil on you from the roof. Raise the drawbridge! Release the Mongolian Terror Trout!"

Richard Sennett, a professor at New York University, says that architects hate the way American buildings are now being designed and constructed, but few ever publicly complain because they need the work in the wake of the financial crisis and recession. "Nobody wants to design a fortress," said Sennett. "People are very frustrated by it. It is against the direction that the profession wants to go. Before 9/11, the trend in urban design was to make big buildings more street friendly." Yet today, Sennett believes that 9/11 has reinforced a long-standing strain of insularity in the American culture. "The security obsession fits into a longer, broader way Americans inhabit space."

America remains on combat footing in the global war on terror, without realizing that the war that was declared after 9/11 is all but over. The main adversary in that war, Osama bin Laden, is dead, and al Qaeda is broken. What is left are shattered remnants and splinter groups.

Individual extremists, connected through the Internet or by fighting with Islamic insurgencies in other countries, often motivated by anger over American military actions, now pose a bigger domestic threat than organized Islamist terrorism aimed directly at the United States. "Lone wolf" terrorists, like the brothers responsible for the Boston Marathon bombing in 2013 that killed 3 and wounded about 180, can sow fear and generate national headlines with sporadic small-scale attacks. But they lack the power or capability of a significant terrorist organization. While the possibility of such incidents means that the nation has to remain cautiously on guard, they don't amount to the kind of existential threats initially feared in the wake of 9/11. They are best treated as criminal matters.

The sudden success of ISIS in Iraq attracted foreign fighters and raised the potential for a new terrorist threat, but the group's primary focus was on its immediate enemy in Baghdad. President Obama's decision to launch airstrikes against ISIS in the summer of 2014 raised the potential for a completely new war on terror, without ever having declared an end to the previous one. It also signified a questionable "whack-a-mole" strategy, in which the U.S. targets Islamic militant insurgencies before they ever attack the United States, just in case they might do so in the future. That strategy would almost guarantee that those groups will eventually turn against us, and that the endless war on terror would remain endless.

Boston stoked outsized fears largely because the American psyche has remained fragile in the years since 9/11. After Boston, of course, many political leaders revived post-9/11 fears and began calling once again for greater limits on privacy, freedom of movement, and the constitutional rights of Americans. Boston was actually shut down for a day during the manhunt for the suspects, an unprecedented action that led to a renewed debate over the limits of security in the post-9/11 era.

In the wake of Boston, Major League Baseball directed that all of its teams impose strict new security procedures for ticketed customers entering the nation's baseball parks, and by 2015 each team must use either handheld or walk-through metal detectors. For fans of America's most traditional national pastime, taking in a game was being transformed into a grim trip to the airport.

The level of resources devoted to fighting terrorism still remains out of proportion to the actual threat level posed by terrorism. So it is only natural that the FBI, Homeland Security, and state and local law enforcement agencies have to find ways to fill their days. In late 2012, the Partnership for Civil Justice Fund, a civil rights group, obtained a series of FBI documents that showed that the FBI had been spying on the Occupy Wall Street movement, treating it like a terrorist threat. FBI agents in New York and across the country conducted surveillance on the Occupy movement and shared information with businesses, universities, and local police and other law enforcement agencies. In Indianapolis, the FBI issued a "potential criminal activity alert" even before any protests were scheduled there. In Syracuse, New York, the Joint Terrorism Task Force sent information about Occupy protests to campus police at colleges in the region.

These FBI documents underscore the danger posed by the unbridled growth of the nation's counterterrorism infrastructure, and how easily the machinery designed to catch terrorists can be turned to other targets. Often, counterterrorism resources are just wasted. Homeland Security's so-called fusion centers, which are supposed to bring together federal, state, and local law enforcement officials to gather terrorism-related intelligence, have turned out to be a multibillion-dollar boondoggle. They have produced shoddy intelligence reports that unnecessarily endangered the privacy and civil liberties of American citizens, even as more than $1 billion in taxpayer funds earmarked for the centers could not be accounted for, according to a scathing Senate investigation in 2012. Many of the intelligence reports produced by the centers were so bad that they were withheld from distribution inside the government. Others that were distributed should not have been. In 2011, one Illinois fusion center warned darkly that Russian hackers had tapped into the computer system of a water district in Springfield. In fact, a repairman had remotely accessed the water district's computer system while on vacation in Russia.

Brian Jenkins of the RAND Corporation, one of the nation's most thoughtful terrorism analysts, points out that in the years since the 9/11 attacks, the United States has been remarkably free of terrorism, despite the heightened levels of fear and anxiety. "In terms of domestic terrorism, this has been the most tranquil decade since the early 1960s," says Jenkins. Domestic radicals in the late 1960s and 1970s engaged in far more violence than the United States has experienced since 9/11, he notes.

The post-9/11 fears that al Qaeda would somehow infiltrate America with fifth columnists turned out to be wildly exaggerated. "There are no secret armies of sleepers, no terrorist groups comparable to those of the 1960s and 1970s, no sustained bombing campaigns," Jenkins wrote in a 2011 RAND report. "The few terrorists, would-be terrorists, and active supporters of terrorism are for the most part individuals or tiny conspiracies who connected or tried to connect with terrorist groups abroad or believed they had done so while communicating with government agents."

Jenkins has tried to understand why there has been such a disconnect between the reality—that terrorism is no longer a significant threat in the United States—and the nation's heightened fears. "There is no question that 9/11 left a deep psychological scar, and it has had a long-term insidious effect," he said. He argues that the scars have affected intelligence analysts as well as the media and public. September 11 made even the most farfetched plots seem plausible. Nothing could be dismissed, and that changed the way the nation has judged threats.

"The object of terrorism is to use violence or the threat of violence to create fear and alarm," says Jenkins. "And so terrorism has worked. Certainly, we have been the major contributors to that. We have scared the hell out of ourselves."

The threats and alarms would not resonate so strongly with the public, or have such lasting impact on the country, if they were not reinforced by the network of independent terrorism analysts that has grown up around the global war on terror. They are the most visible and vocal advocates of the war on terror, and they have worked hard to keep the American people on edge for a decade. They have made careers out of television appearances, speeches, book deals, consulting fees, and government contracts. They generate fundraising for their own organizations as well as allied anti-Muslim campaigns. They have developed personal brands, and have burnished their brands by consistently warning that America is under siege.

They have built a cottage industry out of fear.

None have been more influential than Steven Emerson, the founder and executive director of the Investigative Project on Terrorism. For years, Emerson has consistently argued that the United States has underestimated the threat from radical Islamic groups, both at home and abroad. Emerson's credibility originally stemmed from the fact that he loudly warned, through books, documentaries, and journalism, of the looming threat from Islamist terrorism, long before 9/11.

Emerson started as a journalist, first in print and later television. He gained prominence in the 1990s thanks in part to an award-winning PBS *Frontline* documentary, "Jihad in America," which detailed the Islamic militant presence in the United States. Emerson's work impressed Richard Clarke, who was the White House counterterrorism czar in the Clinton administration and the early months of the Bush administration. Frustrated by the FBI's lack of useful information on Islamic groups inside the United States prior to 9/11, Clarke turned to Emerson as an outside researcher and advisor on terrorism, according to an account in *Newsweek*.

But more recently, Emerson seems to have grown overly zealous in claiming to see an unending line of domestic threats from all types of Muslim organizations inside the United States. He denies that he is anti-Muslim, yet his rhetoric and dark warnings that extremists now dominate the leadership of the American Muslim community, that many Muslim organizations in the United States are nothing more than fronts for the Muslim Brotherhood, Hamas, and Hezbollah, make him sound as if he thinks there is a terrorist lurking under every bed in America. Before 9/11, he issued prescient warnings; today, he doesn't seem to want to move on.

"In the end, the mainstream media refuses to recognize that the 'mainstream' Islamic groups are actually radical organizations that teach and imbue their followers with a hatred of the United States and Israel," he wrote of American Muslim groups in 2009. "These groups front as civil-rights groups, but in fact are radical Islamic groups whose constant message disseminated to the millions of Muslim followers is that the U.S. is an evil country engaged in a war against Islam. Once that message takes hold — and after all, these groups control the mosques, the Islamic newspapers, the Islamic schools, and the Islamic leadership from which American Muslims and converts get their ideas about the world — it is not a huge leap for some of them to become committed to violent jihad. We are talking about a situation that is far more rampant than government leaders want to admit because the Islamic groups routinely throw the term 'racist' at anyone who claims there is radicalism in the Muslim community."

Emerson has been able to turn his anti-Muslim rhetoric and research into fundraising prowess. An investigation by the *Nashville Tennessean* in 2010 found that Emerson's for-profit company, SAE Productions, received $3.39 million in 2008 to research connections between Muslims in the United States and foreign terrorism. The funds came from Emerson's nonprofit Investigative Project on Terrorism Foundation, which in turn received donations from contributors seeking to support Emerson's anti-jihadist work. In its 2010 tax return, Emerson's nonprofit foundation reported paying more than $3.4 million to Emerson's SAE Productions for management services, which was more than the $2.6 million the Investigative Project received that year in annual contributions and grants.

Today, Emerson is the godfather of the independent terrorism analytical community, and whenever he publicly takes a stance, his influence is enhanced by like-minded analysts and conservative pundits who follow his lead. He often uses his pulpit to make certain that politicians toe the line on the war on terror, chastising public figures he deems insufficiently sanguine. In 2012, for example, he went after New Jersey's Republican governor Chris Christie, saying that he has "an Islam problem," and that "time and again he has sided with Islamist forces against those who worry about safeguarding American security and civilization." Among Christie's sins, according to Emerson, was that he had criticized the New York City Police Department after the Associated Press, as part of a Pulitzer Prize–winning series of stories, revealed that the department had been unilaterally spying on Muslims in New Jersey.

One of the most prominent of Emerson's protégés is Evan Kohlmann, who was so young when he got into the business that he was nicknamed the "Doogie Howser" of counterterrorism. Kohlmann worked for Emerson's Investigative Project from 1998 until 2003, and has since set up his own firm, Flashpoint Global Partners. He has served as a consultant to the Pentagon, Justice Department, and FBI, as well as foreign governments and international institutions. Flashpoint Global Partners offers its clients "customized online monitoring packages on an array of jihadist groups," as well as "terrorist audio/video/communiqué source retrieval and production" and "forensic analysis of seized digital media" and "custom analytical reports."

Kohlmann has come to prominence through his dual roles as a terrorism analyst for NBC News and an expert witness for the Justice Department in terrorism prosecutions. He has served as a witness in at least twenty-four cases in the United States and another nine in Europe and Australia. During his testimony in one case in Texas in 2011, he said that he is normally paid $300 to $400 an hour by the Justice Department as an expert witness, and that he had been paid a total of about $60,000 by the FBI for his consulting on terrorism investigations since he first began working for them in 2003.

His critics say that Kohlmann's role as a witness for the prosecution has raised troubling questions. The critics complain that while the government relies on him to testify as an expert on terrorism, his knowledge comes largely from researching jihadist websites on the Internet rather than from real-world experience in the Middle East. It is hard to escape the sense that his main attraction as an expert witness for federal prosecutors is that he can be relied upon to paint the terrorist threat in the darkest terms possible to help frighten American juries into convictions. An excellent 2010 profile of Kohlmann in

New York Magazine quoted one critic who described him as working in the "guilty-verdict industry."

Ahmed Ghappour, a clinical instructor at the University of Texas School of Law, has represented defendants in terrorism-related cases in which Kohlmann has been offered as an expert witness. Ghappour said that he and other attorneys have frequently moved in court to bar Kohlmann from testifying. By getting Kohlmann on the witness stand, prosecutors can introduce terrorism threat information into a criminal trial in a way that the actual evidence in the case might not support, Ghappour argues. "His testimony can be the nail in the coffin, because it introduces all these prejudices," said Ghappour. "If you are a prosecutor, all you have to do is get this guy before a jury. All the facts that you can't prove, you get this guy to say as part of his expert analysis, and then you get the jury to hear it. That's very different than saying the evidence will show this. So, in essence, he is a third leg to the government's case."

Kohlmann has also been criticized for hyping the terrorist threat in his other role as a prominent analyst on television. In the aftermath of the Boston Marathon bombing, for example, when the media was being criticized for making frequent errors, Kohlmann was rebuked on air on MSNBC for engaging in loose speculation. As Politico reported, MSNBC's Chuck Todd interrupted Kohlmann when he started describing things that one of the suspects wanted to buy on Amazon. Todd was forced to remind Kohlmann that he could not yet prove that the Amazon "wish list" was really that of the suspect.

Politico recounted their on-air exchange:

> "I want to stress, we don't know for sure, but it is certainly his name. . . ." Kohlmann said, before being interrupted by Todd.
> "I've got to stop you there," Todd said. "Our folks—we don't necessarily want to put this on air yet until we verify it."

Kohlmann then speculated on possible connections between the suspects and terrorist groups along the Afghanistan-Pakistan border, which prompted Todd to interrupt again, according to Politico. "I didn't mean to cut you off, but we don't want to draw so many conclusions," Todd said. (Kohlmann later responded to Politico by stressing that he had not suggested any specific terrorist organization was directly responsible for the Boston bombing.)

Now, new activists have also emerged to take advantage of the fears that have been so thoroughly hyped by Emerson, Kohlmann, and other self-styled terrorism experts. These new activists are culture warriors, rather than terrorism experts, and through their grassroots organizing, they have taken the lead in efforts to block the construction of mosques around the country and to pass state legislation banning Sharia law.

These activists are working hard to make certain that anti-Muslim policies become part of the broader national conservative political agenda. Brigitte Gabriel, a Lebanese American and Christian, is one of the most prominent of these activists, a best-selling author of anti-Muslim books who now leads a group called ACT! for America, which has been involved in state-level campaigns to pass anti-Sharia legislation. Gabriel regularly makes video fundraising appeals to supporters asking for donations to ACT! for America to finance its campaign for anti-Sharia legislation. "Your commitment of $19 a month, just 63 cents a day, will give us the critical funding we need to ensure that American laws only will be used in American courts," she said on one video seeking donations for her 2012 legislative campaign.

Gabriel warns that secret fifth columnists working for terrorist organizations are now undermining the nation. "America has been infiltrated on all levels by radicals who wish to harm America," she told a Tea Party conference, according to a 2011 account of her speech in the *New York Times*. "They have infiltrated us at the CIA, at the FBI, at the Pentagon, at the State Department. They are being radicalized in radical mosques in our cities and communities within the United States."

In the White House and in Congress, during both the Bush and Obama administrations, American leaders have learned that keeping the terrorist threat alive provides enormous political benefits. It lets incumbents look tough, and lends them the national attention and political glamor that comes from dealing with national security issues. As president, Barack Obama quickly abandoned many of his 2008 campaign positions on national security and worked assiduously to burnish his reputation as a warrior president, culminating with the 2011 killing of Osama bin Laden. He continued most of the national security policies of George W. Bush, and even intensified the use of some of the most controversial, including targeted killings with drones. Just to make certain voters got the message, the Obama White House selectively leaked classified information during the 2012 presidential campaign to make Obama look like a hawk and dispel the old image of Democrats as weak on national security.

In Congress, no one learned the lesson of the political advantages of the war on terror better than Rep. Peter King, a New York Republican and former chairman of the House Committee on Homeland Security.

King is an unapologetic advocate of the harshest and most controversial measures that have been employed in the war on terror, from enhanced interrogation techniques to the targeted killings of U.S. citizens overseas. King, a tough-talking Irish-American lawyer from Long Island, revels in his assaults on what he deems to be elitist liberal political correctness, and acts like an angry attack dog against the ACLU, the press, and others he perceives as too soft on terrorism.

While he was chairman, King worked hard to make the Homeland Security Committee an advocate for an aggressive and unbending war against terrorism. In the process, he bestowed congressional legitimacy on the extreme views espoused by independent anti-Muslim pundits.

Through a series of five hearings on the radicalization of American Muslims while he was committee chairman in 2011 and 2012, King transformed the committee into the modern equivalent of the House Un-American Activities Committee of the McCarthy era. One repeat witness who testified at King's hearings was Dr. M. Zuhdi Jasser, the president of the American Islamic Forum for Democracy and the narrator of *The Third Jihad,* a right-wing documentary that was considered so biased against Muslims that the New York City Police Department was forced to stop using it in its counterterrorism training. Democrats on the Homeland Security Committee repeatedly objected to King's hearings, arguing that his decision to focus only on the potential threat from Islamic extremism, to the exclusion of other domestic radical groups, led to a perception that King and the committee were prejudiced against Muslim Americans. "The tone of these hearings, singling out the Muslim community, has undermined religious liberty, and has divided Muslim Americans from the rest of the country," Rep. Hansen Clarke, a Michigan Democrat who is a Catholic of Bangladeshi descent, said during a 2012 hearing. "These hearings are an assault not only on Muslims, but all South Asians. There's not a week that goes by when I don't get stopped here at the Capitol and asked for my identification," said Clarke. "Come on, let's stop attacking religion."

King defended the hearings by arguing that his critics were asking him to ignore the growing threat from radicalized American Muslims. "This committee, along with the Department of Homeland Security, were set up in response to 9/11 and Islamic extremism, and that's our priority," said King at a 2012 hearing. "There is a Judiciary Committee that can look at other domestic threats."

Despite the criticism, King did not pay a political price for his handling of the hearings. As a senior member of Congress with access to top-secret information — and one of the most combative — he has remained a favorite of cable news, where breathless reports of new terrorist threats could always be counted on to help move the needle on ratings.

In fact, rather than dial back the anti-Muslim rhetoric in the wake of King's hearings, another polarizing House Republican, Michele Bachmann of Minnesota, tried to up the ante. Bachmann alleged that the Muslim Brotherhood had deeply penetrated the U.S. government and called for investigations throughout the national security community, echoing the accusations leveled by Brigitte Gabriel. In a June 2012 letter to the deputy inspector general of the State Department,

Bachmann and four other conservative Republican House members wrote darkly that "information has recently come to light that raises serious questions about State Department policies and activities that appear to be a result of influence operations conducted by individuals and organizations associated with the Muslim Brotherhood."

The letter went on to warn that Huma Abedin, a close aide to then Secretary of State Hillary Clinton, had three family members connected to Muslim Brotherhood operatives or organizations. As evidence against Abedin's family, the letter cited the work of the Center for Security Policy, a Washington group run by Frank Gaffney, a conservative who has played a prominent role in state-level campaigns to pass anti-Sharia laws and block the construction of mosques.

It did not seem to matter to Bachmann that Abedin was married to Anthony Weiner, the former New York congressman and erstwhile candidate for mayor of New York who, in addition to disgracing himself through digital oversharing, was one of Israel's staunchest supporters while he was Bachmann's colleague in the House.

Fear sustains the multibillion-dollar homeland security industry through both Republican and Democratic administrations. Michael Chertoff, the former secretary of the Department of Homeland Security who founded his own firm, the Chertoff Group, underlined the connection in early 2010, when he went on television news shows to discuss a failed airplane bombing plot and advocated for the installation of full-body scanners at U.S. airports to deter such plots — at the same time that his firm represented a company that made the scanners.

The relationship among terrorist threats, fear, and cash was on full display at the Counter Terror Expo of 2012. At this gaudy two-day trade show for the war on terror, a hundred companies, large and small, paid for booths to display their wares in the Washington Convention Center, conveniently located close to their potential customers at the FBI, the Pentagon, or Homeland Security.

Southwest Microwave was there, with the Intrepid MicroTrack II, a buried cable detection system — "terrain-following volumetric smart sensors that pinpoint intrusion attempts to within three meters." Garrett was there, with the PD 6500i metal detector — "the walk-through of choice for security professionals worldwide." Vertx was there, selling a rugged line of clothing "for the operational athlete," including "OA Duty Wear Pants" and the "Combat Smock," a kind of camouflage jacket complete with "deceptively large concealed chest pockets" and compartments that "fit an M-4 mag or phone." And Flir was there, with the Griffin 460, bringing "chemical analysis out of the laboratory and into the field," and offering "on-site analysis" of "chemicals of interest," thus "giving users the actionable intelligence necessary to get the job done."

"The heightened sense of security absolutely helped our product lines grow," said one company official at the booth for Ameristar Fence, a Tulsa, Oklahoma–based firm that sells sophisticated, high-security fencing. "Prior to 9/11, people were just going with chain-link fences."

Just to make certain that no one missed the connection between terrorist threats and product sales, the Counter Terror Expo featured a series of speeches and seminars on terrorism and homeland security. In addition to a keynote speech by Michael Leiter, the former director of the National Counter Terrorism Center, there was a series of panel discussions that brought together government officials, outside experts, and contractors. During one, a top official from the Transportation Security Administration (TSA) spoke in glowing terms about its first decade: "It's fun to look back at ten years of TSA and see where we've come and our evolution. . . . We have 50,000 people who truly care about aviation security." Considering that many listening were either with companies selling products to TSA or from companies that hoped to sell to TSA, this was probably the most sympathetic forum any TSA official could ever expect. "The next time you go through security at the airport, take a moment to thank the security screener for what they do, they don't hear that often enough," said the panel's moderator.

And in another panel discussion, this one on Iran and Hezbollah, in a side room just off the main Counter Terror Expo showroom floor, Steven Emerson held forth.

By 2014, three years after Osama bin Laden's death, there was still no sign that the business of fear was slowing down. One research and consulting firm predicted that the global market for homeland security and public safety would continue to undergo dramatic growth for years to come, and would reach $546 billion by 2022.

9

THE WAR ON TRUTH

Of all the abuses America has suffered at the hands of the government in its endless war on terror, possibly the worst has been the war on truth. On the one hand, the executive branch has vastly expanded what it wants to know: something of a vast gathering of previously private truths. On the other hand, it has ruined lives to stop the public from gaining any insight into its dark arts, waging a war on truth. It all began at the NSA.

It was early October 2001, just weeks after the 9/11 attacks on New York and Washington, D.C. Bill Binney was a senior official at the National Security Agency's skunk works, an experimental lab at Fort Meade, Maryland, where the NSA's best and brightest were trying to find ways to cope with the new digital age. He had been working at the NSA for more than thirty years and was just one month from retirement.

Binney says that he was in his lab when Randy Jacobson, a contractor who worked with him on some of the lab's most important projects, walked up and quietly revealed the secret new orders he had just received from the NSA's top management. Jacobson was appalled by the orders and had to tell Binney about them, Binney recalled. (Jacobson did not respond to a request for comment.)

Jacobson had been told to remove the Fourth Amendment protections from an experimental surveillance system, one of the most powerful spying programs the NSA had ever developed. The advanced system was still just a pilot project, but top NSA officials wanted to make it operational immediately — and use it to collect data on Americans. They had ordered Jacobson to strip away the carefully calibrated restrictions built into the system, which were designed to prevent it from illegally collecting information on U.S. citizens.

Jacobson had come to Binney because the experimental surveillance system had been developed by Binney and his team, yet Binney had been cut out of the loop by his superiors about the decision to start using the system to target Americans. Jacobson told Binney that his surveillance software was being teamed up with phone lines from the AT&T network, allowing the surveillance system to spy on the phone calls of American citizens.

"I was in the situation room of the lab, looking at papers, and Randy came in, and said, do you know what they are doing?" recalls Binney. "He said that AT&T is now feeding U.S. data into the system, and they are taking the protections for Americans off."

That is how America's post-9/11 Big Brother got its start.

This is the story of the people who tried to stop the NSA's domestic spying program when it first began, in the face of money, power, and greed. It is also the story of how government secrecy — and a crackdown on whistleblowers — has enabled the worst excesses of the post-9/11 era to go unchecked, from torture to data mining on a massive scale. Secrecy has enabled a new class of national security entrepreneurs and wild freebooters. Secrecy breeds corruption.

Dennis Montgomery, Mike Asimos, and others — like Blackwater's founder, Erik Prince — would never have gotten as far as they did without the protection of the government's high walls of classi-

fication. James Mitchell and Bruce Jessen could never have so easily reverse-engineered SERE so the CIA could torture prisoners if the
CIA did not keep it all secret. And Michael Hayden, the director of the
NSA at the time of 9/11, would never have dared to launch the agency's warrantless wiretapping program if he didn't think the White
House would do everything in its power to shield the NSA from the
law and crush any whistleblowers who tried to get in the way. That
same secrecy has surrounded NSA's operations ever since, even as the
NSA has continued to push for greater access to the domestic communications of American citizens.

Secrecy continues to shield the NSA from uncomfortable questions about the growing role of the agency and its contractors in data
mining and the burgeoning field of cybersecurity. The only way the
American public ever learns what the NSA is doing to them is from
whistleblowers, including, most recently, former NSA contractor Edward Snowden, who leaked documents about the rise of the NSA's
massive data-mining operations during the Obama administration.
To keep the war on terror going, the government has tried to make
sure that whistleblowers are isolated and ostracized.

People like Diane Roark. She was perhaps the most courageous
whistleblower of the post-9/11 era, and yet her story has never been
fully told. She fought a lonely battle against the most powerful forces
unleashed in Washington in the global war on terror. She has never
received the recognition she deserves.

Roark's story also explains why, years later, Snowden felt that he
had to go outside the system to let the American people know just
how much the NSA's domestic surveillance programs had grown
since the early days after 9/11, when the Bush administration first
launched the NSA's warrantless wiretapping operation. Roark tried to
work within the system, tried to go through the right channels. She
was persecuted as a result.

Roark's story offers the most in-depth and personal look at the
rise of the NSA's domestic spying program ever provided, and explains how America allowed its most powerful foreign intelligence
service to turn its tools on the United States. It is a lesson to remember as the government cracks down on people like Edward Snowden

at the same time that the NSA continues to expand its spying on the digital lives of American citizens.

When Randy Jacobson came to warn Bill Binney about the new orders he had just received, directing him to alter the surveillance system that Binney had designed so that it could be used to target Americans, Binney knew exactly how significant — and how dangerous — those orders really were. When he built the system, Binney had gone out of his way to create strong protections to prevent its use on Americans. He knew that he had created something so powerful that, if it were ever turned on the United States, it could become the cornerstone of an American Big Brother. So he had made certain that the system would automatically block data about U.S. citizens in order to comply with the laws against domestic spying that governed the NSA's intelligence operations.

Before the 9/11 attacks, in fact, the NSA's own lawyers had told Binney that they were afraid of his new system. They told him that they believed it was too dangerous to deploy, because it was too powerful. The lawyers were concerned because the speed and efficiency with which the new system collected and analyzed digital information meant that it was likely to illegally collect vast amounts of American data, in violation of the Foreign Intelligence Surveillance Act and other laws and regulations that limited NSA to spying on foreigners.

Binney had argued with the lawyers, telling them that he had already built in strong protections to make certain that any data collected on Americans would remain encrypted and blocked by the software. Data on American citizens could never be viewed by NSA analysts using the system. But the lawyers had been adamant that Binney's program was too risky and would put the NSA in legal jeopardy. To the NSA lawyers, Binney was like a mad scientist who had developed a monster that had to be kept chained in the basement. As a result, Binney's system had never been allowed beyond the pilot project stage.

But now, in the wake of 9/11, it was a different story. Now the

NSA not only wanted to deploy the system, but the agency wanted to unleash Binney's monster on the American public. The NSA wanted to do exactly what its lawyers had previously told Binney they feared most. Bill Binney's lab experiment was being turned into a coldly efficient weapon to spy on American citizens.

★

Jacobson told Binney that the NSA's new domestic spying operation was being set up in a big office space just down the hall from Binney's skunk works, on the third floor of Building 2B at the NSA headquarters complex. New AT&T lines were already being installed in the room.

After Jacobson told him about his secret orders and then quietly walked away, Binney immediately understood why top NSA officials had kept him in the dark. He had been making waves inside the NSA for years and had developed a reputation for being a loose cannon in an agency filled with quiet conformists. Binney was outgoing, talkative and curious, a man who found it easy to laugh and who was always eager to share what he knew with others inside the agency. He believed the agency had become too hidebound and was not keeping up with the revolution under way in information technology, and so he had gravitated to the skunk works in order to try to shake things up. He was constantly questioning the way things were done at the NSA.

That made Bill Binney stick out like a sore thumb in an agency of introverts. A stunning 80 percent of NSA personnel have been identified as ISTJ (Introverted Sensing Thinking Judging) types on the Myers-Briggs personality profile test. That meant that the NSA was filled with quiet people who valued tradition, order, and loyalty; who were organized and methodical; who believed in procedures and plans and respected rules. They were people who believed in going by the book. The joke was that an extrovert at the NSA was someone who looked down at your shoes while talking, instead of at his own.

The NSA did not use the Myers-Briggs test to determine whom it would hire. But the agency's screening process, its hunt for math and computer experts willing to work in a secret, highly compartmentalized organization where they would perform abstract, analytical functions that they could not discuss with anyone else, led to a high degree of uniformity. Many of the NSA's ISTJs were eclectic geeks just this side of Rain Man. One was known to park his car in exactly the same spot in the agency parking lot every day—no matter whether the lot was empty—and then walk precisely the same steps from that parking spot to his office. Another would buy secondhand pants, wear them every day to work for two weeks, and then throw them out and buy another pair, so that he never had to do laundry.

In addition to this disarming weirdness, there was a dark side to the predominance of this singular personality type within the agency. The introverts at the NSA never questioned authority. They kept to themselves and remained silent about the agency's secrets, for good or ill. Many NSA employees were married to other NSA employees, and often their children came to work there as well, reinforcing the agency's insular nature, enhanced by its geographic isolation at Fort Meade in suburban Maryland, far from the rest of official Washington.

This quietly obedient workforce, cramped into a zone of absolute secrecy, sometimes had the feel of a cult that was deeply suspicious of outside influences. That made the NSA ripe for corruption and abuse, an organization that wasted billions, refused to admit mistakes, and was a tempting target for leaders eager to wield its awesome technological power however they saw fit.

Bill Binney was one of the NSA's 20 percent who were not ISTJs yet had still found a home in its secret world. He grew up in central Pennsylvania, majored in math at Penn State, and, after joining the army in 1965, was assigned to the U.S. Army Security Agency, where he learned communications traffic analysis. He soon found himself at a U.S. base in Turkey, analyzing Soviet-bloc communications in the midst of the Cold War. In 1967, he was assigned by the army to NSA headquarters, and, after leaving the service in 1969, returned to the

NSA as a civilian in 1970. He stayed for the rest of his career, and by the late 1990s, had risen through the ranks to become the agency's technical director for world geopolitical and military analysis, making him one of the top technical geeks in the agency's main operations directorate. He was also assigned to a special NSA panel that managed the agency's technical relationships with foreign intelligence services around the world.

But he had been frustrated throughout his career with the NSA's bureaucratic ways. For decades, the agency's flaws had been masked by the fact that the NSA's main adversary—the Soviet Union—was a hulking, slow-moving target that made the NSA look nimble by comparison. But after the end of the Cold War, the NSA began to drift, in search of new missions just as the Internet was triggering a digital revolution.

Binney had taken over the agency's skunk works, officially named the Sigint Automation Research Center, or SARC, in order to force-feed change into the agency's bloated system. At the SARC in the 1990s, he realized that the biggest problem for the NSA was that it still did not know what to do about the Internet and the surging growth of digital communications online. In the early 1990s, at the dawn of the Internet age, the NSA had been largely dismissive of the web. The agency had traditionally focused on cracking codes and secretly breaking into the secure communications of foreign governments and armies, and NSA officials saw little value in monitoring the new public websites that were starting to crop up all over the world. If the information wasn't secret, it couldn't be of much interest.

Binney, however, realized that the NSA was facing a paradigm shift but didn't know it yet. There was an ocean of information being created on the Internet, and the new challenge for the agency was not how to break in and collect a narrow band of data that revealed the Soviet order of battle, but how to sift through and analyze massive amounts of openly available information flooding through the world's computers.

The NSA's fetish for secrecy made things worse. The data that the agency did collect was streaming into hundreds of different databases scattered throughout the agency, all compartmented and closed off from each other. There were at least forty major databases used frequently by analysts, each one tied directly to a specific and highly secretive collection program somewhere in the world. If, for instance, the NSA managed to clandestinely access high-frequency Russian military radio traffic, the data would be fed into its own database, separate from data acquired through other collection programs. There were at least fourteen different databases for phone data alone.

Scouring the databases for information was cumbersome and time-consuming. One of the NSA's largest data repositories was known as Pinwale, and its search function was called Dictionary Search. Pinwale was so massive and poorly organized, and Dictionary Search so rudimentary, that it could take hours for the system to provide answers to many basic questions.

In the late 1990s, Binney, along with Ed Loomis and a few other NSA experts in the SARC, began to work on programs to bring the NSA kicking and screaming into the digital age. Their first attempt was a research project called Grandmaster, which was later refined and developed into a program called Thin Thread. Thin Thread was really four programs in one. The most important of the four was called Mainway. It was the primary analytical tool included in Thin Thread, and was a graphing and social network building process that was years ahead of its time. It applied chaining and link analysis to the data that was streaming through Thin Thread, providing one of the most powerful data search tools devised by the NSA up to that time. It allowed intensive web-based data searches without requiring the NSA to store the data first.

And so, at about the same time that Stanford University graduate students Larry Page and Sergey Brin were working on a research project on search engines that they turned into a start-up company named Google, Bill Binney and Ed Loomis were working in a small government lab on a project they thought would revolutionize the way the American intelligence community collected and analyzed data in secret.

Just before the turn of the century, Binney, Loomis, and their team at the SARC were convinced that Thin Thread provided a leap forward for the NSA and would put the agency back in the forefront of web-based technology. They expected NSA's top managers to embrace their program and give them the modest funding required to deploy it throughout the NSA system.

Instead, their ideas and program were rejected. First, the NSA's inhouse lawyers raised objections, saying that Thin Thread would violate the law by collecting too much data on U.S. citizens, dismissing Binney's claims that the protections built into his system would comply with the law. Next, NSA managers said that Thin Thread would not "scale," meaning that it could never handle the enormous volume of data searches that NSA's analysts conducted on a daily basis. Eventually, it became clear to Binney and his team that the real reason for the opposition to Thin Thread was that top NSA officials were already backing a different approach to dealing with the Internet — a huge new program called Trailblazer. While Thin Thread was a small, in-house pilot project developed on the cheap by a few NSA employees, Trailblazer was a sprawling multibillion-dollar program that involved large outside contractors, led by SAIC, a national security consulting firm that was deeply intertwined with the NSA and its management. SAIC was the prime contractor on Trailblazer, and in 2000, SAIC executive Bill Black was named deputy director of the NSA.

Stonewalled by management, Binney decided to go around his NSA bosses and take his case for Thin Thread to Congress, and specifically to Diane Roark.

Diane Roark was a staffer on the House Permanent Select Committee on Intelligence, assigned to handle oversight of the NSA. Born on a farm in Oregon in 1949, Roark had graduated from Catholic University in Washington, earned a PhD in political science from the University of Florida, and then began working for the government in 1981 when she joined the Energy Department. She rose quickly over the next few years, moving first to the Department of Defense and then the National Security Council at the White House in the Reagan administration. She had been at the House committee since 1985. By the late 1990s, her oversight work on the NSA had made her increasingly skeptical of the agency and its hodgepodge approach to coping with the digital revolution. The NSA had no strategy to make sure that its technical research would provide useful tools for its intelligence operations.

"There wasn't any coherent approach to dealing with the Internet and the digital age," recalled Roark. "Everybody just did what they were interested in. There was a big separation between the technical and the operations people, and the technical people didn't seem to care about whether what they were doing helped the operations people. Nobody tracked how they were spending their money. It was pretty bad."

Worse, Roark realized that the NSA didn't really want to change. "They were so used to believing that they were ahead on technology, they didn't realize that they had fallen behind. There was just about no relationship between the NSA and Silicon Valley at that time. They had extreme insularity. I was really alarmed. But they just kept saying we are okay, just give us money and everything will be okay."

A massive computer crash at the NSA that lasted for three days in January 2000 only increased Roark's skepticism, and made her realize that the agency had to undergo fundamental change.

Her doubts made Roark a natural ally for a brilliant maverick like Bill Binney. She had first met him when Binney briefed her on the SARC's work. She had been impressed and stayed in touch with him as she began to investigate the NSA's weaknesses. And so in his battle with NSA management to save Thin Thread in the years just before 9/11, Binney decided to turn to Roark for help.

After Binney briefed her, Roark became excited by Thin Thread's potential, and she began asking top NSA officials uncomfortable questions about the program's status. She was frustrated that the program had not been used before the millennium, when there were reports of possible terrorist plots.

She also began to look more closely at Trailblazer. She realized to her horror that the NSA liked Trailblazer so much in part because it was designed to try to connect the agency's old, existing analog technology to the new digital revolution. Roark insisted on briefings from Trailblazer managers and came away convinced that the program was doomed to become a costly failure.

"Trailblazer was supposed to build an Internet software-based system on top of an analog hardware system, and it just wasn't going to work," she recalled. "They had always felt comfortable with their existing systems. They wanted to use pre-Internet technology for the Internet age. I told them right away that would fail. It was just common sense." (Roark proved prescient. Years later, the NSA abandoned Trailblazer. After spending billions of dollars on the program's development, the agency was finally forced to admit that it would not work.)

By early 2000, Roark's intervention began to infuriate NSA Director Michael Hayden. He had already decided to go with Trailblazer and SAIC over Thin Thread, and he wanted Congress to give the agency the billions of dollars that Trailblazer would demand, no questions asked. He certainly did not want to have to explain himself to some lowly congressional staffer.

Hayden suspected that it was Binney who had been feeding Roark information, and so he called Binney on the carpet, accusing him of insubordination. He then issued an agency-wide directive to make sure that no one else tried to go around him to Congress again. In an April 14, 2000, message to the NSA workforce, Hayden demanded loyalty, compliance, and silence. He made it clear that he considered Congress the enemy, and that giving congressional overseers any unfiltered information was an act of betrayal.

"Some individuals, in a session with our congressional overseers, took a position in direct opposition to one that we had corporately decided to follow," Hayden wrote. "This misleads the Congress regarding our Agency's direction and resolve. The corporate decision was made after much data gathering, analysis, debate and thought. Actions contrary to our decisions will have a serious adverse effect on our efforts to transform NSA, and I cannot tolerate them. I have dealt with the people involved. . . . This was a disregard of decisions we had made together and, as such, could not be tolerated."

"I do not expect sheepish acquiescence," he added, "but I do expect that problems necessitating course corrections will be handled within these walls. I must insist on all of us having the personal discipline to adhere to our corporate decisions, including those with which we disagree."

Binney's efforts to go around Hayden effectively ended his career at the NSA. His lobbying campaign for Thin Thread was now met with deaf ears throughout the entire agency, and the program stalled and then languished, despite Roark's continued pushing. Binney stayed on for another year, but by the fall of 2001, he and two others from the SARC—Ed Loomis and Kirk Wiebe—had had enough. They decided to retire together to start their own company. If the NSA didn't want Thin Thread, maybe they could sell it on the open market.

The 9/11 attacks happened just as Binney, Loomis, and Wiebe were on their way out. Like the rest of the intelligence community, the NSA had failed to prevent the attacks, and a sense of guilt and shame spread quickly among NSA personnel who knew the truth about the agency's failings. Prior to 9/11, terrorism had been a low priority within the NSA, which was still fixated on listening to the secret communications of foreign governments. Its dismissive pre-9/11 view that there was little intelligence to be gained by monitoring open communications on the Internet proved disastrous.

In the immediate aftermath of 9/11, the Bush administration scrambled for answers, and CIA Director George Tenet sent out a secret directive to each intelligence agency to move aggressively to bring any tool they might have available into the fight against al Qaeda. At the NSA, Trailblazer, the agency's long-term answer to the new digital age, was still little more than a proposal on a series of PowerPoint presentations.

But there was Thin Thread.

Three days after 9/11, Ed Loomis was working in the SARC when he got a call from Maureen Baginski, one of Hayden's top lieutenants. She was looking for Binney, but he was out for the morning, so she asked Loomis to come to an urgent meeting, Loomis recalled. When he arrived in a conference room at the agency's general counsel's office, Loomis was met by a whole team of NSA lawyers, including some of the attorneys who had previously rejected Thin Thread on the grounds that it would illegally collect too much information on Americans. He was also met by Ben Gunn, a senior NSA analyst who was familiar with Thin Thread.

The lawyers asked Loomis whether the SARC had any programs that could have helped to uncover the 9/11 plot. Loomis immediately reminded them about Grandmaster and Thin Thread, and how they had been rejected on legal grounds. The lawyers then turned to Gunn and asked him about Mainway, the part of the Thin Thread program that might have helped connect the dots among al Qaeda operatives. Baginski and the NSA lawyers never met with Loomis again to discuss Thin Thread or Mainway. But Loomis later realized that for Gunn, the meeting was something of a job interview; Gunn went on to become one of the technical managers of the NSA's domestic warrantless wiretapping and data-mining program.

In October, just as Randy Jacobson approached Bill Binney, Kirk Wiebe also began to see evidence that something unusual was going on around him. First he saw lines of large boxes stacked in the hallway outside the SARC, filled with Dell computer servers. They seemed destined for a mysterious locked room down the hall, which from past experience Wiebe knew had work space for as many as a hundred people. Next, Wiebe accidentally walked into a meeting in the SARC's conference room being run by Gunn, and was quickly told that the meeting was secret and that he had to get out. That was strange for Wiebe, because he thought he knew everything that was going on inside the SARC.

Finally, Binney told Wiebe what Jacobson had told him, and Wiebe realized that he had walked in on one of the first meetings of the technical team in charge of setting up the NSA's warrantless wiretapping program. Wiebe also realized that the Dell servers stacked in the hallway were going to connect the Mainway software to the AT&T phone lines streaming into the locked office space just down the corridor. Mainway was to become the heart of the NSA's domestic spying program.

When Bill Binney had been frustrated by the NSA's rejection of Thin Thread before 9/11, he had turned to Diane Roark, and it had cost him his career. Now, after 9/11, Binney realized that the NSA was taking the key component of Thin Thread—Mainway—and perverting its use in an unconstitutional program. And so he turned to Roark once again. Not long after Randy Jacobson first told him about the NSA's decision to start spying on Americans, Binney called Roark and told her that he needed to meet with her, without going into any details on the phone. After work, he drove to her house in Hyattsville, Maryland, a few miles from NSA headquarters. He then told her what he had learned about the secret NSA warrantless wiretapping program.

After listening to Binney, Roark believed strongly that the operation he had just described violated the Constitution. She also knew that it went against the core principles of the NSA. Ever since the Church Committee investigations of intelligence abuses and the reforms that followed in the 1970s, the NSA had been explicitly barred from spying on Americans. The idea that the NSA only looked outward, not inward on Americans, had become deeply ingrained in the agency's culture. But now, Binney was telling Roark that the agency was secretly violating its most fundamental directive.

At first, Roark was sure that this had to be some kind of rogue operation, completely unauthorized by either Congress or the Bush administration. "What he told me shocked me," recalled Roark. "I thought this was a rogue operation, I couldn't believe this was approved, because it was clearly illegal and unconstitutional. The big thing was that the protections had been removed. NSA had been rigorous on protections before that."

Roark knew she had to do something about it. What she didn't realize was that her efforts would turn her into a pariah in official Washington.

★

Diane Roark had no experience as a whistleblower. During her career conducting congressional oversight, people had always come to her to report problems, rather than the other way around. And so when Binney told her about the NSA's warrantless wiretapping operation, she did what came naturally—she reported it to the House Intelligence Committee. She was certain no one on the committee knew about it.

Roark wrote a memo describing what she knew about the wiretapping program and submitted it to Tim Sample, the Republican staff director of the committee, and his Democratic counterpart, Mike Sheehy. Sample reported directly to the chairman of the committee, Porter Goss, a Florida Republican congressman and former CIA case officer who later became CIA director. Sheehy worked for Nancy Pelosi, a California Democratic congresswoman who later became Speaker of the House but who was then the ranking Democrat on the intelligence committee. Roark wrote that she wanted to warn the committee's leaders from both parties that an illegal operation was under way at the NSA.

Roark was confident that her memo would be met by outrage by the congressional leadership; instead, it was met by stony silence. After reading her memo, Sheehy meekly replied that, while he did not know anything about it, this NSA spying operation must explain why Goss and Pelosi had recently been called to a secret meeting at Vice President Cheney's office. He then dropped the subject and did not talk to Roark any further about it.

Sample's response was even more chilling. He had obviously talked to Goss about Roark's memo. Sample admonished her to drop the matter, and to stop talking about the NSA program. She was not to tell anyone else what she knew, Sample demanded, not even other staffers on the House committee. Roark now realized that she and Binney had not stumbled upon a rogue operation but rather on an unconstitutional domestic spying program approved at the highest levels of the government and sanctioned by at least some congressional leaders. That knowledge only made her more determined to stop it.

Despite the warning from Sample not to talk with anyone else on the committee about the program, she privately warned Chris Barton, the committee's new general counsel, that "there was an NSA program of questionable legality and that it was going to blow up in their faces." In early 2002, Roark also quietly arranged a meeting between Binney, Loomis, and Wiebe and Rep. Richard Burr, a North Carolina Republican on the House Intelligence Committee. Binney told Burr everything they had learned about the NSA wiretapping program, but Burr hardly said a word in response. Burr never followed up on the matter with Roark, and there is no evidence he ever took any action to investigate the NSA program. He was later elected to the U.S. Senate.

After getting nowhere with Burr and being shut down by Sample and Sheehy, Roark finally began to realize that if she was ever going to stop the illegal operation, she was going to have to go outside of the House committee, her institutional home. That meant that she was going to have to start taking risks. As she reached out to her network of contacts throughout the government, she gradually realized, to her horror, that there was a cover-up under way to protect the NSA's illegal operation, and it involved far more people than she could ever have imagined — including many she knew and trusted.

Roark first met with a former senior NSA executive who had been trying to help her improve her relations with Hayden and the rest of the NSA's top management. When Roark told the former official about the warrantless wiretapping program, he seemed shocked and agreed to talk with NSA officials about it. But Roark never heard from him again.

Roark then tried to set up a meeting with U.S. District Court Judge Colleen Kollar-Kotelly, who was also the chief judge of the so-called FISA court, the secret Washington-based federal court that was supposed to authorize electronic surveillance in national security cases inside the United States. Since the purpose of the Bush administration's warrantless wiretapping program was to avoid the legal process established by the Foreign Intelligence Surveillance Act of 1978 — and to skirt the secret court established by that law — Roark assumed that Kollar-Kotelly would be outraged when she learned about the secret program. So Roark called Kollar-Kotelly's Washington office and left a message with her secretary, identifying herself and asking for a meeting to discuss "an illegal NSA program." The judge's secretary called Roark back to tell her that the judge could not meet her or discuss the matter with her. Chillingly, the secretary added that the judge had called the Justice Department to inform officials there that Roark was asking questions, and that Roark should expect a call from a Justice Department lawyer. Roark was horrified and believed that Judge Kollar-Kotelly had betrayed her. Later, a Justice Department lawyer did call Roark, but, suspecting a trap, she refused to talk to him. What Roark did not realize was that Kollar-Kotelly had been told about the program by the White House, and she had agreed to keep the fact that the NSA was going around her own court a secret, even from the other judges on the court. When the NSA program later became public, one of the other FISA court judges, James Robertson, resigned in protest.

Next, Roark approached Charles Allen, a legendary figure in the CIA and one of the few top CIA officials who had displayed genuine interest in the NSA and its problems over the years. Over lunch, Roark told Allen about the warrantless wiretapping program, and said that she believed the operation was illegal. Allen said nothing, and by the end of the lunch, Roark realized that Allen already knew about the program and had not objected to it.

In perhaps her most naive move, Roark next called David Addington, an old acquaintance from their days working together on the House Intelligence Committee. Addington had long since left the House committee and become one of Vice President Dick Cheney's most powerful aides. From his post at Cheney's right hand, Addington had become one of the architects of the Bush administration's policies in the war on terror and was a fierce advocate for the NSA domestic spying program.

Roark could not reach Addington personally, so she left a voice-mail message for him at the White House, telling him that it was very important that they meet, that she had been handling the NSA account for the House committee, and that she was very troubled by something that had happened post-9/11. Addington never called back.

Frustrated by her inability to stop the NSA program and depressed by discovering that so many people she knew were protecting the secret, Roark decided to retire from the House committee in April 2002. But she wanted to make one more push to stop the NSA program. On March 20, 2002, just before she left the committee, she arranged to have breakfast with committee chairman Porter Goss. After small talk, Roark brought up the warrantless wiretapping program. She told Goss that she knew that he must have been briefed about the program, but she said she wanted him to know that the operation was of "questionable legality" and was unsustainable. "This cannot go on forever," she told Goss. "It's going to leak and the committee is going to look bad" for not trying to stop it, she warned him.

Haltingly, Goss defended himself, saying that he had not been allowed by the White House to have any staff with him during the secret briefing that he and Pelosi had received on the program, adding that he had also not been able to receive an independent legal review. He said he had accepted the White House's assurances of its legality, and instead had tried to evaluate the program purely on national security grounds. Roark then told him that the NSA had no reason to remove the protections for American citizens from the collection system. She said those protections could even help make the intelligence collection more efficient, and urged him to try to get the NSA to restore them.

Goss agreed that the secret program would eventually leak, and that it would be bad for the committee. He added that the Bush administration's repeated extensions of the NSA program—the White House and Justice Department were reauthorizing it every forty-five days—were beginning to worry him. Roark passed on information she had recently learned, that the NSA had already doubled the number of large computer servers devoted to the wiretapping program, increasing the program's scale. Yet only a small number of NSA analysts were assigned to sift through the massive amount of data because top NSA officials were trying to minimize the number of people who knew of the program's existence. As a result, Roark told Goss, the Bush administration was taking a huge legal risk to operate the program, but it was not being used effectively.

Roark made an impression on Goss. That same day, Goss went out of his way to publicly praise Roark's work, when he took to the House floor to mark her retirement and laud her aggressive approach to conducting oversight of the NSA: "If it were not for the efforts of Ms. Roark, I do believe that our committee's efforts to oversee and advocate for NSA would have been much less effective, and for that she has my personal thanks," he said.

"Recently," Goss added, "one of the senior managers within the community commented on her performance by saying that our staff is very aggressive in their oversight and has a very serious and in-depth knowledge of our programs, sometimes a better understanding than some of the senior managers do. I think that this is the type of oversight capability that the American people are entitled to and should demand."

Secretly, Goss also began asking the NSA more questions about the warrantless wiretapping program. Goss later told Roark that Hayden did not like the fact that Goss was starting to press him.

Just five days after her meeting with Goss, Roark decided to go to Hayden directly, and she had the first of two meetings with the NSA director to discuss the domestic spying program. Over the course of their two secret meetings, Hayden and Roark engaged in a fierce debate over the NSA program—the kind of debate that the Bush administration was desperate to avoid having in public.

Roark used a pretext to get the first meeting with Hayden, but he was a step ahead of her. As soon as she arrived, he quickly raised the issue of the warrantless wiretapping program because Goss had already told him that she opposed it. Hayden defended the program's legality, claiming that it had been endorsed by lawyers "from three branches," and specifically cited David Addington.

Yet for Roark, it was their second meeting that was far more memorable and dramatic. By that time, Roark knew more about the NSA program and was better prepared to challenge Hayden.

Hayden probably suspected that Goss's increased questioning about the program had been driven by Roark, whom he had not trusted since the battle over Thin Thread and Trailblazer. So, in July 2002, after she had already retired from the House committee, Hayden called Roark and asked her to meet him at NSA headquarters.

Taken aback, Roark called Goss for his advice. He encouraged her to meet with Hayden "because you both speak the same language." There was tension in the air as soon as Roark arrived in Hayden's office at NSA headquarters on July 26, in part because of the power imbalance between the two. Hayden was an air force general, the director of the largest agency in the U.S. intelligence community, and a confidant of Bush and Cheney. By contrast, Roark was merely a government retiree. But from Hayden's perspective, Roark was a retiree who knew too much.

They first went over old ground—the contracting war between Thin Thread and Trailblazer—but soon launched into a detailed discussion of the domestic surveillance program. Roark began by asking Hayden why they had taken the protections for U.S. citizens off the Mainway system, but he refused to answer. She repeated her question. Why did they remove the protections? Finally, Hayden blurted out the harsh truth. "He said we didn't need them because we had the power," recalled Roark. "He wouldn't look me in the eye when he said it."

"I said that the protections would not hurt and might even assist analysis by making it more rules-based and automated, especially since only a very small number of analysts were cleared for the program and its massive amounts of data," Roark told Hayden, according to notes she kept of the meeting. She had raised the same issue in their meeting in March, but it was clear to her that Hayden had not followed up to get more information on her arguments.

"I pushed hard and repeatedly about why he had dropped the protections" for American citizens. "He avoided answering until finally he said again that they didn't need them because they had the power." Roark was stunned by Hayden's brutally candid answer.

Roark then told Hayden that she had heard that the domestic surveillance program was already expanding, and Hayden told her it was true. This expansion, coupled with what Roark had previously heard about the doubling of the number of computer servers assigned to the program, indicated to her that the NSA was heading on a path toward unleashing its full surveillance powers on the United States. In her unclassified notes from the meeting, she said that Hayden confirmed that additional forms of data collection were taking place. She then replied that the expansion meant that restoring protections for American citizens was more important than ever.

Prodded further by Roark, Hayden admitted that "we are not in the business of minimizing U.S. citizens." That meant that the NSA was now in the business of spying on Americans. She then asked Hayden how long the program was going to run and when it would end. He shook his head no and said, "It is now among us."

Roark also pressed him on the limits of the program, and Hayden suggested that the only real limit had been imposed by Rep. Nancy Pelosi in exchange for going along with the program and maintaining her silence about it. Hayden told Roark that "Pelosi had repeatedly warned him not to go beyond the CT [counterterrorism] target, and for now they were adhering to that." In other words, the Bush administration and NSA eventually wanted to use the domestic spying program for purposes that had nothing to do with the global war on terror.

Roark asked him if he had a court order approving the program, and Hayden said no. Roark countered that if the NSA received court authorization, it would be much easier to disseminate the data throughout the intelligence community for wider analysis and more efficient use. But Hayden again said "that they did not wish to draw attention" to the program by seeking legal authorization either from new congressional legislation or through the courts. Hayden told her that the lawyers had approved the warrantless wiretapping program based on the president's wartime powers as commander in chief. He added that even if the secret program ever became public, he would still "have the majority of nine votes." Roark took that to mean that Hayden believed that the Supreme Court would back him and the Bush White House in a constitutional showdown over the program.

"I insisted that he needed a court order, that opinions about the constitutionality and SCOTUS votes are simply opinions, not fact, and he was placing himself and his agency at great risk. He again demonstrated supreme confidence the powers were there. He realized it would leak, but believed he would come out looking well, and indeed would like to reveal parts of it himself."

Finally, Hayden explained why he had really asked Roark to his office. He told her that he wanted the program to run as long as possible, that he wanted more time. In other words, he wanted Roark to keep quiet about the program and not leak its existence. Roark looked back at him and quietly told Hayden that she was not going to go to the press. She had no intention of divulging what she knew about the wiretapping program to a reporter.

But that was not good enough for Hayden. He said he did not want her talking to any members of Congress about the program, either. Roark realized that Hayden considered providing information to Congress a leak. He wanted knowledge of the program's existence to be limited to the few congressional leaders who had already been officially briefed. He insisted that he was confident he was "well within constitutional powers."

Roark left Hayden's office more alarmed than ever, and found his statement that he believed that the Supreme Court would go along with the NSA program particularly chilling. Roark decided that she needed to try to get to the Supreme Court before Hayden.

Bill Binney and Kirk Wiebe told her that they knew a government contractor who had mentioned to them that he knew the daughter of Supreme Court Chief Justice William Rehnquist. So Roark took a chance. Using official stationery from the House Intelligence Committee to help verify her credentials, Roark wrote a note to the chief justice, stating that she wanted to meet to tell him about an NSA program that appeared to be unconstitutional. She then arranged for the contractor to hand deliver the letter to Rehnquist's daughter with instructions for her to give it to her father. Roark never heard back from Rehnquist.

Increasingly depressed, she realized that she was fighting the entire Washington power structure. She had gone to all three branches of government — Congress, the White House, and the courts — and had discovered that there was a conspiracy of silence among the nation's most powerful public officials to protect an unconstitutional operation. "It was very clear to me that there were all these people who had signed over their lives, and that they had pledged not to talk about it."

Roark tried one last time. In September 2002, she joined with Binney, Wiebe, and Loomis to file a formal complaint with the Defense Department's inspector general about the NSA's decision to go with Trailblazer over Thin Thread, accusing the agency of wasting taxpayer money on Trailblazer. When they met with investigators from the inspector general's office to discuss their complaint in detail, Roark asked Binney and the others whether they wanted to bring up "the other issue"—the NSA's domestic spying program. Binney shook his head no, and Roark dropped the matter.

She had reached a dead end. In 2003, she moved back to her native Oregon, tried to work with Binney, Wiebe, and Loomis to start a new company to commercialize the Thin Thread technology, and finally settled into retirement. She was still depressed that she had not been able to stop the NSA program, but she had abandoned her efforts to raise the alarm.

★

Thomas Drake, a senior NSA manager, heard about the NSA's warrantless wiretapping program soon after its inception, too. Like Diane

Roark, he decided that he had to do something. But just like Roark, Drake found it difficult to find anyone within the government willing to take action.

Drake had come to the NSA by an unconventional path. Earlier in his career, Drake had served in air force and naval intelligence and spent time as an analyst at the CIA. He was working for an outside contractor when he was hired in 2001 by the NSA as part of an effort by Hayden to bring in young managers to foster change. It was Hayden's answer to the obvious signs that the NSA was bloated and moribund. But the problem was that Drake and the dozen newcomers Hayden recruited were never given any real authority. They kept running into brick walls whenever they proposed changing existing practices. Rather than directly confront the entrenched bureaucracy, Hayden seemed content to turn over more and more of the NSA's operations to large outside contractors like SAIC.

Eventually, Drake became convinced that Hayden had brought in the newcomers just for show. It had been a token effort to make it appear as if he was serious about change, Drake was convinced. Most of Hayden's newcomers quickly became frustrated and left the agency.

Drake was still there at the time of the 9/11 attacks, still serving as a kind of free-floating management troubleshooter, and that job gave him a remarkable ability to roam around the NSA in the immediate aftermath of one of the greatest intelligence failures in American history.

Drake had developed a reputation inside the NSA for being curious and approachable, so in the days after 9/11, he became a sounding board for angst-ridden NSA employees who told him stories about how the NSA could have — and should have — prevented the attacks. One distraught NSA analyst showed him a report his unit had prepared months earlier about al Qaeda that Drake said identified many key players in the terrorist network — including the names of some of the hijackers. The analyst told him that NSA management had refused to disseminate the report outside of the agency, and so the report had never been sent to the CIA, FBI, or the White House. Others told him that after the attacks, they had reviewed the available data and discovered dozens of communications that held clues that had been ignored.

In the days after the attacks, Drake was assigned by Maureen Baginski to scour the NSA for any programs that could be brought into Bush's new war on terrorism. Like Roark, Drake had been impressed by the possibilities of Thin Thread, and so he wrote a memo to Baginski urging that Thin Thread, along with several other programs, be deployed as soon as possible. But in a cryptic reply, Baginski returned the memo with a handwritten note simply saying, "They don't need it any more. They have gone with a different program."

What she meant was that the NSA had taken the protections off Mainway and turned it into something very different. Drake realized this after he began to hear from several NSA officials about the agency's warrantless wiretapping and domestic data-mining program, which now had its own code name—Stellar Wind. One of the NSA officials who told him about the program was a supervisor on Stellar Wind; he was troubled by it and not certain it was legal. Other NSA personnel who had fragmentary knowledge of Stellar Wind also approached Drake, figuring that he was close to top management and so might know more about what was going on.

Drake approached Ben Gunn, the technical manager on Stellar Wind, and Drake came away from their conversation convinced that even Gunn privately had qualms about the program and the agency's new direction. (Gunn did not respond to a request for comment.) Finally, Drake confronted Baginski about it. In an awkward conversation in her NSA office, Baginski would say only that the decision to launch the warrantless wiretapping program had already been made and was out of her hands. But Drake persisted. "I said, do you realize what you are saying?" recalled Drake. "I said, they are bypassing FISA. And she just looked away." (Baginski declined to comment.)

Drake said that Baginski told him that if he had a problem with what was going on, he should talk to the NSA's lawyers. So Drake arranged a meeting with Vito Potenza, then the NSA's acting general counsel. Potenza told Drake that "the program," as he called it, was perfectly legal and had been approved by the White House. When

Drake persisted, Potenza made it clear to Drake that the matter was really none of his business.

Drake was still frustrated, so when he was asked to talk about the NSA's performance by two early congressional probes into 9/11 — one by a House intelligence subcommittee and another by a joint House-Senate inquiry formed specifically to investigate 9/11, a precursor to the official 9/11 Commission — he seized the opportunity. He met privately with staffers for the House subcommittee and from the joint inquiry, and told them about Stellar Wind. Drake was disappointed when they failed to follow up and never mentioned it in any report.

After Roark and Drake tried and failed to stop the NSA's warrantless wiretapping program, the Bush administration still had to scramble on other fronts to keep the existence of the NSA program secret. Senior Justice Department and FBI officials were the next to rebel against the NSA's domestic spying operation, nearly triggering a constitutional crisis that threatened not only to force the entire domestic surveillance program out into the open but also to topple the Bush administration.

In 2003, John Yoo, the Justice Department lawyer who had originally rubber-stamped many of the Bush administration's counterterrorism policies, from enhanced interrogation techniques to warrantless wiretapping, left the government. After he resigned, Justice Department lawyers reviewing his work were appalled by what he had done for the White House. They concluded that they could no longer provide the White House with assurances that all aspects of the NSA's domestic surveillance operations were legal, triggering a dramatic series of events that climaxed in a showdown in Attorney General John Ashcroft's hospital room in March 2004. The hospital room confrontation is now considered the dramatic highlight of the most serious constitutional crisis in the post-9/11 era.

The showdown developed because a hospitalized Ashcroft had temporarily turned over his duties to Deputy Attorney General James Comey, just as it was time for the attorney general to give his approval for the reauthorization of the NSA's secret warrantless wiretapping program. But Comey had been persuaded by Justice Department lawyers that not all of the elements of the program were legal, and so he refused to give his approval. Angered by his refusal, White House chief of staff Andrew Card and White House counsel Alberto Gonzales went to see Ashcroft in his hospital room to try to get him to sign. Tipped off, Comey beat them there, and Ashcroft sided with him and told the White House officials to deal with Comey. Card and Gonzales left with no agreement, triggering an escalating crisis between the White House and Justice Department.

During the course of an intense legal showdown over the next few days, Comey, FBI Director Robert Mueller, and other senior Justice Department officials threatened to resign after the White House insisted on going ahead with the surveillance operation without the legal imprimatur of the Justice Department. Finally, President Bush personally resolved the crisis by agreeing to modify some aspects of the surveillance operation to satisfy Comey and Mueller.

A 2009 NSA inspector general's report later leaked by Edward Snowden revealed for the first time that Comey and the other Justice Department and FBI officials were concerned about the legality of one particular component of the domestic surveillance program — a data-mining operation to collect and analyze Internet metadata from American citizens. The report said it was one of the four components of the NSA domestic surveillance program that Bush had first approved in October 2001. In addition to the main warrantless wiretapping of phone calls, the NSA domestic surveillance program included the collection of the content of e-mails and the collection of the calling log data of phone calls and the metadata of e-mails, which included the e-mail addresses and IP addresses of both senders and recipients of the e-mails.

Comey was not opposed to the main warrantless wiretapping program but, based on the legal advice of his lieutenants at the Justice Department, refused to reauthorize the Internet metadata collection operation. To satisfy Comey, Bush rescinded his authorization for the bulk Internet data collection on March 19, 2004. Then the White House and Justice Department began to look for new legal justifications to use to resume the Internet data collection. They finally decided that they could authorize it by claiming that it was a form of "Pen Register/Trap and Trace," a long-established process used by the FBI to keep calling and e-mail logs in criminal cases. This new legal theory was a big stretch — the Pen Register/Trap and Trace procedure was used to monitor specific individuals under criminal investigation, and had never been used to justify the bulk collection of the records of millions of American citizens.

But the compliant chief judge of the FISA court, Colleen Kollar-Kotelly — the same judge who had betrayed Diane Roark to the Justice Department — secretly went along with the plan. She issued an order on July 15, 2004, authorizing the resumption of the Internet data collection program based on the new theory. She issued her order in secret, without telling any of the other judges on the FISA court, who still were not aware of the existence of the NSA domestic spying program.

And so, despite the drama surrounding the confrontation in Ashcroft's hospital room, the crisis between the White House and the Justice Department subsided without bursting into public view. Comey and the other Justice and FBI officials backed down from their threats to resign, and the NSA domestic surveillance operation continued in secret, largely intact and with only a brief interruption.

The NSA program's existence was finally revealed by the *New York Times* in December 2005, only after the Bush administration mounted an intense campaign to convince the *Times* not to publish the story. The administration's point man in dealing with the *Times*'s editors was Michael Hayden, the same man who had pressured Diane Roark to remain silent. The paper agreed to hold the story for more than a year.

When it was finally published, the story set off a firestorm of protest on both the left and right. Civil liberties advocates accused the Bush administration of violating the Constitution with a high-tech invasion of the privacy rights of American citizens, while conservatives attacked the *New York Times* for publishing the story and damaging national security in the midst of the war on terror.

Within days, President Bush ordered a leak investigation to find out who had talked to the *New York Times*. The Justice Department convened a grand jury, and the FBI assigned a task force of agents to hunt down the paper's sources. It did not take long for the Justice Department and the FBI to focus on Diane Roark as a prime suspect.

Roark was living quietly in Oregon when she got a call in August 2006 from the general counsel of the House of Representatives. The lawyer told her that the FBI was looking for her, and that the agents wanted to know whether she would be willing to talk to them as part of their NSA investigation. Roark replied that it was about time that someone investigated the program — but the lawyer quickly explained that the FBI was investigating the leak to the *New York Times,* not the program itself. Roark said she would be willing to talk with the FBI, but she was taken aback when the lawyer told her that the House of Representatives would not provide her with a lawyer.

Roark finally met with a prosecutor and two FBI agents in February 2007. With a shock, she realized that she was a target of the investigation. Roark denied that she had been a source for the story in the *Times* — a story that I wrote along with Eric Lichtblau — and also said she had not been a source for my book *State of War,* which also included a chapter revealing the existence of the NSA program. The prosecutor then asked her whether she knew who had talked to me or Lichtblau about the NSA, and she said she had no idea.

An incessant pounding woke Diane Roark from a sound sleep. She stumbled out of bed, went down to the front door of her Oregon home, peered out a window, and asked who was there. It was the FBI. It was 6 A.M. on July 26, 2007, and a phalanx of FBI agents, pouring out of a convoy of cars that filled her driveway, had come to raid her house.

As she opened the door, at least a dozen agents filed in. The lead agent quickly asked if she had any guns, and she said no. He then showed her a search warrant and stood next to her while she called her lawyer in Washington, who told her to ask the FBI agent to let her see a copy of an affidavit in support of the search warrant. The lead agent told her it was under seal and that she couldn't see it. With that, the FBI began to pick apart Roark's house.

While other agents started to carry out her computer and other electronic equipment, one female agent accompanied Roark back upstairs, watched as she got dressed, and then followed her outside when she decided to get out of the house and work in her garden while the FBI rifled through her belongings. The FBI search took five hours — conducted mostly by women wearing hair nets and gloves — and even extended to the apartment of a tenant who was renting rooms in Roark's house. They took fifteen boxes filled with Roark's belongings, made her sign for it, and then left.

On that same day in Maryland, FBI agents raided the homes of Bill Binney, Kirk Wiebe, and Ed Loomis. A few months later, in November 2007, the FBI raided the house of a fifth member of what the government was convinced was a conspiracy of leakers — Thomas Drake, the only one of the group who was still working at the NSA.

A previously sealed FBI affidavit filed in support of the raid on Drake's house shows that he and the others were all targeted because the government believed that they had conspired together to reveal all that they knew about the NSA domestic surveillance program to the *New York Times*. The affidavit is from an FBI agent ironically named Jason Lawless, who stated that he was assigned to a "task force that is conducting an investigation into the unauthorized disclosure, 'leak,' of classified information to two New York Times (NYT) reporters, James Risen and Eric Lichtblau, who work in the NYT's Washington, D.C. Bureau, concerning alleged activities of the National Security Agency (NSA), including the Terrorist Surveillance Program (TSP)."

All five told the FBI that they had not talked to the *Times* about the NSA program, and all said that they did not know who did. One reason they had been targeted as a group was because they had jointly signed a letter to the Defense Department's inspector general calling for an investigation of the waste and abuse in the NSA's Trailblazer contract.

After Drake denied talking to the *New York Times*, he told the FBI that he had only spoken with a reporter from the *Baltimore Sun*, who had written stories about the NSA's contracting problems with Trailblazer, which had been published after the *New York Times* stories about domestic spying. Embarrassed by the fact that they had devoted enormous resources to investigating the wrong people, the Justice Department was forced to grasp at straws. Prosecutors decided to charge Drake in connection with leaking to the *Baltimore Sun*, based on his own statements. Eventually, that case collapsed when the government failed to prove that he had leaked any classified information at all. (In fact, Drake was not even the original source for the *Sun*'s stories on Trailblazer. Drake did not talk to the *Sun* reporter until after she had already written her first stories on the subject.)

But while the Drake case collapsed, and the other four were never charged, the investigation had a devastating impact on all of them. Just as she was being targeted by the Justice Department, Diane Roark was diagnosed with breast cancer. She had to begin treatments as prosecutors threatened her with jail for perjury for lying about not being a source for the *Times*'s NSA story. When word that she was under investigation began to spread, Roark was ostracized by her former friends and colleagues on the House Intelligence Committee.

Drake's wife, who also worked at the NSA, was furious at her husband for putting their family at risk. Pressured by the NSA to cooperate or else risk losing her job, she talked to the FBI about her husband, despite the marital privilege that gives spouses the right not to testify against each other. They separated for a year but then decided to stay together for the sake of their youngest son.

Bill Binney has been suffering from diabetes that he believes was triggered by a case of hepatitis A he contracted from food he ate in the NSA cafeteria. He has suffered four episodes of MRSA since 2008, and has lost his right foot and left leg below the knee. He now must use a wheelchair. Whether stress from the federal investigation was a factor in his health problems is difficult to determine. "Actually, my medical problems seemed to make the government crap trivial," he now says.

After his home was raided, Ed Loomis felt betrayed by the system that he had been a part of all his life. He became so embittered and traumatized that his wife left him. "Her departure was of my own making along with the able assistance of the U.S. Government," Loomis says now. "My personality metamorphosis was created solely from being dishonored by NSA. . . . It embittered me to the point where I had virtually withdrawn from most friends and family out of utter shame and embarrassment. I morphed into a curmudgeon, purchased a couple of handguns to test whether the Men in Black would allow the purchase to go through."

Today, Thomas Drake has emerged from the wreckage of the government's case against him and is trying to put his life back together again. In a deal to end the case as rapidly as possible, he agreed to plead guilty to a single misdemeanor charge related to the improper handling of a document that the FBI found at his house during its raid. He served no jail time.

Drake has since become celebrated and was awarded the Ridenhour Prize for Truth-Telling, given annually to whistleblowers. It is named for the soldier who blew the whistle on the My Lai massacre in Vietnam. Drake works in an Apple store in Bethesda, Maryland, in order to help make ends meet. In October 2013, he traveled to Moscow to meet with Edward Snowden and participated in a small ceremony in which Snowden was presented with an award as an intelligence whistleblower. (Snowden has said that the government's persecution of Drake was one reason he decided to leave the United States before leaking documents to the press.)

Diane Roark, by contrast, has received almost no public recognition for her repeated efforts to try to stop the NSA program. She still lives quietly in Oregon and has been relying on alternative medical treatments to deal with her breast cancer. "I know I did the right thing in challenging the completely unnecessary threat to our liberties and to our very Republic," Roark now says. "It was, after all, what

I was paid to do and what was rightly expected of me. I will never regret it."

★

Stellar Wind was the start of a modern American Big Brother, but the surveillance state certainly did not end with the public disclosure of the NSA's domestic spying by the *New York Times*. Edward Snowden's disclosures in 2013 revealed that, more than a decade after 9/11, the capacity of the NSA and the rest of the U.S. government to spy on American citizens has gone far beyond the original Bush wiretapping and data-mining programs.

After the *New York Times* disclosed the existence of the NSA program, the Bush administration staunchly defended its actions. Later, the White House reluctantly agreed to have Congress pass an overhaul of the FISA law that largely codified the program. In the legislation, the FISA Amendments Act of 2008, Congress even provided retroactive legal immunity for the telecommunications companies that had been involved with it. Sen. Barack Obama, then the Democratic candidate for president, voted for the telecom immunity provision, angering many of his liberal supporters in the midst of the 2008 presidential campaign while providing a preview of his hawkish embrace of the Bush approach to the war on terror that he would display as president.

In the years since, the government's surveillance capabilities have expanded radically, as the NSA documents leaked by Snowden reveal. In fact, the ability of both government and business to track the daily activities of Americans, in something close to real time, has been developed, refined, and expanded over the past few years, with little public debate. A decade of technological change and the rise of social media have shredded the traditional concept of privacy in America. One NSA contractor observed that Americans are now living in a "post-privacy age."

Once the NSA embraced the Internet and a drift-net style of data collection, the agency was transformed. The bulk collection of phone and e-mail metadata, both inside the United States and around the world, has now become one of the NSA's core missions. The agency's analysts have discovered that they can learn far more about people by tracking their daily digital footprints through their metadata than they could ever learn from actually eavesdropping on their conversations. What's more, phone and e-mail logging data comes with few legal protections, making it easy for the NSA to access.

One 2012 NSA document leaked by Snowden provides an overview of how the NSA views the new digital world. The document, titled "Sigint Strategy, 2012–2016," makes it clear that NSA officials believe that things have never been better for electronic surveillance—and they are intent on keeping it that way. The strategy paper proclaims that the NSA is now living through "the golden age of Sigint," largely because of the explosive growth in digital information ripe for NSA collection. Between 2006 and 2012, total digital information grew tenfold.

The strategy paper shows that the NSA is determined to influence U.S. policy in ways that allow it to retain its vast powers of data collection, and even expand them further. The NSA will "aggressively pursue legal authorities and a policy framework mapped more fully to the information age," the paper states. "For Sigint to be optimally effective, legal, policy and process authorities must be as adaptive and dynamic as the technological and operational advances we seek to exploit."

The NSA has been flourishing by taking advantage of the fact that the United States has not yet had a comprehensive national debate over how to properly strike a balance between the government's powers of domestic surveillance and the privacy rights and civil liberties of American citizens. That is because the NSA's powers have been expanded in secret, and the public has only learned about domestic spying from a series of whistleblowers forced to risk their careers and sometimes even their lives in order to reveal the truth. As a result, the public debates have been ad hoc and piecemeal, and government officials have only grudgingly engaged, loudly proclaiming that the media leaks that sparked the debates are damaging to national security.

In fact, a draconian crackdown on leaks by the Obama administration has made it far more difficult for the public to find out how electronic surveillance and domestic spying have grown. Few are willing to face what Diane Roark, Tom Drake, or Edward Snowden have endured.

That fear has even extended to the floor of the U.S. Senate. Before Snowden's disclosures, one of the few people in official Washington who rebelled against the growth of the surveillance state was Sen. Ron Wyden, an Oregon Democrat. As a member of the Senate Select Committee on Intelligence, Wyden had been briefed by the Obama administration and the intelligence community on the extent of the government's domestic surveillance apparatus, and he became convinced that if Americans knew as much as he did, they would be shocked. Wyden was upset that the Obama administration had followed the same course as the Bush administration by using secret Justice Department legal opinions and secret court opinions to pervert the law in order to get away with massive domestic spying operations.

For years before Snowden began to leak documents, Wyden tried to sound the alarm. He publicly warned that the Patriot Act was in reality two laws, one that American voters knew about, and the real one that the government actually used. Specifically, Wyden said that the Obama administration had secretly reinterpreted the provision in the Patriot Act that covered searches of the business records of Americans—and its interpretation of that provision had given the government far greater surveillance powers than ever intended. "It is almost like there are two sets of laws, one the public can read, and one the government has developed in secret," he complained. He said he met privately with Vice President Joe Biden to warn him that the Obama administration was going down the wrong path on domestic spying.

But Wyden refused to publicly explain how the administration was manipulating the law, and would not say exactly why he thought what the government was doing would shock the nation. He said that because the information was classified, he could not publicly detail his complaints unless the Obama administration and the intelligence community agreed to declassify the material, and they refused do so.

Wyden could have gone to the floor of the Senate to discuss the domestic spying openly, since he had legal immunity as a member of

Congress. But the Obama White House and top intelligence officials would almost certainly have pressured the Senate's leadership to strip Wyden of his membership on the Senate Intelligence Committee, and he would thus have lost access to any further information on the subject. Wyden was left in the bizarre position of warning the public about something that he couldn't discuss.

Most ironically, it was only after Edward Snowden began to leak documents that Wyden felt free to say publicly exactly what he had been warning about for years. After Snowden's disclosures revealed that the NSA was relying on secret law to obtain the private data of millions of Americans, Wyden confirmed that Snowden's leaks had disclosed what he had been concerned about. That meant that a low-level whistleblower had achieved what a U.S. senator could not, proving just how dysfunctional Washington had become. Wyden's experience offered conclusive proof that Snowden could never have triggered a national debate by working within the system.

Threats and alarms about terrorism gave the NSA room to expand domestic surveillance in the aftermath of 9/11; now threats posed by cyberattacks have given the NSA maneuvering room once again. And once again, government secrecy has prevented the public from understanding the true nature of the cyber threat or knowing the full extent of the government's intrusions into their online privacy in the name of cybersecurity.

With Osama bin Laden dead and terrorism on the wane, *cybersecurity* is the new buzzword in Washington, the latest justification for the expansion of the government's surveillance powers, and the new cash cow for defense contractors.

Rod Bergstrom tried to warn Washington about what was coming. As director of the National Cybersecurity Center at the Department of Homeland Security in the late Bush years and the early months of the Obama administration, he saw evidence that the NSA was maneuvering to take control of the government's cybersecurity efforts. Bergstrom feared an NSA takeover of cybersecurity because he knew that would mean that an agency whose primary responsibility was the collection of foreign intelligence would now be in charge of policing the domestic Internet.

Bergstrom was a Silicon Valley entrepreneur, not a Washington lifer, and so he had little interest in fighting a prolonged turf war. When he realized that he could not stop the NSA's power grab, he resigned in protest. He warned that if the NSA became the arbiter of cybersecurity, it would have access to all of the digital data of all Americans.

Bergstrom returned home to northern California and put his time in Washington behind him. But his warnings proved prophetic. During the Obama administration, the NSA did exactly as Bergstrom predicted, maneuvering to take control of cybersecurity. The Pentagon created a new U.S. Cyber Command that was nominally supposed to be separate from the NSA. But Gen. Keith Alexander, the director of the NSA, was given a second title as commander of U.S. Cyber Command, which was of course based at Fort Meade, the home of the NSA. In 2012, Alexander shed his uniform and donned a T-shirt and jeans to address a hacker convention in Las Vegas, where he tried to convince the nation's leading hackers to cooperate with the NSA's push into cybersecurity.

By 2013, as the number of reported cyberattacks on private companies and government agencies increased, the national debate about the need for greater cybersecurity intensified. But while the threat was real, the attacks led politicians and intelligence officials to begin to use increasingly apocalyptic rhetoric to describe the threat, hoping to justify a surge in government spending on cybersecurity as well as new legislation that would give them greater control over cybersecurity operations inside the United States. That would mean big new government contracts for outside contractors who have rebranded themselves as cybersecurity experts.

Cyber spending has surged even as the rest of the federal budget has faced severe cuts. In 2012, federal agencies spent $14.6 billion on cybersecurity, up from $13.3 billion the year before. And where there is an open spigot of federal money, lobbyists are not far behind. A report compiled in 2013 by the Center for Responsive Politics for CNNMoney found that a total of 1,968 lobbying reports filed with the government in 2012 mentioned the word *cybersecurity* or variations of the term multiple times, compared with 990 lobbying reports in 2011.

The government's scramble into cybersecurity also means a rush to build even more programs that could threaten the privacy of American citizens. One NSA cybersecurity program that has already raised concerns among privacy advocates comes complete with its own Orwellian-sounding name—Perfect Citizen—and a $91 million contract for Raytheon, a defense and intelligence company. The program reportedly is supposed to prevent cyberattacks on the nation's most critical infrastructure like power utility grids. But the NSA has refused to publicly explain exactly how Perfect Citizen will work, or how much it will intrude in private, domestic networks.

A Homeland Security program designed to protect government networks, called Einstein 3, has also raised concerns, since it has the capability to preempt attacks against government and contractor networks by searching out and disabling potential threats. But privacy advocates worry that it might become a kind of preemptive hunter-killer, analyzing data to determine whether it poses a threat, reading e-mails as well as detecting malware, and intercepting data before it reaches government or contractor networks.

Supporters say Einstein 3 needs to be able to roam the Internet to protect government networks before attacks occur, while critics say that its technology is derived from the NSA and is similar to spy technology used by authoritarian regimes to monitor Internet use. Either way, there has been little public debate in Congress about the privacy concerns raised by Einstein 3, Perfect Citizen, or any other cyber programs; instead, money has continued to pour into cybersecurity at a record pace with few questions asked.

Documents leaked by Snowden now make it plain that, for the NSA, there is little real difference between cybersecurity and domestic surveillance. Both rely on broad access to Internet metadata and both intrude on the digital privacy of American citizens to achieve their objectives. But because the concept of cybersecurity has gained such widespread public acceptance, the NSA's involvement has proved far less controversial than its role in domestic spying.

The intense campaign to ramp up cybersecurity and pour money and resources into mysterious new programs, while limiting online privacy, sounds eerily similar to the debate after 9/11 over security versus civil liberty, in which security always won. In Harvard Law School's *National Security Journal*, Jerry Brito and Tate Watkins, technology experts at George Mason University, warned that the cyber threat is being hyped by government officials seeking greater power and by outside contractors seeking more money. "A cyber-industrial complex is emerging, much like the military-industrial complex of the Cold War," they wrote. "This complex may serve not only to supply cyber security solutions to the federal government, but to drum up demand for those solutions as well."

Mike McConnell, the former director of national intelligence at the end of the Bush administration, provides a case in point. After he left office, McConnell became a senior executive for Booz Allen Hamilton, one of the top three contractors in defense cybersecurity, according to data compiled by Bloomberg Government in 2012. While at Booz Allen, McConnell has used the media platform provided by his status as a former director of national intelligence to publicly argue that much more needs to be done to protect the nation from cyberattacks. In one op-ed, he argued that cyberwar "mirrors the nuclear challenge in terms of the potential economic and psychological effects."

But a fact rarely mentioned in the rush to grant the NSA more power over cybersecurity—and greater access to the Internet—is that the NSA is now one of the world's leaders in the use of offensive cyberattacks. The NSA has been behind some of the most sophisticated and damaging cyberattacks ever mounted, including the Stuxnet and Flame viruses that targeted the Iranian nuclear program.

But when the *New York Times* reported the fact that the NSA was behind Stuxnet in 2012, the government reacted in a depressingly familiar fashion. It launched a leak investigation, one that this time turned on Obama's inner circle.

AFTERWORD

One day in the summer of 2007, my wife, Penny, called me to say that a FedEx envelope had arrived at our home.

It was from the Justice Department. Inside was a starkly worded letter from a federal prosecutor notifying me that the Justice Department and the FBI were conducting a criminal investigation into my 2006 book, *State of War: The Secret History of the CIA and the Bush Administration*. The letter stated that the government was investigating the "unauthorized disclosure of classified information" in my book. The letter demanded my cooperation.

The letter was sent to satisfy the requirements of the Justice Department's internal guidelines that lay out how prosecutors should proceed before issuing subpoenas to journalists to testify in criminal cases. The letter was essentially a warning from the Justice Department. Cooperate now, or a subpoena will follow.

I didn't cooperate, and in January 2008, I was subpoenaed by the Justice Department to testify before a federal grand jury in Alexandria, Virginia, in the government's leak investigation into my book.

I again refused to cooperate, and my lawyers and I moved to quash the subpoena.

That was the start of my marathon legal battle waged first against the Bush administration and later against the Obama administration.

As my legal battle against the government dragged on year after year, eventually making its way to the Supreme Court in 2014, I became convinced that I was fighting to protect press freedom in the post-9/11 age. But in the process, I discovered that I was no longer merely a journalist and author covering the war on terror. I had joined the many people whose lives had been upended by its excesses.

Undeniably, *State of War* had a huge impact — in some ways even before its publication in January 2006.

As an investigative reporter for the *New York Times* covering intelligence and national security, I have covered the war on terror ever since 9/11. In 2004, I discovered my biggest story of the post-9/11 age.

In October 2004, Eric Lichtblau and I wrote a story for the *Times* that disclosed the existence of the National Security Agency's warrantless wiretapping program. The story showed that President George W. Bush had secretly directed the NSA to engage in domestic spying on a massive scale, skirting the post-Watergate law Congress had enacted thirty years earlier to curb the intelligence community's domestic abuses. The NSA program was the biggest secret in the U.S. government, and many of our sources believed it was illegal, and possibly unconstitutional.

The story was explosive, and the Bush administration was frantic to kill it. Top officials at the White House, the NSA, and the CIA pushed back hard.

The White House launched an intense lobbying campaign designed to convince Bill Keller, then the executive editor of the *Times,* and Phil Taubman, then the paper's Washington bureau chief, that the story would severely damage national security. Senior government officials, including then NSA director Michael Hayden, argued that the NSA program was the "crown jewel" in America's war on terror.

That October, in the face of the mounting White House pressure, Lichtblau and I, along with our primary editor, Rebecca Corbett, met in New York with Keller to try to convince him to run the story. But Keller, accepting the government's national security arguments, killed the story about two weeks before the 2004 presidential election between George W. Bush and John Kerry.

Immediately after Bush's reelection, Lichtblau and I convinced Keller and Taubman to let us try again to get the story in the paper. In November and December 2004, we did more reporting and more rewriting, while Corbett did more reediting. There were more discussions with the government.

In mid-December 2004, we turned the story in again, and Lichtblau and I, along with Corbett, again argued to run it. But the story was killed once more.

The NSA story had now been killed twice by the *Times,* and the decision this time seemed to be final.

I was frustrated and deeply concerned that the truth about the war on terror was being covered up. Before the invasion of Iraq, my stories that revealed that CIA analysts had doubts about the prewar intelligence on Iraq were held, cut, and buried deep inside the *Times,* even as stories by other reporters loudly proclaiming the purported existence of Iraqi weapons of mass destruction were garnering banner headlines on page one. I decided I wasn't going to let that happen again.

In late December 2004, just after the NSA story was killed a second time, I took a leave from the *Times* to write a book about the war on terror. I decided to include the NSA story in my book, along with another story that the *Times* had killed at the request of the White House about a botched CIA operation involving a harebrained scheme to give nuclear weapons blueprints to Iran.

Because we had worked on the NSA story together, I told Eric Lichtblau that I was planning to include the story in my book. He approved.

After my manuscript was completed in the late summer of 2005, I told the editors at the *Times* that I was planning to include both the NSA story and the story about the CIA's botched Iran program in my book.

They were furious. For several weeks, the editors refused to reconsider running the NSA story, which, of the two stories, was freshest in their minds and which became the focus of our tense internal negotiations.

Finally, the editors agreed to reconsider. Months of additional meetings between the editors and top government officials followed. Finally, after an Oval Office meeting between President Bush and Arthur Sulzberger, Jr., the publisher of the *Times*, the NSA story was published in December 2005. It ran about two weeks before the publication of *State of War*. The *Times* story sparked a firestorm of protest against the White House and the NSA.

Meanwhile, top White House officials launched a last-minute effort to block the publication of *State of War*, according to the recent memoir of the CIA's former acting general counsel. But after its release in early January 2006, it triggered a huge national debate, not only about the NSA program but also a wide range of other intelligence abuses detailed in the book. I now believe that *State of War* played a significant role in the history of the post-9/11 era, because it was the first book to really force Americans to seriously reconsider the basic tenets of the war on terror.

But the twin controversies surrounding the *Times* NSA story and *State of War* also prompted Bush to order the Justice Department and the FBI to launch a pair of criminal leak investigations.

Immediately after our NSA story ran in the *Times*, Bush ordered the first leak investigation to find out who had talked to me and Lichtblau for our story. After *State of War* was published, the government launched a second leak investigation into the book as well. It was this second investigation into *State of War* that ultimately led to my prolonged legal battle with the government.

In 2009, when the new Obama administration continued the government's legal campaign against me, I realized, in a very personal way, that the war on terror had become a bipartisan enterprise. America was now locked into an endless war, and its perverse and unintended consequences were spreading.

And so my answer—both to the government's long campaign against me and to this endless war—is this new book, *Pay Any Price*.

Pay Any Price is my answer to how best to challenge the government's draconian efforts to crack down on aggressive investigative reporting and suppress the truth in the name of ceaseless war.

My answer is to keep writing, because I believe that if journalists ever stop uncovering abuses of power, and ever stop publishing stories about those abuses, we will lose our democracy.

—JAMES RISEN

INDEX